Routledge Revivals

Doing Philosophy

First published in 2012, *Doing Philosophy* presents the basics of how 'to do' philosophy – what philosophy is, how we can think, the nature of logic, some special terms – in a straightforward and easy to understand style. Then, using questions and exercises as well as everyday examples, the author takes the reader on a wide-ranging tour of key philosophical topics which, as well as the 'standard fare' of logic, epistemology, mind, God etc., also includes ethical, social, scientific, cultural and human issues such as time, cosmology, war, animal rights, euthanasia, abortion, genetics, evolution, and the meaning of life.

The author's emphasis throughout is that philosophy is accessible to anyone keen enough to try and do it and that, as a subject, philosophy is practical, fascinating and exciting. By encouraging independent critical thinking and being succinct yet informative, the book involves the reader with the history, the breadth of subject matter, the skills of philosophising and the benefits that philosophy can offer to the enquiring individual.

The book accesses major philosophical topics briefly, breaking them down into convenient points, with challenging questions throughout and exercise questions at the end of each chapter, whilst introducing major thinkers and their ideas. There is an extensive further reading list to help those who wish to take this absorbing subject further.

Doing Philosophy

Gerald Rochelle

First published in 2012
by Dunedin

This edition first published in 2020 by Routledge
2 Park Square, Milton Park, Abingdon, Oxon OX14 4RN

and by Routledge
52 Vanderbilt Avenue, New York, NY 10017

Routledge is an imprint of the Taylor & Francis Group, an informa business

© 2012 Gerald Rochelle

The right of Gerald Rochelle to be identified as author of this work has been asserted by him in accordance with sections 77 and 78 of the Copyright, Designs and Patents Act 1988.

All rights reserved. No part of this book may be reprinted or reproduced or utilised in any form or by any electronic, mechanical, or other means, now known or hereafter invented, including photocopying and recording, or in any information storage or retrieval system, without permission in writing from the publishers.

Publisher's Note
The publisher has gone to great lengths to ensure the quality of this reprint but points out that some imperfections in the original copies may be apparent.

Disclaimer
The publisher has made every effort to trace copyright holders and welcomes correspondence from those they have been unable to contact.

A Library of Congress record exists under ISBN: 9781780460048

ISBN: 978-0-367-50362-8 (hbk)
ISBN: 978-1-003-04969-2 (ebk)
ISBN: 978-0-367-50373-4 (pbk)

Doing Philosophy

Gerald Rochelle

for Pauline
a truly mighty

Contents

	Introduction	xvii
1	Doing Philosophy	1
2	Some Philosophical Terms	6
3	Argument and Logic	12
4	Possibility	21
5	What Do We Know?	26
6	Perceiving the World	33
7	Mind	40
8	Right and Wrong	50
9	Equality	62
10	God	74
11	Science	85
12	Time	95
13	Human Rights	104
14	Freedom and Determinism	115
15	Politics, Political Equality and the State of the World	124
16	War	136
17	Punishment	152
18	Abortion	161
19	Euthanasia	175
20	Animal Rights	183
21	Genetics	196
22	Life, Death, Immortality and Reincarnation	208
23	Evolution	220
24	Cosmology	234

25 The Meaning of Life	241
Annotated Bibliography	245
Extended Reading	248
Internet Resources	250
Index	252

Introduction

Who is this book for?
Doing Philosophy is for anyone interested in thinking. You could be someone who just wonders what doing philosophy is, or you could be someone with some experience of it who wants to broaden their range, you could be a student, someone who likes arguing, or someone who is interested in a challenge, or you could be someone who wants to keep their minds alive and their brains active. In any of these cases, or in any others, this book will help you start doing philosophy. It will get you involved in topics that have interested philosophers and thinkers for more than 2,500 years.

Why do philosophy?
There are no right answers but there are many conclusions that can be drawn from our careful reflection on ideas presented to us. Many of these conclusions can be satisfying because of how we have arrived at them, exciting because of what we have come to know, and influential in the ways they may affect our future thinking and lives. In other words, doing philosophy is good for you! Our lives are complex and our individual circumstances different from all others. Doing philosophy can help us understand better the world we live in as individuals, it can help us lead a more useful and fulfilling life, it can help us move towards something Socrates (470–399 BC) called the 'good life'. In short, doing philosophy can make us a little wiser and help us flourish as human beings. It can point us towards what Aristotle (384–322 BC) thought the object of life — living and doing well, flourishing.

Introduction

Why this particular book?
Philosophy is practical — it is something we do. This book is assembled in such a way that you will be continually involved in doing philosophy. Some of the topics introduced are strongly identified as philosophical areas (Chapters 2, 3, 4, 5, 6, 7), some deal with ethical issues (Chapters 8, 9, 13, 14, 15, 18, 19, 20) and some are more broadly interesting (Chapters 10, 11, 12, 16, 17, 21, 22, 23, 24, 25). Many more subjects of philosophical enquiry lie beyond these pages (for example, linguistics, aesthetics, the nature of being and existence, the nature of reality). The mixture has been chosen not only to provide the basic ideas of philosophy but also to afford opportunities to do philosophy and excite interest in doing philosophy across a broad range of human interests and concerns not normally thought of as philosophical. *Doing Philosophy* will show you that there are no subject limits to philosophy, and it will enable you to deal with any of them in a thoughtful and productive way.

What are you supposed to do with it?
It is a good idea to look at Chapters 1, 2 and 3 before any others — there is useful grounding here and it will be helpful throughout. After that, choose as you wish. If something interests you, pursue it. If you want to look more at a topic outside this book (a website, a film, a piece of art, a newspaper article, for example), follow it, pick up whatever information you want from it and return later. *Doing Philosophy* often takes you beyond the normal range of conventional philosophy and into many other areas of human interest — do not hold back from looking into them.

How should you work?
Whether you work alone, with another or with others, be yourself. If you talk to others about your ideas, ask them their views and try to explain yours. Always allow them to express their ideas fully. Take up their ideas by developing them or rejecting them. Learn to express your ideas in a reasoned way and develop an ability to modify or strengthen your own case. Every question raised, either as an outcome of discussion with others or from specific questions introduced here, should be used to encourage this process. Always test your thoughts (and the thoughts of others) against the standard logical form presented in Chapter 3, 'Argument and Logic'.

Summarily, this is that we should ask of any argument: 'How is it justified?', 'What makes it true?' and 'Why should I believe it?'. In answer to these questions you should look for true reasons, a logical framework and valid conclusions. If your own arguments or the arguments of others fall outside this logical form, they should be challenged on their formulation as opposed to their content. If you work by yourself, note down the main elements of your thinking process and try and refine it. Look at what you have produced later and, if it makes less sense, try to find out why. Always challenge yourself. Ask yourself why you have decided on a certain view, how you reached it and if it is truly defendable. Do not be afraid to take on new ideas and concepts — step outside your normal thinking habits. Doing philosophy is exciting; it can bring about challenge and novelty, and sometimes a little wisdom.

Using the book
The text of each topic covers some fundamentals of that area, referring to examples and citing important contributing philosophers. Try to form a response to the *Initial question*, which appears immediately beneath each chapter title. It provides a starting point from which the rest of the chapter proceeds. Generally, you will find yourself supporting or opposing (more or less strongly) what you read if you have formed an initial response. There is nothing wrong with this. The forming of an opinion causes you to want to argue for it, and this makes you think about the reasons you have for arguing this way and the conclusions you draw from them. Remember to work out how others would argue against your opinion as this allows you to see flaws in your own case. *Questions* [?] within the topics provide natural breaks in the form of opportunities for focused thought or to take some discussion to friends or relatives. These questions could form topics for a discussion group or philosophical café. Whatever is the case for you, pause at these points and allow some of your own philosophising to take place. *Further questions* consolidate the contents of each chapter. Again, use them as discussion points with others or as subjects for your own philosophising. Do not try to work through all the questions in one go. Give each one you tackle your fullest attention; finding things you agree or disagree with may not only be in the content but in the way the questions are formulated.

When reflecting on questions try to bring in examples of your everyday experience. This is particularly important when thinking of abstract concepts like cosmology or God (where we have no direct experience) or on ethical issues (where we tend to have ready-made opinions). For example, thinking about whether God is male or female and whether this would make any difference to the way he or she behaved puts the question into an understandable human context.

There are no answers given to any of the questions posed here, though there is sometimes supplementary information or definitions given in *Notes* following the *Futher Questions* to each chapter.

Do not forget, you bring your own experience to doing philosophy.

1
Doing Philosophy

What do you think philosophy is?

Introduction
We make our lives fuller when we reflect on them. Philosophy gives us some basic thinking tools and a ready-shaped framework of ideas into which we can fit our thoughts. To know why it is that we do things, to be able to fit our motivations into an ethical code and to project our ideas into the abstract world of mind, allow us to experience the best of life. Philosophy is a huge body of knowledge. Tapping into it can help us interpret all aspects of the world that cause us to ask questions, and it can provide solid, well-thought-out concepts against which to match our moral actions and worth. In short, philosophy can help us understand and attain the good life.

Understanding information
There is a difference between manipulating information and understanding it. Whereas a computer helps us to manipulate information, philosophy helps us to understand its content and, in so doing, encourages us to reason. Human beings have a unique facility to reason, it stems from our self-conscious ability to know that we exist. We are not like computers that simply manipulate information and are not self-aware. The test for artificial intelligence applied to computers (the 'Turing test') demands that the machine's replies to questions should be indistinguishable to those of human beings. No computer has yet passed this test.

> **?** Is a computer cleverer than a human? What information did you use to arrive at an answer?

What is philosophy?

Philosophy is thinking, not just thinking in the way that every day we say we think (e.g. about where I should go this afternoon and whether or not it will rain tomorrow) but a special kind of thinking. It involves us in abstract thought and ideas (e.g. not where I should go this afternoon but why I am here at all, not whether or not it will rain but what do I mean by the sensation of wetness when I talk about rain).

This sort of thinking helps us to ask questions about the often-puzzling world in which we find ourselves. First, it allows us to work out whether the question is meaningful (and that we are justified in pursuing an answer), second, it helps us work through the problem, obtain a conclusion and decide whether that conclusion is valid. Whether or not the conclusion is true will depend on the truth contained in the argument.

The method of philosophy, as a way of thinking, can be (and is) used in all fields of human enquiry: scientific, ethical, religious, political or any other matter psychologically important to us as individuals or members of society. We may say that philosophy is a systematic method of asking valid questions about uncertainties.

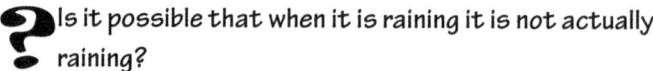 Is it possible that when it is raining it is not actually raining?

Doing philosophy

We do philosophy (in its weakest sense) all the time because we are continually taking in information, thinking about it and coming up with conclusions. But, although we all do this, our results can sometimes be misleading (e.g. we turn left when we should have turned right) or confusing (e.g. 'Why did I say that? I knew it would upset her'). This sort of thinking may lead us to reasoned conclusions but more often than not, in this sense, we use 'conclusion' to stand for the last thing we thought in a connected chain of thoughts. Whether that conclusion is entailed by (relies upon) the thoughts that preceded it is another matter.

Even if we do come up with results that seem to work or make sense, it is common that we come up with different results from other people. This is so even though we start out with the same question and try to balance the same sort of information or evidence. The variations in this process could, for example, lead me to thinking that X is good looking while someone else thinks they are not, or me sitting on a jury and thinking someone guilty of a crime while someone else on the jury thinks them innocent.

Human difference is valuable and important — the world would be a dull place if everyone thought X was good looking — but sometimes human difference is a result of different people tackling thinking in different ways. This might not be so important for X (though it may be if X wishes to be admired for her good looks) but it may have serious consequences for the person accused of murder whose future is dependent upon the thoughts of a jury.

The reason to philosophise need not be abstract. Primitive people were doing philosophy when they thought about the best ways of trapping animals for food. Should they dig a hole, cover it to make a trap or should they make a net, chase the animal and throw the net over it? How we come to conclusions about such questions involves us in thinking rationally and so involves us in philosophy. There is no gain in thinking about this sort of thing in an irrational way.

> **?** Because I like digging holes in the ground and I like eating wild duck for my dinner, I conclude that if I dig holes in the ground I will be able to catch wild duck (and have a satisfying dinner). Does this make sense? If not, why not? Explain carefully your reasons for holding this view.

Philosophy (in its strongest sense) first started when human beings began to wonder why their world was like it was. For example, human beings did not philosophise (in this strong sense) when they assumed that God created the world (if this was the case then no amount of thinking about it would alter the conclusion). Philosophy in the strong sense began when people started to wonder about the nature of God himself (e.g. Who is he or she? Where is God? Is God completely powerful? Is God good?). We call this sort of thinking 'metaphysics' and is to do with thinking about what things 'really are'. All philosophy, in some way, connects to this central metaphysical theme.

What is the best approach to philosophy?
We can approach philosophy by looking at its history and what philosophers in the past have said (e.g. the Ancient Greeks, Descartes (1596–1650)) or we can study it by topic (e.g. philosophy of science, philosophy of mind). Both of these have their merits and different individuals will have differing success with differing routes. Whichever we choose, it is important to have an understanding of what philosophers have already thought about. Without this, we would waste too much time trying to think over the same ground. However, philosophical thinking is not in itself a historical process. It is to do with using our imagination to come up with new ideas and argue in their defence, or to challenge existing ideas by providing rational arguments against them. It is an activity. To argue effectively we need to be aware of what it is to reason. There is little (or nothing) to be gained by proclaiming we have a 'philosophy' about this or that without supporting our ideas by reason, or if we have no declared reasons for holding a view to simply state 'That's what I believe and that's all there is to it.'

Further questions

This introductory exercise offers a broad-ranging set of questions to help you explore expressing yourself abstractly. Focus on the formulation of argument more than the ideas pursued or the conclusions reached. Use a checklist to measure the reasoning of your argument: 'How is it justified?', 'What makes it true?', 'Why should I believe it?', 'Have I used true reasons?', 'Is there a logical framework?', 'Have I reached valid conclusions?'.

For each of the following decide how you wish to respond to the question, then work out:

> Why do you think this?
> What reasons do you have for thinking this?
> Where do these reasons come from?
> Why do you believe your reasons?
> Would you change your view, should someone convince you otherwise?

1. Do you believe that war is wrong?
2. Do you think that criminals should be punished for their crimes or helped to lead better lives?

3. Do you think the earth is flat?

4. Do you think that water goes down the bath plughole in different directions according to whether you are in the northern or the southern hemisphere?

5. Do you think computers are intelligent?

6. Do you think that everyone in the world should have the same amount of money?

7. Do you think philosophy is worthwhile? If so, why? If not, why not?

Further reading

Bertrand Russell, *The Problems of Philosophy* (Oxford: Oxford University Press, 1986), Chapter 15.

Roger Scruton, *Modern Philosophy: an Introduction and Survey* (London: Pimlico, 2004), Chapter 1.

Nigel Warburton, *Thinking from A to Z* (London: Routledge, 2007).

2

Some Philosophical Terms

Does it matter what words we use to represent things or concepts?

Introduction

As with all areas of thought, philosophy has a broad and sometimes complex vocabulary. Some terms we use in everyday life may have a more specific meaning in philosophy. Understanding some of these terms makes for more certain progress in doing philosophy. This is not an exhaustive list by any means, but these terms are used regularly in philosophy and in particular ways that if not explained may cause confusion.

Metaphysics

Philosophy tries to deal with (and possibly answer) questions about the nature and reality of things in the world such as God, time or causality. This so-called 'metaphysical' aim is the main thrust of philosophy and all its other areas are in some way connected to, or elaborations of, this central theme.

Nature

By 'nature', we mean the 'way something is', its character and the qualities it has. We do not mean nature as the content of the universe regulated by universal laws (outside of which may be God who is by his 'nature' *super-natural*), nature as the living (not inorganic) world (which may be past or present and so includes 'natural' history) or 'nature' in the sense of everything in the (especially) organic world which is not subject to the influence of human beings (i.e. 'nature' the way it is). In the philosophical sense, the nature of something which is 'natural' is the character of something which is accessible to scientific study and the nature of something non-natural is an attempt to describe something which is abstract or beyond the reach of space and time.

Reality
By 'reality', we mean the ultimate nature of the sum total of the universe (and its constituent reality). We do not mean 'real' as opposed to 'fake'. Something which is fake, although an improper imitation of the 'real thing' will still constitute something real in the universe (it will still be a 'real' fake).

Epistemology
Philosophy concerns itself with what we know (if indeed we are entitled to say we know anything) and we call this enquiry 'epistemology'. When faced with a concern about our knowledge of something, we call it an 'epistemic concern'.

Scepticism
Much epistemological philosophy leads to doubt about whether we know anything. This doubting of our knowledge we call 'scepticism'. Epistemological scepticism about what and how we know anything drives us back to the central metaphysical aim and either supports further philosophical scepticism (if doubt remains) and consequently more enquiry, or leads to the generation of accepted certainty (and so becomes part of scientific 'fact' or 'law'). When we establish facts in this way and formulate laws sufficient to constitute a body of knowledge, a new science arises. When this happens, philosophy concerns itself more with the methods that the science uses rather than the substance of the science itself. For example, physics was once part of philosophy but now stands alone as the central natural science.

Things
By 'thing' we mean any entity or being the existence of which has been tested by some investigative process. 'Things' can be particular (pens and paper) or universal (stationery items). They can be abstract (emotions or wishes) or concrete (have some spatial place). The traditional philosophical term 'substance' stands for more or less the same. Because 'thinghood'

is also linked to the notion of the 'subject' (that is how it is that we, as subjects of an experience, describe the thing that we experience), it is both a language problem and a problem for the philosophy of mind.

The world

The 'world' is the universe that contains not only all apparently real or less tangible things but also all possible things, or things that we can only possibly imagine. The world contains things that we cannot possibly imagine, for example, a square circle, because although we cannot form a picture of a square circle (which is self-contradictory because nothing can be both square and round at the same time without each definition contradicting the other), we can imagine the contradictory nature of this impossible thing. Imagining an impossible thing, although not bringing that thing into existence (because it cannot exist if it is impossible), somehow 'cuts beneath' our format for imagining things that are (on one definition or another) only possible. The world also includes things that may be known or imagined by entities of which we have no knowledge, and our ignorance of them or their possibility does not exclude them in any way from the world. An alien may know something I do not know or even entertain, and this is also the case for God. In order to investigate the nature of the world to its limits, philosophers imagine 'possible worlds' which are not governed by any law or process which we understand but which we can nevertheless conceive of. The 'world' here does not mean the planet that we inhabit that revolves around the star we call the sun.

Logic

In all its undertakings, philosophy utilises a systemised way of thinking called 'logic'. Logic can be justified because it makes a certain way of coherent thinking possible, though checking it against some known prototype cannot prove it. Logic is simply a method supported by made-up rules that themselves only make sense if we apply the same rules to the rules we wish to support. In this way, you might say that logic is a self-justifying system, but if you think that logic is not a good idea just try imagining how we could think otherwise. Being 'illogical' or trying to think in ways that do not abide by the rules of logic is possible (e.g. 'lateral thinking') but it would be difficult to communicate our ideas to others and very hard to justify them without an alternative set of commonly agreed (illogical) rules. In doing this, we would end up with what logic offers anyway — a commonly shared and agreed method of thinking about things. In addition, logical rules seem to have a definite 'logic' of their own; they appeal not only to the constraints of their own system but also to what seems an inherent 'common sense'. Though we must remember that anything that has been in operation for well over two thousand years would by now almost certainly have become part of the human folklore of inherited good sense anyway, and so would seem intuitively 'self-evident' or 'natural'.

Idealism
Many philosophical concerns relate to the world as we experience it. Some sceptics hold that instead of the world being truly physical it is 'ideal'. 'Idealism' in this sense means that we can only have an 'idea' of what the world is: that is, that we only ever experience the world as an idea in our minds. We can think of ideas as deriving from our senses having contact with a world of objects, contained in our minds in the absence of any objects, or contained in only one mind ('solipsism').

Necessity
In philosophy, the word 'necessity' has a number of different meanings.

We say something exists necessarily if no natural process leads to its cessation (e.g. God, the immortal soul) as opposed to existing contingently where the thing's existence relies on natural processes that can cause its cessation (e.g. heat, movement). When we make a conditional statement such as 'If p then q', the p is said to be a sufficient condition of the state of affairs of q, whereas q is said to be a necessary condition of the state of affairs of p. If the conditional statement is true, for example, 'If the object is green all over (if p) then it is not red all over (then q)', then the conditionals are logically necessary and logically sufficient. Weaker senses of truth, for example, 'If I cut my finger then it will bleed', imply that cutting my finger (in this case) is a causally sufficient condition of my finger bleeding.

Necessity is also used in an epistemic sense to show what is entailed by what a thinker assumes (e.g. 'My finger is bleeding so I *must* have cut it'), what is supposed (e.g. 'My finger is bleeding so I *may* have cut it') or what is held to be certain (e.g. 'My finger is bleeding so I am *certain* that I have cut it').

Logical necessity is what follows in accordance with the laws of logic. Logical necessity in its narrowest sense is true in respect of its logical form (i.e. propositions which can be reduced to statements of the type 'If p then q'). In its broadest sense, it may be said to be true in every 'possible logical world' (e.g. 'God exists' is logically necessary in this sense because it is true not by virtue of its logical form but true because of the contents of the proposition itself).

Whereas logical necessity is known a priori (that is, it is knowledge not needing empirical evidence), metaphysical necessity is known only a posteriori (that is, it is knowledge built on the basis of empirical evidence). 'Water is H_2O' is necessarily true in every 'possible world' where water exists. However, we can only know that water is necessarily H_2O a posteriori (as a metaphysical necessity) but, because this is inductive evidence, we *might* be wrong in thinking this (epistemic necessity).

Nomic necessity refers to the high level of order and regularity we observe in the world (which we commonly describe as laws of nature).

Words

Human beings invent words to stand for things. In English, we call a tortoise a 'tortoise' because we all agree that we will call it a 'tortoise'. This is its 'designation', and the word 'tortoise' is how we 'denote' the thing that is a tortoise. If we agreed to call a tortoise something else (as indeed it is called by other names in other countries which use different languages), for example, a 'toliton', there would be no problems with this as long as we all kept to our agreement. Nothing about the tortoise would alter, because when we said 'toliton' we would still be 'connoting' that particular type of land based four-legged animal with a shell that moves slowly and eats lettuce leaves.

Further questions

Clarity and word meaning are crucially important in philosophy and an ability to define clearly the meanings of words is important. Use this exercise to test out your ability to explain what we mean when we use certain terms. Question 4 asks you to think about the application and limitations of logic in human life by enquiring about an emotion that often defies abstract description.

1. What is the difference between 'belief' and 'scepticism'?
2. Does denoting something differently affect the way that thing is? Give examples.
3. Explain how we are using the term 'nature' in the following contexts:
> 'It's just human nature.'
>
> 'It's a law of nature.'
>
> 'Nature is beautiful.'
>
> 'It's just his nature.'

4. Does logic only apply to certain human situations? For example, is it logical to fall in love?
5. Is there anything ambiguous about the word 'ambiguous'?

Notes

Question 1:

'belief' – a mental state based on either a true or false proposition that directs and controls our voluntary behaviour;

'scepticism' – a mental state which doubts our achievements and ability to obtain reliable knowledge.

Question 5 ~ There is nothing ambiguous about the meaning of the word 'ambiguous'. It has a well-defined meaning: that is, anything that has an obscure or double meaning or is difficult to classify. However, there is something implicitly ambiguous about anything classified as 'ambiguous' which, in this case, is not the word 'ambiguous' itself.

Further reading

John Hospers, *An Introduction to Philosophical Analysis* (London: Routledge, 1997), Chapter 1.

Nigel Warburton, *Thinking from A to Z* (London: Routledge, 2007).

3

Argument and Logic

In Star Trek when Mr Spock is referred to as being 'logical', it is usually taken to mean that he is without emotion. Sherlock Holmes is considered similarly 'cold'. Why is this? And what is being 'logical' anyway?

Introduction
Before being able to reason adequately, we need some foundation in the principles upon which reason rests. This foundation is logic. It would take us a long time to work out why 2+2=4 from first principles; it is much easier to learn that 2+2=4 then try to find reasons why this is so.

There are essentially two different forms of logic: modern, born of mathematical logic in the mid nineteenth century and influenced largely by Gottlob Frege (1848–1925) and Bertrand Russell (1872–1970), and traditional, originating with Aristotle (384–322 BC), sometimes called 'syllogistic logic'. Modern (symbolic) logic consists in two main strands: the propositional calculus and the predicate calculus. From this, other forms of logic have appeared, including: modal logic which deals with necessity, possibility and impossibility; tense logic which deals with matters related to time; and many-valued logic which assigns truth-values other than merely true or false. Both modern and traditional forms are concerned with sound reasoning and the rules that apply to it.

The philosophical process
There are two stages in the philosophical process. First, is there a meaningful question? In other words, is it possible to ask such a question? For example, 'Do I want to catch food?' is meaningful, whereas 'Do I want to defy gravity by the power of thought alone' is, under normal circumstances, not. Second, is there a method for working towards a conclusion?

In other words, is it possible to formulate valid stages from the basic question to some sort of resolution? For example, 'If I want to catch food then I can dig a hole, cover it with leaves and wait until I trap something' is a valid thinking process. However, the fact that I live in a world where all animals except human beings spend all their lives in flight may make the conclusion practically meaningless (assuming I am not a cannibal). In this case, it would be reasonable to test such a plan by arguing about its contents, for example, a basic test would raise the question of whether or not there were any land-based animals other than human beings.

Argument

We argue in different ways: we quarrel, debate or persuade. In a philosophical (or generally academic) sense, we use argument to persuade others of our point of view. Although quarrels may not have rules, persuasion arguments do. An argument consists in a group of statements (premises) some of which purportedly provide support for another (the conclusion). For an argument to be convincing it must use true reasons, blend them into a logical framework and draw valid conclusions from the reasons used. Any sound argument must show how it is justified and what makes it true, as well as providing reasons why I should believe it.

There are two categories of argument, divided according to the degree of support they provide for their conclusions: deductive and inductive. A deductive argument provides conclusive support for its conclusion as long as it is valid. An inductive argument provides probable support for its conclusion providing it supplies strong evidence.

Deductive argument is a method of ascertaining validity. A properly constructed deductive argument is valid, so if all its premises are true then its conclusion *must* be true.

Inductive argument is a method of ascertaining the degree of certainty the premises confer on the conclusion. A properly constructed inductive argument has strength, so if all the premises are true then the conclusion is probably true.

> **?** If you wanted to persuade someone that the earth is round, what sort of argument might you present? Would this be deductive or inductive? Which is the most successful in this case?

Deductive argument
There is nothing God-given about deductive argument. Aristotle invented it and prescribed the three laws that govern it. These are: things are what they are (the law of identity), nothing can be both what it is and what it is not (the law of non-contradiction), and everything is either something or something else (the law of excluded middle).

Aristotelian logic (unlike modern logic) quantifies the subject using the ordinary words 'all', 'no' and 'some' and has only two truth-values: 'true' and 'false'.

A deductive argument follows this pattern:
>All x are z
>There is an x
>Therefore it must be a z

Or, in other words:
>The general case is such and such.
>There is something that is included in the general case.
>Therefore, that something must be such and such.

❓ Can you construct a simple deductive argument that follows the pattern, all x are z, there is an x, therefore it must be a z?

Inductive argument
Inductive argument is what we might call the 'logic of science' or the 'logic of everyday life'. It is based on experience and, based upon that experience, provides us with a means of predicting what will happen next. If I hold my pen away from a surface and let it go it always falls downwards (though describing something 'falling' implies 'downwards' anyway because 'falling' means 'going downwards'). Because everyone else who has ever lived (as far as we know) has always found the same thing happening (though not necessarily to pens), I have strong evidence to allow me confidently to predict that the next time I drop my pen (or the next time anyone else drops a pen) it will fall downwards.

However, scepticism leaves me in doubt that this will always be the case. It is perfectly reasonable that for say the last 15 billion years (or since the universe began) things have always tended towards the centre of a gravitational force (that is 'fall' towards it) but that from tomorrow and for the next 100 billion years this process might be reversed. If this turned out to be the case then the time (the first 15 billion years of the universe's life) when things fell downwards would be remembered only as a distant and short-term anomaly.

An inductive argument follows this pattern:

Look, there is an *x* which is a z.
Look, there is another x which is a z. (and so on)
I conclude that the next x will be a z.

? Is there anything that we know by induction that is absolutely certain? For example, are all human beings mortal?

Syllogistic argument

Working through some problems using traditional logic is a good way of looking in detail at statements and conclusions and their meaning in argument.

The syllogism is a simple form of deductive (traditional) logical argument that contains two premises and a conclusion. Distributed between the premises and conclusion are three terms: a middle term ('M'), a second term ('2') and a third term ('3'). A syllogism is useful for checking the validity of a piece of reasoning. To the question 'Is Socrates mortal?' the syllogistic answer would be:

All men (M) are mortal (3) (1st premise)
Socrates (2) is a man (M) (2nd premise)
Socrates (2) is mortal (3) (conclusion)

The conclusion follows from the premise because the middle term 'M' (man) is common to the premises, the second term '2' (Socrates) is common to the conclusion and one of the premises, and the third term '3' (mortal) is common to the conclusion and the other premise.

A valid syllogism will always yield a valid conclusion, but the truth of the conclusion relies on the truth of the premises. For example, a valid syllogism can have the following elements:

1. True premises and a true conclusion, e.g.
   All diamonds (M) are hard (3) (true)
   Some diamonds (M) are gems (2) (true)
   Some gems (2) are hard (3) (true)

2. Some or all premises false and a true conclusion, e.g.
   All cats (M) have wings (3) (false)
   All birds (2) are cats (M) (false)
   All birds (2) have wings (3) (true)
3. Some or all premises false and a false conclusion, e.g.
   All cats (M) have wings (3) (false)
   All dogs (2) are cats (M) (false)
   All dogs (2) have wings (3) (false)

In each of these arguments, if the premises were true then the conclusion would have to be true (as in the first example). It is impossible for a valid argument of this form to have true premises and a false conclusion.

A syllogism can be rendered invalid in a number of ways:

1. The middle term (M) must appear in both premises at least once, e.g.
   All men (M) are human beings (3)
   All women (2) are human beings (3)
   All women (2) are men (M)
   Invalid because the middle term (M) 'men' appears only once in one premise.
2. If a term does not appear in the premises, it must not appear in the conclusion, e.g.
   All cats (M) are mammals (3)
   Felix (2) is a cat (M)
   Felix (2) is friendly (X)
   Invalid because 'friendly' only appears in the conclusion.
3. No conclusion can follow from two negative premises, e.g.
   No dogs (M) are cold-blooded (3)
   No dogs (M) are capable of talking (2)
   Cold-blooded things (3) are capable of talking (2)
   Invalid because both premises are negative.
4. If either premise is negative, the conclusion must be negative, e.g.
   No birds (M) have feathers (3)
   Cats (2) are not birds (not M)
   Cats (2) have feathers (3)
   Invalid because the first and second premise are negative but the conclusion is positive.

5. A negative conclusion cannot follow from two affirmative premises e.g.
   All men (M) are mortal (3)
   Socrates (2) is a man (M)
   Socrates (2) is not mortal (not 3)
   Invalid because both the premises are positive but the conclusion is negative.

When confronted by an invalid argument our intuition tends to let us know that something is wrong (so deeply imbedded in our culture are the rules of logic). When doing philosophy it is necessary to work out what leads us to think this is so in a more rigorous way.

〉〉〉〉See also Further questions 1 〈〈〈〈

Limits and scope — proof and justification

We can justify the laws of logic (because they are presupposed in all discourse and thought) but we cannot prove them without the support of other propositions which themselves rely on the same laws. Even so, we have to rely on them because they alone make proof possible. It seems unsatisfactory that the principles of proof do not themselves rest on something ultimate, but there is no ultimate support available. In the case of logic, we are at the mercy of the rather unsatisfactory conclusion that 'it is because it is'.

Using the laws of logic, we can prove arguments by validly deducing conclusions from our propositions. This is not the same as proving something by giving evidence (the most commonly used form of proof). Evidence in everyday life may contribute to the truth of premises offered, but only deductive reasoning can prove the validity of the argument itself. Whereas the question 'Where were you on the night of the murder?' can be answered together with proof — 'I was in the pub, and I've got witnesses (who were also in the pub) to prove it, so, I could not have committed the murder' — only deductive reasoning will show the argument of the accused to be valid or invalid. For example:

   I was in the pub on the night of the murder. (which is true)
   Plenty of people saw me in the pub and did not see me commit the murder. (which is true)
   Therefore, I did not commit the murder. (which is invalidly drawn

and may not be true as I could have committed the murder at a time when the witnesses did not see me)

▶▶▶▶See also Further questions 2◀◀◀◀

Further questions 1

Working carefully through the examples helps us to make sense of arguments that we recognise intuitively as wrong but cannot immediately understand why. It is also good 'brain-training'.

1. Explain the differences and similarities between the words:
   'correct', 'logical' and 'convincing'.

2. In these syllogisms find the middle term 'M', second term '2' and third term '3', then decide whether the argument is valid or invalid. When you have done this, decide whether the conclusion is true or false. In either case, explain your reason for thinking this.

    a. All cyclists are fit
       All philosophers are fit
       All cyclists are philosophers

    b. All men are things
       All women are things
       All men are women

    c. All vegans are vegetarians
       I am a vegetarian
       I am a vegan

    d. Some Scandinavians are non-drinkers
       All Norwegians are Scandinavians
       Some Norwegians are non-drinkers

    e. Some cyclists are alcoholics
       Some motorists are not alcoholics
       Some cyclists are motorists

    f. No oak trees are roses
       Some roses are not climbers
       Some oak trees are not climbers

    g. Some eyes are not blue
       All blue things can see in the dark
       Some things that can see in the dark are not eyes

Notes

Question 1:

'correct' – true and accurate, right;

'logical' – correctly reasoned, an argument that does not contravene the laws of logic;

'convincing' – to cause another to believe because there is no margin of doubt.

Question 2:
a. Invalid. Middle term M does not appear in both premises. Untrue.
b. Invalid. Middle term M does not appear in both premises. True.
c. Invalid. Middle term M does not appear in both premises. True or untrue according to whom makes the statement.
d. Valid. True.
e. Invalid. Affirmative conclusion derived from a negative premise. True.
f. Invalid. No conclusion can be drawn from two negative premises. True.
g. Invalid. Middle term M does not appear in both premises but does appear in conclusion. True.

Further questions 2

Try to respond quickly to the questions here. It will cause you to come up with less considered ideas. It is a useful experiment in abstract, imaginative thinking. Most of the sentence beginnings have human or social meaning. Note that the conclusions given appear before the reasons that support them (conclusions do not have to be at the end).

Provide connected reasons to support the following conclusions:
1. The earth is round because ...
2. Art is beautiful because ...
3. Art is not beautiful because ...
4. Democracy is good because ...
5. Democracy is not good because ...
6. Murder is wrong because ...
7. Murder is not wrong because ...
8. I am in love because ...
9. I am not in love because ...
10. I think science is good for humankind because ...

11. I think science is bad for humankind because ...
12. I think genetically modified food is good for humankind because ...
13. I think genetically modified food is bad for humankind because ...
14. I think rich people should give away all their money to the poor because ...
15. I think rich people should keep all their money and the poor should look after themselves because ...
16. Murder has always been wrong, so it must be bad because ...

Provide connected conclusions for the following statements:
1. Elephants have four legs so ...
2. I have just paid £5 million for this picture so ...
3. The 'New X' party has just won the election so ...
4. After the murder, he was found standing over the body with a knife in his hand so ...
5. I can feel my heart pounding so ...

Further reading

Bertrand Russell, *The Problems of Philosophy* (Oxford: Oxford University Press, 1986), Chapters 6 and 7.

Douglas N. Walton, *Informal Logic: A Handbook for Critical Argumentation* (Cambridge: Cambridge University Press, 1989).

4

Possibility

Is there a sense in which the force of gravity could start being exerted in the opposite direction? In other words, if I drop my pen it fails to fall to the ground but, under the force of gravity, it rises into the sky?

Introduction

Logic allows philosophers to think seriously about abstract concepts in ways that are usually confined to the realms of science fiction or fantasy. For example, in order to imagine what the real nature of the universe could be, philosophers may think about various sorts of universe (e.g. ones in which there is no matter or time). Doing this allows them to extend the possible 'state of affairs' beyond what seems to be the case. By conducting such 'thought experiments' and imagining such 'possible worlds', philosophers investigate the conceptual limits of reality and what we know. Thought experiments have a reputable lineage. Isaac Newton (1642–1727) did most of his famous work by this method and the concepts (if not the mathematics) of Albert Einstein (1879–1955) were born of the same.

> **?** *What can we gain from trying to imagine something we do not know?*

Logical possibility

A state of affairs is said to be logically possible whenever a proposition that this state of affairs exists is not self-contradictory. For example, to 'fall upwards' is logically impossible because 'fall' means 'go downwards' and to 'fall upwards' would mean to 'go downwards upwards' which is self-contradictory. However, it is logically possible that the direction of gravitational pull could change, in which case (presumably) we would need to reconsider our use of the word 'upwards' which would then more meaningfully denote 'downwards'. In the same way, it is logically impossible to think of a triangular square because the contents of the proposition are self-contradictory (although it is logically possible to imagine the contradictory nature of such a construction).

It is convenient to divide possibility into three sorts: logical, empirical and technical. Logical possibility is constrained only by the laws of logic, empirical possibility is constrained by the laws of nature, and technical possibility by the current state of human technological achievement (and also by the laws of nature). Whereas it may be logically possible to run a hundred miles in a minute it may not be empirically possible because laws of motion, mass and gravity may prevent it, and it is also technically impossible (because no one can achieve it) although in the future, with the use of implants or genetic modification, it may be.

Although it is logically possible to imagine a state of affairs where logical rules would not hold, it is difficult to think about it in anything other than a logical way.

>>>>See also Further questions 1<<<<

Conceivable and imaginable

Logical possibility is different from that which is conceivable or imaginable. Although it is logically possible to think of a 1,000-storey building, a goldfish the size of a whale, or a human being with 18 heads, some people would not be able to imagine these things. At the same time, just because we cannot imagine it does not mean it is logically impossible (it just means our powers of imagination are limited).

>>>>See also Further questions 2<<<<

Possible and probable

There is a distinction between what is possible and what is probable (or likely).

Probability can be mathematical, for example, where there is an equal chance that throwing a coin will ultimately lead to an equal distribution of heads and tails (although this becomes circular if, in an infinite world, there is opportunity for another chance), or statistical, where forecasting is based on the relative frequency found in past data (e.g. most 50-year-old men who smoke 50 cigarettes a day die before they are 70 years of age).

The two processes of probability tend to mix. Mathematical probability requires a possibly infinite length of future time in which to work out, statistical probability never makes probable the specific case ('most' 50-year-old men but not 'the' or 'a particular' 50-year-old man).

Because of the lack of specificity inherent in statistical probability there have been attempts to replace frequency probability with 'personalist' theories based on degrees of reasonable belief. But it is difficult to establish an acceptable view about what is reasonable. For example, the statement that there is enough reason to believe that Mr X who is 50 years old and smokes 50 cigarettes a day *will* die before he is 70 years of age may be sufficient to deter Mr X from smoking from now on, but the reasonable belief may have turned out to be wrongly founded. Even so, statistical probability has great force and is the main tool in social (and, in a large part, scientific) argument.

〉〉〉〉See also Further questions 3〈〈〈〈

Further questions 1

This exercise allows you to carefully unpick the different sorts of logical possibility. Match the five given questions against the three different types of possibility. Prepare a brief defence of your conclusions and test them against the opposite view (ideally argue it out with someone else).

1. Is it possible in any way for human beings to fly by the power of mind alone?
2. Is it possible in any way to travel back in time?
3. Is it possible in any way to build a machine that will think like a human being?
4. Is it possible in any way to be two different people at the same time?
5. Is it possible in any way that there is someone living on earth today who is immortal?

Further questions 2

Are the following logically possible? Justify your answer in each case.

1. To run one hundred miles in an hour.
2. To swim across the Atlantic Ocean.
3. To hear someone speaking on the other side of the earth.

4. To hear a colour.

5. To wish for something without knowing it.

6. To play a computer game that does not exist.

7. To see next week's episode of a TV soap opera.

8. To get up, have your breakfast, leave for work then suddenly find yourself back in bed waking up.

9. To hear without ears.

10. For a lead ball to float in water.

11. For a colour to exist that no creature in the world can see.

12. For a sound to exist if there is nothing in the world to perceive it.

13. For the universe to exist if there is nothing in the world to perceive its existence.

14. For someone to have two blue eyes and two brown eyes at the same time.

15. For the day after tomorrow to follow today without tomorrow in between.

16. For no world to exist at all.

17. To be transported from London to Tokyo in a millisecond.

18. For consciousness to exist without any conscious being to be conscious of it.

19. For time to reverse itself.

20. To think of things after you have died.

21. To fall from the top of a 20-storey building and survive.

22. To go back in time and cause yourself not to be born.

Notes

Most of the propositions are logically possible in some way. The ones that are not (or at least seem unlikely and would require an unusual argument to support them) are 6, 13 (at least not for an idealist), 14, 16 (if this were so then what are we doing asking the question, and what could 'we' be anyway in this context?), 18 and 22 (though not if there in one continuous time).

Further questions 3

These three questions deal with the possible and the probable. Look for the wide-ranging issues present in them all by extrapolating the contents or thinking of analogous examples.

1. 'The roads are congested with cars. If we stop building roads there will be no more traffic congestion.' Is this more possible than probable?

2. Flipping a coin will produce either heads or tails. After one million throws it has only produced heads. Is there a difference between the mathematical and statistical probabilities for the next throw?

3. I think it is possible that it will be warm this summer, but every summer for the last ten years has been warm and my neighbour says we must be due for a change. I told my neighbour that she is probably right but she says anything is possible. Should I buy a new barbecue?

Further reading

John Hospers, *An Introduction to Philosophical Analysis* (London: Routledge, 1997), Chapter 4.

5

What Do We Know?

Is there something you can say with complete certainty that you know? If so, what is it and why are you so certain? If you do not think there is anything which you can know with complete certainty, how do you know this and how certain are you of it?

Introduction

Knowledge is not just a point of view (though we may think we 'know' that we hold such a point of view). Knowledge is not a mode of thinking that is subject to 'correctness', such as political, moral or social attitudes (e.g. 'I know it's wrong to murder another human being', 'I know everyone should have equal rights'). Knowledge (in its strongest sense) is a belief that we can hold with absolute certainty. It is commonly defined as 'justified true belief'. Something I consider I know may seem to be true, and I feel sure I believe it, but it may be difficult to justify (or prove) why it is either true or believable. The philosophical term for the question of what is knowledge is 'epistemology'. Any theory of knowledge leads to sceptical doubts about how we know anything and that, in turn, raises questions about the nature of the world that we believe we may know.

> **?** We believe that the genealogy of the earth is true because we find fossils of creatures that have lived before us. But what if these fossils were placed there to deceive us into thinking the earth has a longer history than we believe is the case?

Theory of knowledge

Varying importance is placed by different philosophical theories of knowledge on the different aspects of knowledge. Broadly, they can be split between 'externalist' and 'internalist' theories. Externalist theories rely on strong connections as they appear in the world. They can be: causal, that is, that something is known only if there is a causal connection between the fact in question and the knowledge we have of it (e.g. 'I see you because you are there'); reliabilist, that is, that something is known only if true belief is justified by a reliable process (e.g. 'I see you because science has proved that light rays are transmitted between you and my senses'); and counterfactual, that is, that we cannot believe something to be true if the thing in question is known to be false (e.g. 'It cannot be you I see if what I am seeing is someone else'). Internalist theories rely on a coherence of fact and belief, this in turn depends on coherent internal/subjective states (e.g. 'I recognise you because of the shape of your nose. The person I am seeing has that distinctively shaped nose and so I believe it is you.').

Plato (c.428–347 BC) was the first to explain a method for investigating whether anything is known or knowable. His method deals with both the process of coming to know as well as the question of how to defend what is believed to be true. Plato claimed that ordinary knowledge is suspect; it is epiphenomenal, that is, produced by other effects such as appearance, our circumstances and our perceptual apparatus. Plato believed that true knowledge could be found by open and critical dialogue. By this means he thought it possible to see beyond the world of appearance and come to know the world of truth, a world he thought made up of the original and perfect 'form' of everything. This sceptical tradition has continued ever since.

> **?** Is it possible to see something truly square? After all, when I look at it from different angles it always appears different shapes.

Scepticism

Scepticism casts doubt on our ability to obtain reliable knowledge. This may take the form of global scepticism that doubts everything we think we know, or more restricted forms which question our knowledge on particular things (e.g. ethics, other minds, the past, the underlying structure of matter, time).

The first task of epistemology is to be sceptically critical. Plato began the tradition in his search for reality by questioning the dogmatic belief in the world of appearance. While Plato's disciples continued and refined his subtle form of scepticism, more radical versions followed. Pyrrho (*c.*360–*c.*270 BC), for example, believed we should suspend judgement on all matters and that we should lead a 'life without belief'. The story (according to Sextus Empiricus (*c.*160–*c.*210)) is that Pyrrho needed protection from the dangers of the world by his friends because he did not believe that the dangers were real.

More than a thousand years later, René Descartes (1596–1650) set out to defeat scepticism once for all and install a reliable set of foundations for science, religion and metaphysics. Descartes' system of doubt exposed the difficulty of distinguishing dreams from the waking world. He also thought up the idea of an evil demon that deceives us into thinking false things (e.g. that matter is really there when it is not). If we cannot tell whether or not we are dreaming, or the evil demon controls everything we know of the world, then everything we know is potentially in error. Descartes' system of doubt led to his assertion that although almost everything we think we know is in doubt, the fact that we think we doubt entails that we know something (i.e. that we are a thinking thing that doubts — *cogito ergo sum*, I think therefore I am).

These days, Descartes' evil demon is commonly replaced by the notion of 'brains in a vat' (Hilary Putnam (1926–)) that depicts our brains as suspended in a vat with wires connecting them to the world outside. Putnam says that sceptical possibilities are themselves self-refuting, that is that even if we were a brain in a vat we could not formulate the thought that we were one (because we would always assume ourselves to be what our sensations led us to believe). Even if we could think 'I am a brain in a vat', this would not have the same meaning that it does to those of us who suppose we are not brains in vats because those who think they are not brains in vats could not conceive of what it is to be a brain in a vat.

David Hume (1711–1776) proposed a strong, global scepticism. He came to the conclusion that our sensual and intellectual faculties are inadequate to deal with the task of discerning reality because our beliefs are based on causal chains for which there is no legitimate basis. For example, we may know that one snooker ball hits another and causes it to move but we do not know of what that cause constitutes. Though this may seem a despairing situation, Hume believed it led us to a sense of modesty and good sense, forcing us to recognise our own cognitive limitations. According to Hume, we should be sceptical of scientific results and keep in mind that our beliefs may stretch beyond the evidence and conclusions that science has to offer; science is a useful activity but should not lead us to dogmatic acceptance of its proclaimed 'knowledge'.

Immanuel Kant (1724–1804) thought that sceptics were asking the wrong question. For him, we do know *something* and the philosophical problem is to find out *how* this is possible. He concludes that the character of the world as it is (what he calls the 'noumenal world of objects') is known only after it has been processed by our minds and is apparent to us as the 'phenomenal' world. In other words, we cannot know objects directly but only as mental phenomena. He accepted that sceptical arguments may indeed cast doubt on what we know about the noumenal world but our task is to understand what knowledge we have of the phenomenal world. From this, he concludes sceptical arguments are irrelevant.

Since the beginning of the twentieth century, 'common-sense' philosophers have attacked this sort of abstract thinking (language philosophers such as Bertrand Russell (1872–1970), G. E. (George Edward) Moore (1873–1958) and Ludwig Wittgenstein (1889–1951), and 'logical positivists' of the Vienna School most notably A. J. (Alfred Jules) Ayer (1910–1989)) . Moore took the view that if I can see two hands in front of me then there is nothing else worth considering in the matter. However, if we attempt a philosophical analysis of the problem (e.g. 'Are these two hands really mine?'), this everyday working proposition is insufficient for the task.

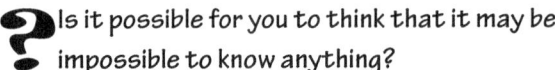
Is it possible for you to think that it may be impossible to know anything?

Rationalism and empiricism
Scepticism leaves us unsure about how we may know something and this leads to the fundamental question of whether in the first place there is anything there to know.

Something in the universe that exists prior to our experience of it is called existence a priori and knowledge of it a priori knowledge. In other words, if we take ourselves (as conscious beings) out of the system, there are entities in the system (e.g. 2+2=4) that still exist even though we are not there to be conscious of them. On the other hand, knowledge that we know by experience (e.g. scientific or empirical knowledge) we call a posteriori knowledge.

Plato, Descartes and Gottfried Wilhelm Leibniz (1646–1716) we call rationalists in that they believed that true a priori knowledge could be discovered by rational thought as opposed to experiment.

Aristotle (384–322 BC) accepts this in part, believing that although we should start out from experience using a posteriori knowledge, true knowledge, or 'science' (as causes, axioms, principles) is logically prior to that experience and so a priori).

On the other hand Hume, John Stuart Mill (1806–1873) and, to some extent, John Locke (1632–1704) we call empiricists in that they believed true knowledge could be discovered by analysis of the world as opposed to simply thinking about it. Such knowledge we have via (or after) our sense experience and is thus a posteriori. However, if according to Hume, there is nothing logically certain about our sense experience and our sense experience is our only way of knowing anything, there is nothing logically certain about anything that we 'know'. Any so-called 'universal' condition (e.g. the Universal Law of Gravitation) may well have held good up to this point in time but there is nothing to say it will hold good for all future time.

Kant took on Hume's damning scepticism and by a sophisticated system of explanation tried to show that knowledge starts out from experience but does not arise from it — that knowledge is dependent on what is given a priori. In this way, Kant harmonises and passes beyond the conflict (and entrenched camps) of rationalism and empiricism.

> **?** If I see something and it looks blue, have I good reason to believe that the object is the same colour that I see?

Pragmatism

Pragmatism came about as a reaction to philosophical rationalism. It upholds a concept of acceptance of the world as it appears to be. These days we generally understand it as some sort of rule system by which we test standards according to how they seem to work out. Pragmatism takes different forms. Charles Sanders Peirce (1839–1914) saw pragmatism as a way of developing impersonal and objective standards tested by empirical results (e.g. scientific prediction or experiment). William James (1842–1910) saw pragmatism as testable by the efficacy and success it bestows on the individual. John Dewey (1859–1952) saw the pragmatic test rooted in the moral and aesthetic beliefs of ordinary people.

> ❓ 'The fact is that's how things are. There is no point in worrying about it.' Is it reasonable to apply this way of thinking to the following: an illness that kills many people that is presently incurable; the disturbance of a persistently barking dog chained up in the next door neighbour's garden; growing civil unrest in a nation torn by social strife?

Certainty

Only something indubitable is certain (i.e. absolutely beyond doubt). Anything we feel 'certain' of remains open to some degree of sceptical doubt. Descartes suspected much of our conventional certainty could be doubted and believed that scepticism would be defeated only if a genuine certainty is available. He thought that the act of thinking provided this certainty, but the analogy of the 'brain in the vat' shows us that even though we may know we are thinking we cannot be certain that what we are thinking is right.

> ❓ Can you be certain that what you are thinking now is true?

Further questions

These questions challenge some of our basic assumptions about how we experience life, our belief in the nature of the universe and our understanding of the nature of self. Try to investigate all possibilities for doubt no matter how this goes against apparent common sense.

1. I stand on a drawing pin with my bare foot and I get a pain. Do I know the drawing pin has caused the pain?
2. If the telephone rings it means that someone is calling me. Is this true?

3. I believe that I am immortal even though there is no human being who has so far been verified as living any longer than 122 years. Is this a reasonable view to hold?

4. I believe the earth is flat. Is this a reasonable view to hold?

5. I believe that the sun will rise tomorrow because it rose yesterday. Is it possible to disagree with this?

6. There are particles that are too small for detection and some, like electrons, that change their position according to whether or not they are observed. Why should I believe in such things any more than unicorns or fairies?

7. How can I tell when I am dreaming and when I am awake? What are the tests I can use to prove this?

8. Would it make any difference to me if when I think I am awake I were really dreaming?

9. Is it possible that when I think I am dreaming I am really awake and when I think I am awake I am really dreaming? If you think it is possible then why do we all think that when we are awake we are not dreaming? If you think it is not possible, explain why you believe this.

10. 'I know that there must be a real world because I am aware of this thought.' Is there any way that such a thought could be wrong?

Further reading

René Descartes, *Meditations on First Philosophy, with Selections from the Objections and Replies*, trans. Michael Moriarty, Oxford World Classics (Oxford: Oxford University Press, 2008).

Edith Hamilton and Huntington Cairns (eds), *The Collected Dialogues of Plato including the Letters* (Princeton: Princeton University Press, 1961).

Hilary Putnam, *Reason, Truth and History* (Cambridge: Cambridge University Press, 1981), Chapter 1.

Bertrand Russell, *The Problems of Philosophy* (Oxford: Oxford University Press, 1986), Chapters 1, 7 and 11.

Roger Scruton, *Modern Philosophy: An Introduction and Survey* (London: Pimlico, 2004), Chapter 22.

6

Perceiving the World

Can 'I' actually touch an object? If I can then this must mean that 'I' am the same thing as my sense experience. Does this make sense?

Introduction

Scepticism causes us to doubt much of what we perceive in the world. However, in our everyday lives we share a view, a common-sense realism, that the world consists in real objects that we sense. If we did not think this, we would find it difficult to live with any degree of reliance on the world around us (e.g. we might decide to sit on a chair we did not think was there) and would soon lose grip on our sanity. Nevertheless, if we ask ourselves how we actually 'know' that these objects exist, the only answer available is that we know they exist via our senses. In other words, if there is an object in the world, 'I' (as the 'knower') do not 'know' it directly; I only 'know' the sensations I have. If anything is in 'contact' with the object, it is not me but the sensing apparatus that sends me the information (the 'sense data'). For example, if I touch something hot and feel a pain, the pain I am feeling is caused by the sensation I am having. My only 'contact' is therefore between the sense data and me, and the sense data are a result of my sensing apparatus (not 'me') having contact with what they sense. This is not so odd as it may seem at first. It would, after all, be unusual to imagine that the pain itself rests in the object I touched and that therefore I 'touched' pain.

> **?** Does it make sense to think that 'I' am somehow separate from the world around me even though my body is part of that world of objects?

Representative realism

Representative realism accepts the difficulty of being separate from the objects of our senses. It proposes that although the picture of the world that I have in my mind is a mental one, it nevertheless represents something that is real.

This was the view proposed by John Locke (1632–1704) — an empiricist who believed in the facts of science. He accepted that although many of our sensations are a product of sensing in itself (e.g. sensing the pain), the objects that we sense are themselves real. An object, on his view, has what he calls 'primary qualities', qualities it has in itself irrespective of it being perceived (like shape). Sensations we have which are derived from our contact with, but are not part of, these objects (like pain) are 'secondary qualities'. Secondary qualities are not held by the object itself and are the subject of perception.

> How can we know that a smooth, round and blue object is smooth, round and blue? Do we have any direct evidence for believing in any of these qualities?

Causal realism

Causal realism holds that the primary fact is that the world exists and that we perceive it (more or less) accurately. Our perceptual processes provide us with information that bears a strong (if not complete) resemblance to the world. On this view, the world exists in its entirety in the absence of any perception and therefore has a reality all its own. This interpretation of the world, however, leaves us wondering how some things that we experience (e.g. love, volition, embarrassment) can possibly have a place outside our mental self. In addition, if the external world is real even without my mental self, what sort of reality can I attribute to the mental experiences that I have?

> If I feel unhappy, what has caused this: the world, my mental self, or a mixture of the two? If it is the world, where is the object 'happiness' that exists in the world? If it is my mental self, where has the emotion come from if not from the world? If it is a mixture of the two,

how is it that the world of objects and my mental self can correspond?

For all realism arguments the problem remains that 'I' do not have direct contact with the objects I sense. Even though I may be strongly encouraged to believe in real objects of the world (by common sense or for the sake of sanity), my experience gives me no certainty of their existence. Because of this, a high level of philosophical scepticism remains and this takes a variety of forms.

Idealism
Bishop George Berkeley (1685–1753) was an idealist (he believed that everything we know is mental). He proposed that the world is unknowable unless it is perceived — *esse est percipi*, to be is to be perceived. He thought that although it may be that the contents of the room remain in existence when I am not in the room (or the room itself for that matter), he was sceptical about how we can possibly know this. He concluded that in order to prevent things jumping in and out of existence according to whether I am there to perceive them or not, things must be perceived all the time by another — God.

> What evidence do we have to prove that what we think is outside this room is truly there? Is any such evidence incontrovertible? If so, how?

Extreme idealism leads us to solipsism, the conclusion that we are the only mind in existence and that all others (and other things) are part of our own mental process.

> Is it possible that everything we think we know is all the content of one person's imagination? For example, could everybody else you are aware of all be in your mind? If this were so, why do you think you are a separate individual?

Our experience of the world is a dream
René Descartes (1596–1650) (a thorough-going global sceptic) supposed that everything we think we know could be a dream, or worse, that an evil demon makes things seem as they are even though they are not.

The difference between the dreaming and waking world seems slight, and our senses provide little conclusive information (our dreams can provide all the experiences we have in the waking world). However, we use additional information from others (people or objects) to check on how our lives progress (e.g. we find continuity in talking to our friends and feel supported by the knowledge they have of us, or by reading books that were the same books we read before). If we returned to the same dream every time we slept (at the point at which we last left off) and 'woke up' into an entirely different world each day (or perhaps sometimes did not 'wake up' for several days at a time), then we might tend to favour the dreaming world as the 'real' world. That this is not the case is our strongest guarantee of the distinction between the two.

> **?** Can you prove that everything you think you know is not just a dream?

Internal realism
Hilary Putnam (1926–) accepts both the real world and the contents of our mind but in various weights according to need. He reinterprets Descartes' evil demon as the 'brain in the vat' — that we are like a brain in a vat with connections leading from our vat to the outside world (or whatever is outside our vat), but with us, as the brain, having contact only with the messages brought in via the connections. All the images we 'see' or 'feel' are, therefore, a product of the sensing system. The origin of those sensations is unknown and could be subject to any sort of deception, trickery or misinterpretation. Our experience is therefore an illusion (that we believe an object has certain qualities when it does not and vice versa).

> **?** Imagine yourself as a telephone exchange with connections to a huge number of subscribers each of whom sends information to you about themselves. You have no other sources of information. How can you tell

that the information your subscribers are sending is in any way true?

Hallucination

When we see or believe something not seen or believed by the 'public' world, we call it a hallucination. As individuals, we are not in a position to check on the experiences of others directly (e.g. I cannot tell whether someone else experiences exactly the same colour or shape that I do), but I can check with others whether they see something that I can agree is more or less the same. This constant checking process allows me to be fairly sure that my world is not my personal hallucination. However, still there remains doubt. Bertrand Russell (1872–1970) suggested it is possible that we all share a commonly remembered though unreal past, a sort of global, group hallucination.

> What reasons do I have for believing that not everything I think I know is a hallucination?

Memory

If we doubt our memories then no explanations of the world and our perception of it are sound. It is certainly possible that we all came into existence ten minutes ago with our supposed memories already built in, though the likelihood of such an extreme case (even though difficult to dispute) seems small.

> Ms X claims that a supernatural being created the world this morning at 9.30 a.m. She says that we only think the world existed before then because the supernatural being also created all our memories. You suspect that she might be mistaken in this belief but what evidence can you offer to disprove her claim?

Phenomenalism

Like idealism, phenomenalism, expressed by John Stuart Mill (1806–1873) as 'eliminative induction', doubts the existence of real objects and acknowledges that what we know is a mental experience. However, unlike idealism (which demands the perceiver to be there perceiving in order to guarantee the existence of the object), phenomenalism accepts the possible existence of objects even when they are not being perceived. However, it is difficult to accept the one principle without the other. It does not seem possible to describe objects that are both reliant on sense experience and have an identity (albeit only a possible one) without the use of sense experience. Like the idealist, the phenomenalist lives in a private world that cannot provide the sort of external checks necessary to guarantee the existence of the outside world.

Further questions

These questions investigate some sceptical ideas. They can be difficult to deal with as common-sense realism dominates our everyday lives and it is hard to abandon the views that go with it. However, scepticism is at the root of philosophical investigation and you should press yourself for imaginative resolutions. There is a tendency to give scientific explanations to such questions as 7. However, philosophical enquiry must go beyond this. The best overall conclusion to this exercise would be that though we may not believe a particular sceptical view, at the same time we have no true reasons to accept that our common-sense experience is real.

1. If everything I know is a dream, would it make any difference to me?
2. If everything I know is a dream, would it make any difference to everyone else?
3. What is the difference between being awake and having a dream? Work out ways of checking this.
4. Here are three ways that might help us distinguish between being awake and dreaming. Assess each one.
   a. I wake up from my dreams into the same world in which I went to sleep but I do not necessarily start dreaming from where I left my last dream.
   b. Sigmund Freud (1856–1939) showed that our dreams reflect our waking experiences but that our waking experiences do not necessarily reflect our dreams.
   c. We are all having the same waking experience now but our dreams will be different.

5. What precisely is the nature of a hallucination? How can we prove that a hallucination is not real?
6. How can we disprove that we are not all 'brains in vats'?
7. If I can see things as they really are, then why does an object that is far away from me look smaller than when it is close? What is the actual size of such an object?
8. If there is an apple that we both have an image of, is it the same apple?
9. What would the universe be like in the absence of any conscious perception? For example, would it be dark?
10. If everything I know is in my mind, does that mean that everyone I know is also in my mind?
11. What reasons have you for believing that the world did not come into existence 10 seconds ago?

Further reading

George Berkeley, *Principles of Human Knowledge and Three Dialogues*, Oxford World Classics (Oxford: Oxford University Press, 2009).

Richard Feldman, 'Evidence', in Jonathan Dancy and Ernest Sosa (eds), *A Companion to Epistemology* (Oxford: Basil Blackwell, 1994), pp. 119–22.

Thomas Nagel, *The View from Nowhere* (Oxford: Oxford University Press, 1986).

Bertrand Russell, *The Problems of Philosophy* (Oxford: Oxford University Press, 1986), Chapters 2, 3, 4 and 5.

7
Mind

Am I a body with a brain or a body with a brain and a mind? What is the difference?

Introduction

I speak of 'myself' but what or who is the self that I claim to be 'me'? David Hume (1711–1776) thought that 'we' are nothing but a bundle of perceptions. However, if this is so then why do 'I' think there is a 'me'? 'I' seem able to regard 'my' own bundle of perceptions as if 'I' was in some sense separate from them, but this would seem unlikely if 'I' actually were them.

The concept of 'me' is difficult to analyse. If I think, then 'I' am not only the thought of thinking but also the object of my thoughts, or if 'I' wish, then 'I' am not only the wish of the wishing but also the object of my wishing. But my thoughts and wishes change from moment to moment whereas 'I', the thinker and wisher, do not — 'I' am the constant presence, 'I' am my self-consciousness, 'I' am myself as the subject of my experiences, the holder of my beliefs, the 'owner' of my own history. In this, we occupy an exclusive position in the world, for although animals and machines may 'know' their environment (e.g. animals respond to their environment and modify it accordingly, machines operate according to external instructions) only a self-conscious being knows that it is the 'knower'.

? *Am I simply what I think, or is it 'I' doing the thinking?*

Being self-aware is puzzling and raises a stream of questions. How can I be both me and myself being aware of me? When I think thoughts like this, in what way can I describe these contents of my mind? Do these thoughts differ from sense impressions or ideas? Are thoughts truly not extended in space and time? If they are not, then can we assume that they are indestructible? If they are indestructible, then do they constitute a soul or spiritual self? And still after this, where do I find me?

> **When I think something what does that 'something' constitute?**

As the knower of myself, I have both the ability to be myself and to regard myself as an entity as if I was separate. The peculiar sensation of somehow being able to regard myself as both subject and object is what Thomas Nagel (1937–) calls the 'view from nowhere'.

> **When I talk about 'me', to whom or to what am I referring?**

Dualism
Those who believe the mind a substance separate from the body are called dualists. St Augustine (354–430) believed 'I' am a soul 'chained' to a body. René Descartes (1596–1650) believed my mind to be a mental 'substance', separate but somehow in contact with my body. Dualists regard the mind (the soul or spirit) as the source of consciousness. The mind is, according to Plato (c.428–347 BC), the rational element of our being, the higher order of existence that allows us to transcend the physical world of appearance.

Although we all feel we have or are a mind, the nature of mind itself is elusive. It cannot be scientifically investigated (no one has ever held a mind in their hands). In addition, it is difficult to fit in with evolutionary theory, because if our distant ancestors (as single-celled creatures) did not have minds then it is hard to see where our consciousness came from. After all, how can the mind, which is apparently so different from physical existence, emerge from physical existence? In addition, if mind and body have completely different qualities, it is difficult to see how they interact.

There have been a number of attempts to get around these problems: mind/body parallelism, in which the mental and physical are separate but work together in coincidental parallel; occasionalism, which is like parallelism but where, instead of mental and physical operations being coincidental, they are directed by the hand of God; and epiphenomenalism, which states that mental events are caused by physical ones but not the other way around: in other words, that the mind is some sort of shadowy epiphenomenon of the body.

If we can accept that mind and body do interact in some way (which, if dualism is true, seems the case), dualism still poses a problem because the idea that thought itself brings about something physical contravenes a basic scientific principle. For example, if thought can allow my will to affect my bodily movements, then why can I not will other things in the world to move?

> **?** If I have a mind and a body, it seems reasonable that they are in some way connected. However, if my mind is not physical how can it 'connect' to my body?

Physicalism
As the dominance of scientific thinking continues to consolidate on the everyday thinking of human beings, we increasingly interpret everything in the world as something physical. Those who believe that all our mental functions are in some way part of our physical nature we call 'physicalists'.

Type-identity theory
Type-identity theory states that mental states are themselves merely brain processes. However, if this is the case, how is it that we know mental states as thoughts (as well as 'our' thoughts, and 'our' selves) but not brain processes? On this argument, thoughts must be located where brain processes are so we should be able to find them, but this has never been the case. In addition, thoughts are always about something yet brain processes do not seem to be about anything, they are simply the states the brain is in according to the information received and the processing in progress. Brain states themselves also seem to ignore what it is like to feel sensations (e.g. of pain, love, embarrassment), whereas 'me' as my mind seems deeply involved in such things. Ignoring this is ignoring what separates us from other living species that do not have consciousness.

On this account, brain processes are the same as mental states. If two different people had the same brain state (e.g. they were both exclusively thinking about the same weather), then their mental states should be the same. But, under such circumstances, each individual retains their 'own' thoughts of the weather that are typically different from the other's 'own' thoughts about the same weather.

Token-identity theory
Token-identity theory tries to get around the problem of different thinkers experiencing different thoughts about the same thing by distinguishing between 'type' (which is the species) and 'token' (which is the individual instance). Therefore, individual tokens of a particular type of thought (e.g. my thoughts about the weather) are not necessarily physical states of precisely the same type (e.g. the weather that me and others are thinking about). This is because mental properties, such as my mental response to the weather, supervene (i.e. go above) physical properties and cause individual experiences to be different. However, this reintroduces a distinction between mind and body that seems even more mysterious than (and not all that different from) mind/body dualism.

> **?** If two people had exactly the same experiences from birth, would they have identical minds?

Behaviourism
Behaviourism claims that the mind/body problem is a pseudo-problem, a fixation on a fictitious distinction. Gilbert Ryle (1900–1976), in his *Concept of Mind*, called it 'the dogma of the ghost in the machine'. Ryle proposed that what appears to be mental (and so private) is in fact a description of a person's public behaviour and that is an outcome of the circumstances that influence the person. On this account 'I' am merely a product of the world around me.

However, behaviourism does not allow for the feeling that I am 'me' — what it feels like to be in some particular state. It does not explain how 'I' come to know things by introspection and it cannot distinguish between genuine and pretend behaviour. On this view, someone completely paralysed should not have any mental experience (there is no physical behaviour to provide the experience), but this is clearly not the case.

The behaviourist thinks that behaviour itself (influenced by the world) causes belief, but often our experience is that this is the other way around. For example, I *believe* it will rain so I *will* wear my raincoat.

> **?** A certain view would claim that nothing was truly my fault (e.g. the car crash happened because of

the weather, the murder happened because someone else made the gun). Are there limits to such a view?

Functionalism

Functionalism ignores the problem of the brain and its states. It concentrates on the relations between different sorts of thoughts and behaviour in much the same way that one might concentrate on the relations between different software in a computer (as opposed to how the software relates to the hardware). In this way, it sidesteps the mind/body relation problem and reduces mental states to functional manipulation of information.

Nevertheless, functionalism does not provide an adequate account of what it is like to understand. John Searle (1932–) proposed a thought experiment he called the 'Chinese room'. Alone in a room, you receive information through a window, process it according to laid down rules and pass it out of another window. If the process is conducted in Chinese and you do not understand Chinese then you would not come to understand it by fulfilling your role in the process. There seems a clear distinction (even if the connection is blurred) between manipulation and understanding which functionalism does not take into account.

> *A functionalist believes that if we could analyse all the information that constitute the thoughts of an individual then we would know that individual's mind. Is this reasonable?*

Other minds

Because 'I' am intimately involved with 'myself', I say with some confidence that 'I' know 'I' am 'me'. However, because of the interlinking of mind and body (or its identity) and the body's isolation from others, it is difficult to be sure that other minds actually exist and that, if they do, their experiences of others are in any way similar to my own.

This is not a problem for the behaviourist (who attributes mental experiences to others on the basis of their behaviour which can be externally observed), or for the functionalist (who believes that the manipulative processes of another mind can be established by analysing its output) but, by any other account, there is no direct experience of other minds.

Most of our evidence for other minds comes from analogy. Because others seem to act (more or less) in the same ways that I do I conclude that they must be (more or less) similarly conscious and have a mind (more or less) like mine.

However, analogous arguments require a lot of supporting evidence, and in the case of mind, the only support comes from myself (that is, 'I' am the only comparative example). In addition, others often act in more ways differently from me than they act in ways that are the same (e.g. others get more upset about the same thing, others feel happier about the same thing). Apparent evidence of the behaviour of others is insufficient: people can lie about what they think; they can pretend, or perhaps they can be programmed by an evil demon to seem conscious beings when they are not. Added to which, the argument from analogy is only inductive and so cannot provide conclusive proof. However, on balance, it is more reasonable to adopt the view that there are other minds than to adopt solipsism (that is, that we are the only mind and everything is the content of that one mind).

> **?** Describe how it would be possible to guarantee that someone else is having exactly the same thought or image that you are.

Memory

It may be that 'I' am simply the total or the content of my memories. Recollection of my previous experience may compose itself into a system of experiences I conveniently call 'me'. After all, it would be difficult and long-winded to have to recount all previous experiences in order to demonstrate selfhood, in the same way that it would be difficult and long-winded to fix points in past time without a measure of time (e.g. 10 years ago) by using references only to what point in time we want to establish as being before certain events and after others (e.g. before the Battle of Waterloo and later than the Roman occupation of Britain).

> **?** Could I possibly claim to be 'me' if I could not remember anything?

▶▶▶▶See also Further questions 1◀◀◀◀

When is it still me?
Bodily continuity (as opposed to mental continuity) is the usual test for deciding whether it is 'I' that continues to be 'me'. But this is not always convincing. For example, a dead body continues to exist even though we consider the 'person' no longer 'there'.

Even so, if continuous bodily existence is interrupted we have problems justifying continuity of the person. For example, we could suppose that we pass out of existence when we are in dreamless sleep. In *Star Trek*, characters are 'transported' from one place to another by being broken down into their molecular parts then reassembled elsewhere. In this case, the person has passed out of existence and then come back into existence; by all accounts this amounts to being dead then coming back to life. In this case, we would also want to know if when Captain Kirk is reassembled it truly is Captain Kirk's body, after all, 'continuous' bodies do not travel between points in space without covering the distances in between those points.

Mental continuity or memory does not seem so important. In cases of amnesia, where a person has no recollection of their previous history or, in the case of complete short-term memory loss, where even knowledge of self-identity is lost, the person still continues as a recognisable individual. Someone in a persistent vegetative state who shows no mental or behavioural activity may be considered 'brain-dead' but is still a living bodily existent that we recognise as a person.

Cases of multiple personality (real or fictional) corrupt the view that 'I' am only one person, discrete and separate from all others. In Corbett H. Thigpen's (1919–1999) and Hervey M. Cleckley's (1903–1984) *The Three Faces of Eve*, three separate personalities inhabit the same body. In Robert Louis Stevenson's (1850–1894) *Dr Jekyll and Mr Hyde*, two separate personalities struggle for supremacy in one body. In Franz Kafka's (1883–1924) *Metamorphosis*, a person's mind moves from a human body into the body of an insect.

▶▶▶▶See also Further questions 2◀◀◀◀

Further questions 1
These questions look at aspects of all the central mind/body theories. Try to test out your ideas fully here. With advances in cognitive science, our understanding of the working of the brain and the linking of brain activity

to higher level thinking causes us to question much of how we view mind. This is an area where there remains a great deal of philosophical uncertainty and research. It is a good example of the premature release from philosophy of an insufficient body of knowledge to the new science of psychology in the late nineteenth century. The subsequent return of many of these insufficiently worked theories to philosophy in the late twentieth century indicate the 'questioning service' which philosophy provides to all human enquiry.

1. Who is the 'I' that I refer to when I talk about myself?
2. Is the word 'mind' interchangeable with the word 'brain'? Give examples to back up your opinion.
3. If the mind is not physical then how does it interact with the body? After all, a physical effect like lifting my arm requires a physical cause and if my mind is not physical then how can it bring about a physical effect?
4. If my own non-physical mind can affect my own physical actions, can it also directly affect the physical actions of others? For example, could I will some else's arm to rise?
5. If the mind is not physical then it cannot have a physical position in space. If this is so, then where is my mind? If it is 'inside' my body then it must be physically confined, but how can this be the case for something non-physical? If it is 'outside' my body, then how can I think it is mine?
6. How can I know what is going on in someone else's mind?
7. If mental telepathy is true, could I experience someone else's embarrassment directly?
8. If a person in a persistent vegetative state is considered 'brain dead', must that person also be considered 'mind dead'?
9. Could I genuinely claim to have one body and two minds? Could I genuinely claim to have two bodies and one mind?
10. Would it be possible for a mind to exist without a body?
11. If my body disappeared, would I still think I existed?
12. If my body disappeared and I lost all my memories, would I still think I existed?
13. How can we prove that we are not part of a computer program (e.g. *The Matrix* (1999)) or in a deceiving TV programme (e.g. *The Truman Show* (1998))?

Further questions 2

This question tests our ability to think in detail about ideas that do not form part of the everyday world of experience. This type of abstract thinking is essential to philosophy. The question follows a theme by bringing in further examples, all of which should be answered in some way, without losing track of the initial question about personal identity. As such, it is an example of how to pursue a tight philosophical line.

Generally speaking, if I continue to have the same body and memory then I am accepted as 'me'. Would it still be 'me' in the following cases? If you think not, then who would 'I' be?

a. If I completely lost my ability to remember anything.
b. If I completely lost my memory say an hour ago but could remember everything since the point at which I lost my memory.
c. If I suddenly lost all my memories but they were replaced with someone else's memories.
d. If I had 'my' memories on Mondays, Wednesdays and Fridays but someone else's memories on all the other days of the week.
e. If I had not only my own memories but also someone else's memories at the same time.
f. If my body suddenly changed into someone else's but I retained my own (original) memories.
g. If my body suddenly changed into someone else's and, at the same time, I took over all their memories and lost mine.
h. If I turned into an insect but retained my own memories.
i. If I turned into an insect but took on the memories of another human being.
j. If I turned into an insect and took on the memories of the insect, and lost all my own memories.
k. If I took over the body of another person whom, though previously thinking herself an insect, now thinks she is me.
l. If I disappeared and reappeared instantly in another part of the world still with all my memories.
m. If I disappeared and reappeared instantly in another part of the world having lost my memory.
n. If I disappeared then reappeared 10 years later with no recollection

of the intervening period but still with all my memories before my disappearance.
o. If I disappeared and lost all my memories but still believed I existed.

Further reading

Paul M. Churchland, *Matter and Consciousness* (Cambridge, MA: MIT Press, 1988).

David Hume, *A Treatise of Human Nature*, 2nd edn, (ed.) P. H. Nidditch (Oxford: Oxford University Press, 1978), Book 1, Part 4, Chapter 6.

Thomas Nagel, *Mortal Questions* (Cambridge: Cambridge University Press, 1979), Chapters 11 and 12.

Hilary Putnam, *Reason, Truth and History* (Cambridge: Cambridge University Press, 1981), Chapter 1.

Roger Scruton, *Modern Philosophy: An Introduction and Survey* (London: Pimlico, 2004), Chapter 4.

8

Right and Wrong

What is the worst thing a human being can do? Why is this so bad?

Introduction

We should always be suspicious about any view that purports to illustrate what is right or wrong. According to Friedrich Wilhelm Nietzsche (1844–1900), most moral philosophers end up justifying 'a desire of the heart that has been filtered and made abstract' (*Beyond Good and Evil*).

It is useful to distinguish between 'ethical', meaning what it is that constitutes the good, and 'moral', which is the term we can use to describe how we act or to describe the rules of conduct that govern those actions. These terms are often interchanged but sometimes this can be confusing.

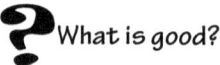What is good?

Good

The root of all ethical enquiry is what is 'good'. Aristotle (384–322 BC) believed that 'good' is a state of happiness. This idea underlies most ethical theories that vary more in respect of how and, most importantly to whom, happiness should be applied, than whether or not happiness itself is the ethical goal. If I think it is my state of happiness that should be the measure of good, then I am an egoist. If I think it is the state of happiness of others, then I am an altruist.

Moral dilemmas

Moral judgement is bound up with some notion of proportionality and it is the desire to attain some sort of moral symmetry between competing views that guides our moral thinking. Moral doubts occur when the negative aspects of the means seem greater than the positive aspects of the ends. When this occurs the essentially physical aspects of a situation take on a moral character. For example, someone may wish to kill himself or herself because he or she is terminally ill and in great pain — the end would seem justified — however, there is a competing claim for this person's life in the form of a religious claim on the sanctity of life. If the latter case is made strongly (as it is), then the simple situation becomes a moral dilemma.

> **?** Is there any reason why someone terminally ill and in great pain should not be allowed to take his or her own life?

How we should act

There are three major groups of theories that describe how we should act or behave (philosophers call them 'first-order' theories): duty-based, consequence and virtue. Though the different theories have separate starting points, when we start to consider their application their distinctions tend to blur.

Duty-based theories

Duty-based theories propose that some things are right or wrong irrespective of their consequences. According to duty-based theories, the most important thing about moral action is its application according to a deeper inner sense of responsibility to the wishes of God or to ethical standards deemed unassailably right. The two most prominent examples of duty-based ethical theories in the Western world are Christian ethics and Kantian ethics.

Christian ethics

Christian ethics are based on God's law distilled into instructions for conduct: 'love your neighbour as yourself', 'do unto others as you would have them do unto you' and so on. These rules do not have to prove themselves right because God's wisdom is perfect and so his wish that these instructions be followed is unchallengeable. Examples in Christian writings vindicate the application of these rules. Nevertheless, primarily, a sense of duty to Christian ethics is reliant upon the existence of God. If God does not exist then not only must anything be permitted (a view expressed by Fyodor Dostoevsky (1821–1881)), but also following his will when he does not exist is ethically perverse.

Even if God does exist, can we really be sure of God's will? We are often faced with conflicting views concerning the same issue both of which God's will seems to approve (e.g. it is wrong to kill someone because you don't like them, but it is right to kill them in a just war). It is usual, in cases like this, to assume that God wishes the conflict to be the case (perhaps as a test) or that we are confused about his wishes. In addition, as far as we know, the rules have been created arbitrarily by God's will. We do not know what led up to his deciding on the rules or whether or not they have some underlying universal quality of good. Utilising God's will to shape our moral actions requires that God exists, that we believe him to exist and that he is truly good.

> **?** If God had declared killing praiseworthy would it have been good because God had willed it and because God is good, or only because he willed it and we therefore think it is good (just because it is his will)?

The application of these principles raises many questions. For example, who is my neighbour? Is it someone who I know or everyone in the world? If I am a masochist or a liar should I do unto others as I would wish them to do unto me, that is, do others harm or always tell lies? Christian rules rely on my 'wants' because these measure how I should treat others. I cannot do unto others as I would have them do unto me without my 'want' to be treated in a certain way. Because of the variation in individual 'wants' this view is difficult to apply.

> **?** Is it right that I should steal things that belong to other people (because I want to) as long as I do not mind that they steal from me (perhaps I consider myself a better thief and so assume I will always gain overall)?

Kantian ethics

Immanuel Kant (1724–1804) held views on how we should behave which are sometimes unfairly seen as cold or inhuman. Kant believed that people should be treated as ends in themselves, never as means to ends. In other words, in our dealings with people we must always recognise their humanity. In this context, Kant believed that we should be responsible for our actions but not for the consequences of our actions which may be out of our control. This is based on the idea that although we may think we can know many of the consequences of how we act, we only have to imagine a few years into the future to realise that this connection (of action to consequence) soon becomes impossible to plot.

Because of this, Kant believed that the only way to govern our actions is by the use of a 'categorical imperative'. The categorical imperative is an instruction to be carried out as an absolute and unconditional duty: 'Act only on maxims which you can at the same time want to be universal laws.' In other words, you should only do something if you would be happy that everyone else did it too.

However, there are many difficulties with the categorical imperative. Though it is not hard to work out moral rules for me, it is more difficult to work out acceptable rules that can be applied to everyone. We might think that such imperatives as 'always tell the truth', 'always keep promises' or 'never kill another human being' are reasonable moral duties, but even these are difficult to apply universally. Should we tell the truth if it means that our friend would be unfairly punished? Should we keep a promise when this means that others will suffer? Should we hold back from killing anyone even though killing them is the only way of saving our friend or our own child?

The categorical imperative cannot cope well with conflicts of duty, for example, applying the maxim 'always tell the truth *and* protect a friend' when I am confronted by a psychopathic killer with an axe demanding to know the whereabouts of my friend. In addition, although there may be a dominant human perspective on moral action (e.g. most people would agree that lying was wrong or killing was bad) there will still be those who would not agree (e.g. the pathological liar or the psychopathic killer). Also, it is possible to universalise seemingly immoral acts (e.g. 'kill anyone who does not keep promises') without having a method of measuring such rules against any other ethical standard.

Overall, categorical imperatives lack a regard for human emotions (e.g. our affection for others may affect our moral view) and an absolute measure against which to test the imperatives themselves.

> **?** You are in an aircraft hijacked by terrorists. You know that your friend is a terrorist target and before the flight you promised her that you would never reveal her identity if a situation like this arose. A terrorist says to you that if you reveal the identity of the person they are looking for (your friend) then they will let everyone else go free. If you do not then they will kill everyone else on board. What do you do?

Consequence

Although all societies have categorical rules by which their citizens are expected to abide, the strongest influence in contemporary Western society on how we should act morally is based upon the prospective consequences of our actions.

Utilitarianism

Utilitarianism was a view formulated by Jeremy Bentham (1742–1832) and John Stuart Mill (1806–1873). For both of them the ultimate aim of moral action is hedonistic (an increase in happiness). However, even though they had different views about what happiness is — Bentham thought it a blissful state whereas Mill believed it found on an ascending scale of lower to higher pleasures the more refined pleasures (e.g. music or art) being higher on the scale — they both believed that 'amounts' or 'degrees' of happiness could be calculated. For example (on both their views), happiness is the absence of pain. So, if action X will bring about '+4' amount of happiness and '–3' amount of pain, the potential net gain in happiness of '+1' means that action X is the correct moral path to follow.

Not only is it hard to know if such calculations are using equivalent qualities (e.g. does one unit of happiness equal one unit of pain?) but calculating probable consequences is notoriously difficult. How do we know that an action we take will lead to particular consequences (particularly in the long or very long term)? We cannot see into the future so we can only extrapolate from known circumstances. This means that we do not know future events that influence later future events (e.g. child A, born in 50 years' time, influences the fate of the world in 100 years' time). The question of whether our moral actions should also apply to non-human species further complicates the issue. For example, we do not know at present whether or not the human race will be superseded by a species of creatures that currently we victimise and who may remember this in their future regard for human beings.

> **?** Is it appropriate to use inductive reasoning to establish moral actions? For example, killing animals to eat has always been acceptable so it must continue to be acceptable.

Utilitarianism also suffers from the same ethical vacuity as the categorical imperative. It can readily be used to justify actions that seem intuitively immoral (e.g. killing someone to deter violent crime, going to war for nationalistic reasons) or it can produce results that vindicate the happiness of the individual as more important than the happiness of the many. For example, millions of people may be only slightly troubled by the raising of a small tax against them (they may not even know it has been levied) by a ruler who uses the money to purchase a work of art the ownership of which gives him great happiness. Not paying back debts may lead to a net amount of greater happiness for the one who has avoided the payment, particularly if the one to whom the debt was owed was very rich and repayment was of little consequence.

If a 'blissful state' is the only aim, then drugs could be added to the public water supply to achieve this, and although utilitarianism might be able to calculate the net gain or loss of happiness, it could not resolve whether such action was moral or immoral.

> **?** Should we choose to save the life of one person who we know to be important to the welfare of society or 100 people who we know will have little influence on society's wellbeing?

Negative utilitarianism

Whereas ordinary (positive) utilitarianism tries to achieve an increase in happiness, negative utilitarianism only wants to reduce the amount of pain or suffering. For example, in order to achieve the greatest net gain in happiness, the positive utilitarian would share a fixed amount of money between 1,000 people (each of whom would gain a very small but calculable amount) against giving it all to a sick one (with great personal needs). On the other hand, to reduce the total amount of suffering, the negative utilitarian would give all the money to the sick one (whose suffering would be reduced) and ignore the others (whose well-being would be relatively, though positively, unaffected).

> **?** Is it possible to apply either negative utilitarianism or positive utilitarianism as separate principles irrespective of circumstances, or do circumstances dictate which one we should choose? Think of examples to back up your view.

Virtue

Aristotle believed that our actions should be dictated by inner reflection on the question 'how should I live?' He thought that if we encourage our virtuous self then it would lead us to a virtuous life and cause us to act morally to the highest ethical standards.

But, as well as being culturally influenced over time, our personal estimation of what is virtuous and good tends to be different from the estimations of others. Few of us get pleasure from exactly the same thing as others. Aristotle's theory assumes that there is such a thing as an absolute standard of virtue, but it is hard to see where this comes from. The application of such a principle could easily become (as Nietzsche points out) simply an extrapolation of our own wishes.

> **?** Can you think of something that is a true virtue? Could such a virtue be applied universally?

Applied ethics

Since the advent of utilitarianism and the obvious problems of both categorical imperatives and virtue theory there has been more concentration on the application of ethical theories (what philosophers call 'second order questions' or 'meta-ethics') than on what is ethically right in itself. In applied ethics (as moral conduct) we are forced to question the meaning of 'right' in human behavioural or evolutionary contexts.

We find the main thrust of this in 'naturalism', which draws its interpretations of what is moral from scientifically discovered facts about human nature (i.e. the way that most human beings behave or have behaved). On this, we act in a certain way because that is how we are (or have been). Exceptions to this, for example, someone who kills human beings for their own reasons, we consider aberrations from the 'norm' because we think that to kill someone is psychologically destructive. In just the same way someone who does not want to go to a state-condoned war and kill people for nationalistic reasons would be considered aberrant because (in these circumstances) not to kill someone would be considered psychologically destructive.

Existentialism

Existentialism is a form of individual naturalism that considers psychological destruction part of the innate nature of self. Jean-Paul Sartre (1905–1980) explained that human nature, in the way it is interpreted by science, is a self-deception and that we alone, as individuals, can make value judgements about how we act. The test for how we act is our response to an inner sense of what he called 'good faith' and our conduct should be guided by this alone.

> **?** How can I resolve the conflict of being asked to go to war for my country (and in the process protect my friends and family from the enemy) while, at the same time, believing that killing other human beings is wrong?

>>>> See also Further questions 1 <<<<

Is anything absolutely wrong?
It may be that our views about right and wrong are entirely human: that is, human beings invent them to deal with human problems. It may be that there are no truly right or wrong acts: in other words, there is nothing absolutely right or wrong. An 'ethical relativist' would say that nothing is absolutely right or wrong. For example, slavery was considered right at the time of the Greeks but wrong now. Our sense of right and wrong in this case is not dictated by God, imperative or virtue, but is derived from the way society views the activity of slavery. A.J. (Alfred Jules) Ayer (1910–1989), on a view called 'emotivism', said that ethical statements are meaningless, they are just expressions of emotion (like smiles or frowns). Therefore, if you say that slavery is wrong that is just your emotional response and you are articulating an emotional 'frown'.

>>>>See also Further questions 2<<<<

Further questions 1
The questions here tackle human problems, most of which we should be able to identify with or imagine, or for which we can readily find contemporary examples. A contemporary Western view is generally to reduce moral questions to a matter of consequence. To test this it is useful to argue the philosophical case for both duty and virtue-based theories, even though they may be considered less important in our own society.

1. Would it be morally right to cause another human being harm in any of the following circumstances?
  a. To protect my children.
  b. To protect a distant cousin who I liked.
  c. To protect a distant cousin who I did not like.
  d. To defend a national principle, for example, the retention of a national currency.
  e. To defend a friend whom I know would not defend me.
  f. To protect people I did not know on the weaker side in a conflict in a foreign country.
  g. To protect people I did not know on the stronger side in a conflict in a foreign country.

2. Some people would classify the following situations differently, for example: murder, attempted murder, manslaughter (unintentional killing), corporate killing (where a company, not an individual, is held responsible), suicide, euthanasia (helping someone or yourself to die), or accident. How would you classify them? Explain your reasoning.

    a. A friend is terminally ill, in great pain and wants to die. You help her die by giving her a fatal dose of poison that she bought herself for the purpose.

    b. A friend is terminally ill, in great pain and wants to die. You help her die by pushing her off the top of a 20-storey building when she is not looking.

    c. A man crashed his car into a wall in order to commit suicide but the crash caused the death of some children who were playing behind the wall.

    d. A child, while swinging on a rope suspended from a tree, falls and is killed. Later, it is discovered that the rope was manufactured from inferior-quality materials.

    e. An escaping prisoner shoots at a pursuing police officer but kills an innocent passer-by.

    f. In order to cut costs and keep shareholders dividends at an acceptable level, the signals at a busy railway junction are dimmed at night. A train crashes in the fog and all the passengers are killed.

    g. A man forgets to tell his wife that the brakes on their car are not working very well. At the bottom of a steep hill, she cannot stop and is killed when the car goes over a cliff.

    h. A woman is trapped on the twentieth floor of a burning building. She can see that the fire crews cannot reach her because their ladders are too short. She cannot bear the idea of being burned, jumps and is killed.

3. Are there any circumstances in which it is right to commit murder?

4. Are there any circumstances in which it is right to commit suicide?

5. In 2012, an 89-year-old Polish Nazi collaborator is discovered living in England where he has been since escaping from the Allied forces in 1944. It is said that he was responsible for the deaths of hundreds of Polish civilians in 1943. His life in England has been blameless and he is active in much charity work. Should he be made to stand trial?

6. Why do we consider slavery wrong? After all, for most of human history it has been considered right.

7. I want to give away £1 million. Should I give it one person and make her very happy or should I share it out between all the human beings on earth so that each would receive approximately one seventieth of a penny?

8. Because I do not know how the future will be affected by what I do now, should I be concerned with doing anything right? For example, I may help someone in a road accident and save his life, but 10 years later he is responsible for starting the next world war in which 100 million people die.

Further questions 2

The questions here invite you to think about the very nature of ethics; are they real or merely human constructs? If they are real in any sense, then they should be real in a universe without consciousness. If they are human constructs, themselves drawn from analysis of human behaviour, we must question their true meaning both as applied standards (all forms of behaviour do not carry moral purpose) and their reliability as absolute standards (when they themselves have not been derived from an absolute source).

1. If you were the only person in the world, would you need any ethical standards?

2. If there were no conscious beings in the universe would it still be possible to imagine that there could be a concept of right and wrong?

3. Other forms of life on earth do not seem to have any ethical standards. If we are part of an evolutionary process, and have evolved from species with no ethical standards, why should we believe that our human standards have ethical meaning?

4. Can you define 'good' and 'bad' without referring to human beings?

5. If you were a negative utilitarian, the best way to reduce all suffering would be to eliminate all sentient life. Does this make sense in any way?

6. Can a society set truth in morals? Define what you mean by a 'society' first.

7. Are there degrees of right and wrong or is something either 'just right' or 'just wrong'?

8. Should we ever put the consequences of our actions above our own desires?

Further reading

Susan Haack, 'Pragmatism', in Jonathan Dancy and Ernest Sosa (eds), *A Companion to Epistemology* (Oxford: Basil Blackwell, 1993), pp. 351–7.

Roger Scruton, *Modern Philosophy: An Introduction and Survey* (London: Pimlico, 2004), Chapter 20.

Peter Singer, *Ethics* (Oxford: Oxford University Press, 1994).

9

Equality

What does the state do to benefit us as individuals?

Introduction

Equality is to do with how individuals in a society are treated similarly. It therefore hinges on the moral position that individuals hold relevant to each other and to the society of which they are part.

Equality

Different people have different views of equality: its nature (whether it concerns wealth, opportunity, health, fame and so on), to whom we should be equal (those entitled to more benefits than us or those entitled to less), and whether that means us increasing the quality of our own situation or others decreasing theirs. Because true equality between humans is impossible (we are all naturally different), the state often sees its obligation more in how to reduce inequality using equal rights and so provide equality of conditions.

> **?** In an ideal world should we all be as rich as the richest or as poor as the poorest? Is either possible or desirable?

Natural and not-natural inequality

The diversity of humankind means there is a natural inequality. Accident of birth and a mixture of chances beyond our control largely dictate our fortune. We all have an idea about how our lives would be ideal, and this tends to be either at our existing level or above it to some degree or another (it would be unusual to wish for a less fortunate life). Because of this, our view about equality tends to lead us to the belief that everyone's life would ideally be at the point that we set for ourselves. Consequently, we may wish that everyone had good health, adequate food, opportunity for meaningful leisure and so on, because that is what we would wish for ourselves. Because we are all at different positions in society this leads to a plethora of ideal equalities.

Some inequalities are not natural; they are created by humans and can be corrected. For example, our modern view asserts that discrimination because of race, gender, age and the like is not natural (although primitive peoples may not have considered this the case). However, much inequality is still beyond our control and cannot be corrected by our own endeavours. A problem for the state is to decide whether pursuing social policies with an aim of increasing equality is an appropriate not-natural aim or is going against acceptable natural differences. Equal opportunity for different people with different abilities will produce different (and unequal) results.

A utilitarian view sees equality as having no value in itself, only in the benefits it can produce (in increasing happiness). On this basis, the redistribution of wealth downwards has positive effects in that, according to the principle of diminishing marginal utility, wealth transferred from rich to poor has a greater beneficial effect on the poor than it has a harmful effect on the rich.

> **?** Do we truly want everyone to be equal or do we only want what others better off than us possess?

It is a common (though probably mythical) view that, before societies became organised, individuals lived in an individual 'state of nature'. Such a state allowed individuals to express themselves, freely unhindered by the demands or rules of others. However, people progressively abandon the state of nature as they group together to trade for things they cannot produce themselves or because they need protection from other groups or from other individuals who do not share the same goals or aspirations. Ultimately this leads to the formation of a 'social state' — a 'state' composed of many.

> **?** What do you think it would be like to live in a 'state of nature'? What would be the main problems and what would be the main benefits?

The social contract

Most people these days live in a society made up of many individuals; most of us are part of a 'state'. Being a member of a society means we have to accept rules and responsibilities. As individuals we sometimes feel that some of the rules of the state are rules that we ourselves do not need; they are, we think, for everyone else. Sometimes this ends up with a compromise that does not work to our benefit. For example, we may think that we can drive safely at speeds above the speed limit but have to abide by the rules because the speed limit dictates the generally safe optimum speed for 'most people'. In order to benefit from membership of the state we have to accept the rules as willing participants. Life in a society demands that we contract with others. Accepting the social contract means giving away some of our rights in order to gain the protection of the state.

Our situation is made plain by a widely used game theory with many variations (constructed as the 'Prisoner's Dilemma' by Albert Tucker (1905–1995)). Two prisoners are put in separate cells. A proposition is put to them separately in this way. If neither confesses they will both go free. If one only confesses then he will go free while the other will be charged with a serious offence. If both confess each will be charged with a lesser offence. Each prisoner reasons that it is better to confess if the other confesses and better to confess if the other does not. Therefore, each confesses regardless and in so doing produces an outcome that is worse for them both had they each remained silent.

The Prisoner's Dilemma illustrates the problem of being part of a society: we do not know what everyone else is doing or thinking (e.g. we assume they are driving within the speed limit and thinking that everyone else is) and so give up many of our rights (or personal inclinations) on false beliefs. For example, we drive within the speed limit because we think that everyone else is doing the same even though we feel that we would be safe to drive above the speed limit.

A contract that we make has been viewed in different ways. Thomas Hobbes (1588–1679), having lived through the English Civil War, suggested that citizens contract to empower a sovereign who has supreme authority to enforce rules (laws). By doing this, citizens exchange 'war for peace', but have to accept their submission to a sovereign. John Locke (1632–1704) called the agreement we all make when we willingly accept membership of the state, the 'compact'. He believed this agreement enables citizens to exchange 'natural freedom' for 'civilised life' in a 'civil society'. According to Locke, we still submit to a sovereign, but individuals retain 'natural rights' such as the right to protect life, limb and property. Jean-Jacques Rousseau (1712–1778) built his theory on the idea of man's original 'state of nature'. He thought that by nature man is both good and free. For him, the social contract meant that the individual's innate freedom could only be overridden if every citizen together with all others takes every decision. This means that if no one chose to override their own individual freedoms then their freedom could not be overridden. In such a state, the sovereign's powers are limited to that of an executor of the people's wishes.

> **?** Is it right that you should not do something you wish to do because the state thinks that doing such a thing is not in your interest? Give examples.

Degrees of equality

Equality can be of different kinds (e.g. money, choice, access to health care) and for different reasons (e.g. out of respect for others, as a means of bringing about the most happiness, as a means of reducing suffering). It is not possible to be equal in all respects; for example, it is unlikely that we could attain human equality in height, weight, good looks, health, good luck or good fortune. We can only sensibly use the term 'equality' if it has a context. In other words, equality is only attainable in a conditioned as opposed to an absolute sense. So, although it may be worth striving for equality of opportunity or equality of access to health care, it is not worth striving for 'human equality' as a thing in itself.

> **?** We may all be equal in the eyes of God but does that make us equal in any real sense?

Economic equality — equal distribution of money

We might justify equal distribution of money on utilitarian grounds as a means of maximising happiness and minimising suffering. However, in practical terms, equal distribution of money is probably impossible.

Quickly the clever, deceitful or strong would gain over the ignorant, foolish and weak; some would save, some would squander, some gamble and some steal. The only way of controlling this would greatly reduce the individual's freedom and this in turn may lead to a reduction in overall happiness. At best, money can probably only be marginally more equally distributed (e.g. a single set wage for everyone, a tax system that penalised the rich and benefited the poor).

Some argue against the principle of equal distribution of money, saying that different financial rewards are necessary for different work functions or responsibilities, for the different levels of contribution individuals make to the state, in order to attract appropriate people to important jobs, or to fill vacancies where applicants are in short supply. It is also the case that some individuals need more money than others do. For example, those in need of expensive medical care or even those who would become clinically depressed if they could not lead a lifestyle dependent upon extra wealth. Equal distribution of money in itself may violate the individual's basic right to hold onto his or her property: that is, to save, attain goods by choice and become wealthy. Such a right has been thought by some (e.g. Robert Nozick (1938–2002)), a natural right and by others a nonsense (Jeremy Bentham (1748–1832) dismissed such a right as 'nonsense on stilts').

> **?** Someone who was brought up in a wealthy environment would be very unhappy if he or she had to live like most 'other people'. Is it right that the 'other people' should support this person's lifestyle?

Economic equality — equal opportunity in employment

Most Western democracies encourage equal opportunity in employment. Even so, although application procedures can afford increased equality of access to some jobs, job discrimination will always tend to take place according to aptitude, genetic makeup, social background or simply being in the right place at the right time. However, it is common to assert that no one should be discriminated against on racial or gender grounds, even though certain opportunities will always be gender-based. For example, a sperm donor will always be male and a human egg donor will always be female.

At any one time in a society, it may be that certain jobs are dominated by one gender or race. To adjust this imbalance an advocate of reverse discrimination would say that of two applicants the minority-applicant should be given the job. Generally, this would apply to equally qualified applicants, but some would say that, in order to redress an existing imbalance, a less qualified or less experienced applicant from the minority group should get the post. Reverse discrimination therefore discriminates against the majority-applicant. Reverse discrimination can only be a temporary measure until the same proportion as the proportion of the minority group to the whole of society is reflected in the particular employment group. In the case of gender, this is usually taken to be 50 %.

But, even with sophisticated monitoring, it is both difficult to accurately calculate the proportional balance (e.g. keeping figures up-to-date) and apply it appropriately (e.g. because of specific demographic differences). Selecting people in this way is not driven by the employment needs of an organisation but is a form of social manipulation (or engineering). Because it supports the minority-group, it can lead to a build up of resentment in the majority-group (because they consider it democratically unrepresentative) and this can be counter-productive.

> ❓ Race X is 90% of the total national population and race Y is 5%. In town A race X is 5% and race Y is 90%. For a job in town A, an employer decides to apply reverse discrimination based on the national statistic. Accordingly, she appoints the (national) minority applicant from race Y who is less well qualified than the (national) majority applicant from race X. What is your judgement on this?

Political equality — democracy

❓ What do you understand by the term 'democracy'?

Political democracy may take the form of a direct democracy where individuals express their views about how the state should be run by an ongoing system of voting, or it can take the form of a representative democracy where representatives are voted for at regular intervals to run the state. Democracy is in contrast to a monarchy or dictatorship that is ruled by one person or an oligarchy that is ruled by a few. No state allows everyone to vote (e.g. children, the mentally incapable, the constitutional monarch may be excluded), but such restrictions need to be limited to generally accepted categories and not used for political gain. For example, it would not be appropriate to restrict the voting rights of people who hold views against the state.

The best examples of early direct democracies were in Ancient Greece where many city-states brought everyone together to discuss the issues at hand before voting on them. These days, in large democracies, this method is considered impracticable (though a similar system still exists in Switzerland) and the favoured method is that (usually politically selected) individuals are 'voted in' for a known term as representatives of the electorate.

In a representative democracy, representatives are selected in a variety of ways (e.g. proportional representation, first-past-the-post, alternative vote) to represent the views of those that voted for them in a restricted forum (e.g. a parliament, a house of representatives). It is the representatives who discuss the matters of the state and vote (on behalf of the people) to decide issues that affect the running of the state. While representatives are in office, they are not responsible to those who elected them (in the sense that they do not ask the electorate how they should vote on any particular issue), but regular voting for the representatives ensures that they do things more or less in accordance with the wishes of the electorate. Representatives are deemed to be operating in the best interests of the individuals in society even though, for much of the time, they may be unaware of the best interests of every individual in society.

> **? Why should the rights of the majority count against the rights of the minority? What is it about a large number of people thinking the same thing that is in any way right?**

Although democracies provide a strong basis for economic wealth and appear to satisfy the demands made by individuals to have a say in the running of their state, there are a number of drawbacks. Karl Heinrich Marx (1818–1883) considered a representative democracy flawed. He believed the wishes of an undereducated electorate could be too easily manipulated by self-interested propaganda, or they could be duped into believing that a choice was on offer when there was actually no meaningful choice available. Plato (c.428–347 BC) believed that direct democracy would always bring about poor decision making because those who vote cannot possible be experts on everything upon which they vote. In addition, representatives present themselves to their electorate in such a way that they are often elected for reasons that have little to do with serving the best interests of the individuals in the state (e.g. personal popularity, good looks, attractive children).

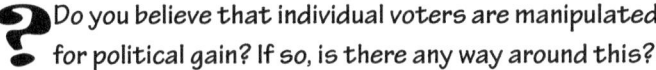
Do you believe that individual voters are manipulated for political gain? If so, is there any way around this?

Sexual equality

Much of the movement for sexual equality in the West has been driven by feminism. Feminism is concerned, in the narrowest sense, in attaining political rights, legal rights and justice for women, and in the broadest sense, in attaining equal status for either sex in the face of oppression and subordination.

Mary Wollstonecraft (1759–1797) wrote in defence of women as rational beings entitled to equal rights and responsibilities as citizens (though her belief involved how women should attain this from 'within the home'). Feminism in its broadest sense (radical feminism) takes on a strongly political aspect that is committed to the destruction of all individual oppression. The term itself is difficult because of its gender connotation, since philosophers such as John Stuart Mill (1806–1873), who have denied the existence of natural distinctions between men and women, are described as 'feminist'. However, many philosophers (including Plato, Aristotle (384–322 BC), Immanuel Kant (1724–1804), Georg Wilhelm Friedrich Hegel (1770–1831) and Rousseau have argued that there is a natural difference between men and women (e.g. men are rational and women are emotional). But even if gender differences are not rooted in biology they are evident in the apportionment of domestic responsibility, political involvement and work opportunity. Mill and Simone de Beauvoir (1908–1986) both argue that as long as there is equality of opportunity, although some differences would remain, those differences would not be prejudicial to either sex.

In feminist philosophy, there is a distinction made between the private and public realms (e.g. domestic work as opposed to paid employment) which highlights a private environment in which women still dominate that is immune from the beneficial effects of the workings of the state. Because of this, domestic violence and marital rape have a problematic status. The conception of equality in the narrow sense seems difficult to apply to these different worlds that still tend to be apportioned according to gender.

> **?** A female is genetically different from a male. Does this mean that they are different species and therefore may be appropriately treated in different ways?

Sexual inclination
Christianity and the Ancient Greeks condemned homosexuality. Plato argued that there was no evidence of homosexuality in animals therefore it was unnatural for humans. St Thomas Aquinas (1224/5–1274) believed homosexuality worse than rape as rape transgressed only human law whereas homosexuality transgressed natural, and therefore God's, law.

> **?** Homosexual sex cannot naturally lead to propagation of the species. Does this mean that this sort of sex is unnatural?

Since the psychological interpretation of Sigmund Freud (1856–1939) and the statistical analysis of the later *Kinsey Reports* (1948, 1953), it has been recognised that homosexuality is not an aberration but an aspect of natural human nature. Michel Foucault (1926–1984) believes homosexuality a social construction brought about by a medical profession seeking to label homosexuals in need of a cure. It is still the case in some countries that homosexuality is considered abhorrent.

> ❓ Is it reasonable to stigmatise homosexuality because of its connection with AIDS (acquired immune deficiency syndrome) in the same way that smokers are stigmatised because of the connection between smoking and cancer?

Pressure from gay and lesbian communities has in some countries led to social and legal recognition of homosexuality: socially by deeming stigmatising because of sexual orientation and preference discriminatory and a contravention of basic human rights, legally by granting the same rights to homosexuals as those held by heterosexuals to enter into same-sex marriage or formal partnerships that attract full civil property rights and obligations (e.g. taxation, benefits, pensions, inheritance, parental responsibility and custody).

> ❓ Is it possible to uphold the view that heterosexual orientation is the only foundation for civil rights?

Although same-sex marriage existed in Ancient Greece and Rome, and did occur in ancient European times, it has not existed as part of civil law until the early twenty-first century. Same-sex marriage was embodied in law in Netherlands, Belgium and Spain by 2005. Since then, it has become legal in Canada, Norway, Sweden, Argentina and South Africa. At the same time, a large part of the world, including much of the USA, Eastern Europe and Russia do not recognise same-sex couples in law, and in some countries (mostly in Africa and the Middle East) homosexuality is punishable by heavy penalties, life imprisonment or death.

> ❓ A central reason for marriage has always been to conceive children and bring them up within a stable family environment. The institution of marriage has always accepted the adoption of children for those unable to conceive their own or for the sake of orphans. Are there any differences between same-sex and different-sex marriage in this respect?

Further questions

The questions in this exercise tackle rights and responsibilities, distribution of money, race, discrimination, democracy and feminism.

1. Explain the differences and similarities between the words:
    'prejudice' and 'superstition'
    'equality', 'similarity' and 'identity'

2. By being a member of a state we give up some of our rights in order to gain the state's protection (e.g. from its laws and law enforcement system, its health service). Because everyone gives up some rights does this mean that:
    a. everyone should have the same responsibilities?
    b. everyone should be treated equally?

3. Should we attempt to redistribute money so that there is no financial distinction between rich and poor?

4. If we decided to redistribute money to eliminate the distinction between rich and poor, should we level everyone's wealth downwards (which could be done quickly via the tax system) or should we strive to bring everyone up to the level of the richest (which would take a lot longer)? Would the result of doing either of these be any different, inasmuch as if everyone was a millionaire would everyone be wealthy?

5. Because I am prudent and save my money, I become better off than someone who squanders her money. Should I give my money to her to make us equal?

6. Should people who hold positions of responsibility be paid more than those who do not?

7. It is easy to distinguish people on racial grounds by counting everyone of each different racial type who is a member of the state. If one race is in a minority and the state decides to apply reverse discrimination nationally, would this make sense if the global balance of these races were the other way around?

8. A state's application of reverse discrimination is so successful that exactly the proportion of a race in the society is reflected in the workforce. Should the reverse discrimination continue in favour of either race (imagining that there are only two races) according to whether there is one person more from one race than from the other (and vice versa)? To deny this would be to deny the rights of the one individual who, at any one time, is in the minority. Would this be right?

9. Does a representative democracy carry out the wishes of the people?

10. How can a representative democracy protect individuals from propaganda?

11. Is it right to allow people to vote for the wrong reasons? What reasons might people have for voting for a certain democratic representative that you consider wrong? Should someone who votes for the wrong reasons still have their vote counted?

12. Is sexual equality a human concept that should be restricted to human beings or should it also be applied to animals?

Notes

Question 1:
'prejudice' – a preconceived opinion, bias or partiality;
'superstition' – a belief in the supernatural associated with an irrational fear of its effects;
'equality' – the state of being equal in any application (for example, rights, responsibilities, wealth);
'similarity' – for one thing to resemble another in kind, nature or amount;
'identity' – the state of being the same in every way; absolute sameness.

Further reading

Edith Hamilton and Huntington Cairns (eds), *The Collected Dialogues of Plato including the Letters* (Princeton: Princeton University Press, 1961).

Robert Nozick, *Anarchy, State, and Utopia* (Oxford: Blackwell, 1974), Chapter 8.

John Rawls, *A Theory of Justice* (Oxford: Oxford University Press, 1971, revised 1999), Chapter VI.

Jonathan Wolff, *An Introduction to Political Philosophy* (Oxford: Oxford University Press, 2006).

10

God

If God created the universe then who created God and where did he get the material for his creation?

Introduction

People hold many different views about God. Some deny God's existence (atheists), some believe that although there is a possibility that God exists there is insufficient evidence to prove this (agnostics), some believe in only one God (monotheists) and some in many Gods (polytheists).

What is God?

Those who believe in one God usually consider that he holds divine attributes: that he is omniscient (all knowing), omnipotent (all powerful), omnipresent (present everywhere at the same time), benevolent (good) and exists everlastingly in timeless eternity. Because God is not evident in the material world, he must be regarded as a supernatural being that is 'beyond nature'.

In the monotheistic Abrahamic religions of Judaism, Christianity and Islam, God's attributes include mostly omnipotence, omniscience, omnipresence and goodness. In these religions, God is male though this is not necessarily the case in other religions (e.g. Mohammed proclaimed one male god against the Meccan al'Uzzah and her sisters, many of the important gods of Greek mythology were female, some beliefs accentuate female attributes such as sexuality, motherliness). Other religions such as Hinduism, Sikhism, many African religions as well as the Baha'i Faith, Mormonism and Zoroastrianism accent different aspects of God including power as creator, combined mortal and spiritual existence, membership of a body of gods, and ability to manifest and intervene in the mortal world.

In Jainism, any human who achieves a sufficiently high state of consciousness is a god. Buddhism, with its stress on moderation and enlightenment, Taoism, which concentrates on naturalness, and Confucianism which accents simplicity, are all non-theistic religions.

The Christian God is usually considered the creator of everything (the universe and all its contents). Such a God must have existed before his act of creation and so did not create himself or the world into which he did his creating. Some ancient religions thought God only gave the universe form by shaping existing materials. Most religions consider God is still in 'attendance', whereas some people think he created the universe then abandoned it. Major religions believe in a God with human characteristics (e.g. Christians, Muslims and Jews), even though they understand that creation must have been more an act of will than of physical manipulation. Indeed, if God had human characteristics, and had been big enough to construct the universe with his own hands, it is likely that we could still see him. Some religions see God more as a cosmic being, a universal consciousness, will itself or a being whose only divine attribute is simplicity.

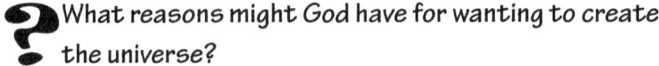What reasons might God have for wanting to create the universe?

Does God exist?
There are many arguments put forward to justify or 'prove' the existence of God.

The argument from religious experience
The argument from religious experience is an a posteriori argument generally put forward by those who already have a strong faith in the existence of God. It proposes that if I have an experience of something then that thing which I have an experience of exists. From this, it follows that if I believe I have an experience of God then God exists. It is certainly hard to imagine that we can have an experience of something that does not exist, but this argument relies heavily on the truth of the experience that I believe I have, that is, the truth of an experience of God. A hallucinatory experience is a real experience (of the hallucination), but my experience of it does not make the hallucination real.

The ontological argument

The ontological argument is an a priori argument first expressed by St Anselm (1033–1109). It tries to get around the problem of checking the veracity of our experience of God used in the argument from religious experience. It says that if we can conceive of God as that which nothing greater can be conceived then God must exist. This argument has great force. Even though it is possible to conceive of something which does not exist (an idea used as the basis of the *reductio ad absurdum* 'Lost Island' criticism by a contemporary of St Anselm, the monk Gaunilo (flourished eleventh century, dates unknown)), it does not seem possible to conceive of something greater than the greatest which can be conceived. However, as pointed out by St Thomas Aquinas (1224/5–1274), we cannot be sure that any conception we are having like this is actually a conception of God. As David Lewis (1941–2001) shows us, concepts are constructions in our minds as they exist in the world we inhabit and this may not be sufficient to validate the existence of something which must, by necessity, exist in all possible worlds (and not just the one we inhabit). It could be that in formulating the ontological argument we are simply constructing something from other concepts and ideas that we already have, as opposed to conceiving something separate from all other influences.

> Human beings have created computers so must be able to conceive of computers, though no one suggests that computers can conceive of a human being. If God created human beings then he must be able to conceive of human beings, but does it follow that human beings can conceive of God?

René Descartes (1596–1650) reintroduced the ontological argument in a revised form in his *Meditations*. He claimed that God is a supremely perfect being which itself implies existence; a perfect being must necessarily be omniscient and omnipotent and existence must accompany such attributes. This argument is considered flawed by what is called the Kant–Frege view (a combination of the thoughts on the subject by Immanuel Kant (1724–1804) and Gottlob Frege (1848–1925)), which shows that existence itself is not in the correct predicate category to be counted perfection.

The ontological argument is by no means resolved and much contemporary philosophical debate continues to pursue the relative qualities of omniscience, omnipotence, perfection, greatness and existence and how these qualities can be applied in all possible worlds. For example, we may conceive of a possible world in which exists a being of maximal greatness, and indeed such a being may exist in all possible worlds, but the existence of such a being still does not imply the existence of God.

> If we know that God exists in our world but not in another world, does this mean that the God we know exists is not really God?

The cosmological argument
The cosmological argument or argument from first cause has been expressed in different ways by the Ancient Greeks and by Jewish, Christian and Islamic philosophers including Plato (c.428–347 BC), Aristotle (384–322 BC), St Thomas Aquinas, Descartes, Baruch Spinoza (1632–1677), John Locke (1632–1704) and Gottfried Wilhelm Leibniz (1646–1716). It can take both a priori and a posteriori forms and concentrates on the notions of a first cause and a cosmic design. A posteriori cosmological arguments always start from the premise that it is possible that something either exists or does not exist.

St Thomas Aquinas put an a posteriori version of the argument. He considered why there is something rather than nothing and concluded that what exists must have been caused by a necessary being. Because it is not possible to establish an infinite regress of causes (not every cause can have been caused), there must be a necessary being that does not depend on anything else for its necessity and that must be God.

Leibniz based his a priori version of the cosmological argument on his 'principle of sufficient reason'. He said that nothing could be unless there is a sufficient reason for it to be that way rather than another. As the world is obviously the way it is, then it must have a sufficient reason and this must be a necessary being who lies outside the world.

> Is it possible that there is something not caused?

The argument from design

The argument from design or the teleological argument (from the Greek *telos* meaning 'end', 'completion', 'fulfilment') has many versions (ranging from those offered by some of the Pre-Socratics, Plato, the Stoics and St Thomas Aquinas) all of which hold (in some way) that the design element evident in the universe is compelling evidence for the existence of a designer. The argument from design is the most widely held view purporting to prove the existence of God. David Hume (1711–1776) puts forward the most interesting version, which, along with Kant, he also criticised.

The argument from design is an a posteriori argument from analogy. It sees in the natural world evidence of the same sort of design processes that human beings put into the construction of machines. To design and create machines, human beings need wisdom, intelligence and rational thought. The analogy extrapolates these human attributes and concludes that anything that created the universe must have similar attributes. It is an 'in-to-out' or 'micro-to-macro' argument.

Hume levels a number of criticisms at the argument from design. If we need to explain the design of the world then, he agrees, there is no reason why we should not imagine that a designer is responsible but, he argues, a designer is not the same thing as God. Because the universe is unique, it is inappropriate to conclude that a human style designer lies beyond it. In other words, the everyday evidence that we use as a basis for the analogy cannot be used for such a unique thing as the universe. Also, he says, if there is a designer there is nothing to say that this designer does not need a designer to have designed him *ad infinitum* and so the argument would never be conclusive proof for one designer. Added to which, the universe may be an organism (like a plant) as opposed to a machine, in which case the analogy fails because the workings of the organic world do not resemble the 'clockwork' of machinery. It may also be the case that the order of the universe could have come about by chance — that there was no design and no designer. Indeed, there is evidence for this because the order we identify in the universe is accompanied by a high degree of apparent disorder.

In defence of the argument from design, it has been argued by Richard Swinburne (1934–) that it is very unlikely that the universe would exist without there being some cause and if God was the cause, and he had taken the trouble to create it, then it would seem strange that he would create something that did not have order.

Even if a version of the design argument proved successful, it would only prove the designer's purpose (to design the universe) and would tell us nothing about the designer's mind (e.g. whether the designer possessed any of the divine attributes accorded to God).

> **?** If we accept Big Bang cosmology, can it be said in any way that the universe is ordered? Explain how it may be possible to reconcile the notion of a 'bang', which connotes sudden and chaotic explosion, with a sense of 'order'.

The argument from miracles

The argument from miracles states that miracles are a proof of God's existence because only God could cause miraculous events. The problem with this argument is not only how to define a miracle but the difficulties associated with establishing whether or not a miracle has ever truly occurred.

Conventionally, a miracle is defined as the act of a supernatural being that violates the laws of nature. In other words, it goes against the whole body of inductive evidence available to us. Hume says: 'That no testimony is sufficient to establish a miracle, unless the testimony be of such a kind, that its falsehood would be more miraculous, than the fact, which it endeavours to establish' (*An Enquiry Concerning Human Understanding*, Section X, Part I). Hume criticised the existence of miracles, saying that belief should be based on evidence and, because sense perception is better evidence than testimony, sense perception should always be favoured as evidence over testimony. Because sense perception reveals evidence of the constancy of the laws of nature (and not evidence of miracles), we are justified in believing in the regularities of nature but never justified in believing in miracles.

In addition, if a miraculous event goes against the body of inductive evidence then how can one have ever happened? If it had happened, it would be part of the body of knowledge and our knowledge of the universe and its laws would have been altered to accommodate it. In this way the occurrence of a miracle is self-defeating.

> **?** Describe something that, if it were to happen, you would consider miraculous. If such a thing actually happened, would it still be miraculous?

The argument from conscience

The argument from conscience is an a posteriori argument based on the idea that man has an innate sense of moral law and this can only be explained by the existence of a superior, moral lawgiver. Justin L. Barrett (1971–) thinks that belief in an all powerful, all knowing God is an inevitable consequence of the way our minds are designed.

The argument from universal consent

The argument from universal consent is based on the idea that human beings have at all times entertained a belief in the existence of a superior being on whom the existence of the world is dependent. This fact cannot be accounted for except by admitting that this belief contains at least some germ of truth.

> **?** Because some people have always believed in God, there must be a god for them to believe in. Does this proposition make any sense? Provide supporting, or counter examples to back up your reasoning.

Pascal's wager: the gambler's argument

Blaise Pascal (1623–1662) set out not to prove the existence of God but to show that to believe in God was the 'best bet'. He compares the agnostic's position with that of a gambler. The gambler calculates the odds of winning the best prize for the least loss, and the agnostic (instead of 'sitting on the fence') should do the same by believing in God. The gambler's argument proposes two different bets that give four possible outcomes. We can bet that God exists. If we win (God does exist), then we win eternal life. If we lose (God does not exist), then we have not lost too much, perhaps we have missed some pleasures that we could otherwise have had but compared to the possibility of eternal life such a loss is relatively negligible. We can bet that God does not exist. If we win (God does not exist), then our worldly life will be free of illusion and we can indulge in any pleasures we think fit without fear of eternal damnation. If we lose (God does exists), then we face the possibility of eternal damnation. Accordingly, the best bet is to bet that God exists.

However, the psychological difficulties are too great to apply this method to belief. We do not choose beliefs as if they were bets. Even if we recognise, on Pascal's argument, that the best bet is to believe in God, this does not automatically cause us to believe that the existence of God is true. Pascal held that if we wanted to believe in something (e.g. because it was the best bet), then as long as we practised that belief we would come to believe it in the end. It is arguable as to whether or not we can condition ourselves in such a way to truly believe in something. Added to which, if such a self-interested view towards belief in God turns out to be ethically questionable it may count heavily against prospective heavenly residence.

> **?** 'The best bet is to believe in God.' 'The best bet is not to smoke cigarettes.' What are the psychological problems associated with propositions like this?

The problem of evil

If God does exist as a supreme being with divine attributes then we have to deal with the problem of evil. The apparently high level of evil in the world makes any claim for an all powerful and good God seem unlikely. This question was much discussed in Ancient Greece by Epicurus (342–270 BC) and Plato, and continues to the present day.

The argument is this. If God is omnipotent then, by definition, he could prevent evil if he wanted to. If God were good then he would surely want to prevent evil if he could. If God exists, and is both omnipotent and good, then he could prevent evil and would want to prevent evil. Why then, if God exists, is there so much evil in the world?

Responses to the problem of evil have traditionally taken the form of theistic arguments called 'theodicies' (a term coined by Leibniz).

According to St Augustine (354–430), evil is only the negative aspect of a pre-existing good released by the human activity of free-will. God knows that ultimately out of free-will good will come. The evildoer will suffer and in the long run the virtuous will benefit from their virtue. The purpose of evil is not to make us happy but to make us virtuous: in other words, we 'learn from our mistakes'. In addition, because we do not see how much the evildoer suffers, the world is not such a morally substandard place as it might appear.

St Thomas Aquinas thought that evil is accidental and caused by human beings as they exercise God-given free-will. God cannot be held responsible for something that he does not intend, and he only intends that human beings should have free-will and not that, by using it, they should cause evil. At the same time, God may permit certain evils that he believes are connected to his ultimately good purpose but this purpose cannot be known to us.

According to Leibniz, God has the power to create the best possible world. No world can be perfect and so God created one with the best possible balance of good and evil. Some good things are only possible because of evil (e.g. compassion is only possible upon witnessing suffering), and God has calculated the balance of good and evil in all possible worlds and so brought out the appropriate and best balance in the world that he has created. Because he weighs up the balance of good and evil God is also just.

Although the existence of evil does not necessarily prove that God does not exist, it does highlight the fact that suffering is an intrinsic aspect of human life. However, there is little evidence to show that non-human life experiences the same tendency towards pain and suffering. It may be that there really is no evil in the world, it may only appear that way to us — it is our psychological perspective, and it is wrong.

> **?** The process of evolution is reliant upon the progressive success of mutated variants within species that drive their less successful competitors (who are also their ancestors) into extinction. Is this evil?

Further questions

Except for Questions 1, 14 and 15, these questions are all to do with the nature of God and so presuppose his existence. 'I don't believe in God' as an answer to any of these questions, although otherwise worth pursuing, is therefore out of place in this context.

1. Explain the differences and similarities between the words: 'faith', 'belief' and 'opinion'.

2. Can God be regarded as supernatural, that is 'beyond nature', because surely nature includes everything?

3. If God is all powerful, then why does he not cause us to know he exists with certainty?

4. If everyone from now on proved to be immortal would that be miraculous or simply a change in the state of the universe?

5. Where was God before he created the universe?

6. If God created time when he created the universe, where did he find the time for the act of creation itself?

7. If God existed before he created the universe then he must have existed in a purely non-physical way. If God existed in a purely non-physical way, why should he want to create something physical?

8. If the universe was created out of nothing (except the will of God), why is there no evidence of 'creation-from-nothing' in what exists? The principle of 'non-emergence' does not seem to be broken in the natural world, and yet if that were at the centre of the universe's creation would it not be reasonable to see some evidence of it?

9. What would be irrevocable evidence of God's existence?

10. If God exists then where is he? Is he separate from his creation or part of it?

11. If a unicorn suddenly appeared in the room and I was the only one who could see it, would you believe that it was there? If a unicorn suddenly appeared in the room and all of us could see it except for you, would you believe that it was there? If a unicorn suddenly appeared in the room and all of us could see it, would you believe that it was there? Can you reapply these statements to God?

12. If the only people that ever won the lottery believed in God, would this prove anything about God?

13. Is it more reasonable that there is one God (omnipotent, omniscient and good), two gods (one good, one evil), or many gods (some good, some bad and some less powerful than others)?

14. Is it more likely that everything in the universe is moving towards good or that everything in the universe is moving towards evil?

15. Describe something that you consider unquestionably evil. Would this be evil in all possible worlds?

Notes

Question 1:

'faith' – a state of complete trust or confidence that supports a belief without logical proof;

'belief' – a state of mind that falls short of certainty and although a firm opinion upon which the holder will act, the state of mind is less compelling than faith;

'opinion' – a state of mind held on unproved grounds that the view held is probable.

Further reading

Paul Helm (ed.), *Faith and Reason* (Oxford: Oxford University Press, 1999).

Roger Scruton, *Modern Philosophy: An Introduction and Survey* (London: Pimlico, 2004), Chapter 11.

11

Science

Is science essential to humankind?

Introduction

When we observe the world, we notice certain regularities (e.g. the sun rises in the east not the west, chickens lay eggs and dogs do not). In fact there are far more irregularities than regularities (e.g. some seasons are rainy and some dry, some dogs are friendly and some are hostile, sometimes the clouds take on a certain pattern and sometimes they take on another). However, some regularities are invariable (e.g. if you are dead you are not alive, objects always fall towards the centre of a gravitational force). On the other hand, some things that were at one time considered invariable turn out to be variable (e.g. when the boiling point of water was first discovered it was not thought that different air pressures would make it variable).

Science is concerned with seeking out genuine invariants in nature. The reason for this is that we are concerned with predicting the future because, if we can do this, we can act in accordance with that prediction. This allows us not only to construct a technology that we can depend on but also to feel comfortable in a world that appears reliable. We might say that science is the systematic search for uniformities in the ways things behave.

> **?** What would it be like to live in a world in which we considered all apparently invariable occurrences variable? How far into the future do we expect something to be invariable in order to call it 'invariable'?

Scientific method

Modern scientific method has replaced our reliance on the simple authority of others. For example, Aristotle (384–322 BC) was considered the authority on all matters 'scientific' until the Italian Renaissance, even though he never conducted scientific experiments (he worked out his conclusions by logic). Scientific method has a number of phases: discovery, which by means of the logical process of induction based on observation leads to justified explanation, this in turn brings about theories which themselves, if sufficiently confirmed, lead to laws of nature.

Discovery

Discovery in itself is problematic because it hinges on human creative reasoning that realistically will not yield to formal rules of method. We cannot usually predict when a certain discovery will be made nor can we forecast with any certainty in what realm of nature it may be found. It is sometimes many years until the importance of a particular discovery is realised.

Often, discovery has only taken place against a distinct social and economic background (e.g. the Italian Renaissance, the Industrial Revolution) which itself sets a particular tone for human belief (e.g. the urge to open up new areas of human understanding, the need to build machines which will undertake repetitive processes). If this is the case, then no discovery is epistemologically neutral. For example, Teflon coating used as a non-stick surface for cooking utensils is a by-product of the US space programme that in turn was driven by the Cold War arms race with the Soviet Union. The development of Teflon could therefore be said to have been an outcome more of circumstances than of the discovery itself, in other words, without the circumstances it may never have come to anything.

> *What do you think is the most important scientific discovery man has ever made? Is it likely that this prime importance will hold in a thousand years' time? If not, why not? If so, what are your reasons for believing this?*

Justification

All scientific knowledge has to be justified in some way. Francis Bacon (1561–1626), who himself saw the advancement of science as a social activity, said that scientific knowledge is gained and justified by induction. Induction (as opposed to deduction) is the inference from the particular to the general (e.g. 'Under these conditions, I have seen it happen a hundred times so I predict that if these conditions are present it will happen again.'). Any gambler knows that inductive method is not always dependable.

Inductive method in its simplest sense (as the counting of instances or the collection of statistical data) is always subject to the potential presence of counter examples. For example, every true crow I have seen so far has been black but this in no way guarantees that the next true crow I see will also be black. David Hume (1711–1776) pointed out that because induction is founded on the future resembling the past, any suspicion that the nature of the world may change would make such an assumption useless. For example, if there is a chance that the next true crow I see will be white then the collection of evidence to date about true crows that are black guaranteeing that true crows are black means nothing. But (as Hume accepted) we could not live in a world where we suspected future occurrences to this degree, not only would it go against common sense but it would make leading our lives impossible.

Criticisms of Hume's view rest on the belief that there is no reason to distrust induction just because it is not deduction, and that because of the past success of induction it is itself inductively vindicated. Karl Popper (1902–1994) rejected such criticisms, saying that science does not rest so heavily on induction from past regularities as we generally think. He believed that the role of science is to make bold generalisations that it then seeks to falsify. In other words, instead of continuing to collect evidence of true black crows by increasing the statistical count, science should confidently assert that 'all true crows are black' until it is able to discover one that is white.

Nelson Goodman (1906–) believes that attempts to justify induction are based on how we define the regularities that we expect to persist. If we define them in different ways (his own example is a colour called 'grue' which is green up to a certain date and blue thereafter), then any system of predictable regularity collapses altogether.

Because of its reliance on inductive method, science can never achieve certain knowledge. All scientific claims, no matter how much testing they have been subjected to, remain, according to Popper, falsifiable (i.e. open to a counter example). Every scientific hypothesis can be potentially disconfirmed and replaced by another.

> **?** Does it make sense to assume that what science says it knows is true? For example, science says it knows the world of appearance is made up of ever-smaller particles and qualities of which we are sensually unaware.

Observation

In order to collect data, the general method of science is to observe the world. The theories it then develops, based on its observations, tell us how things are caused. Justification of cause itself can be found by analogy with the everyday world (e.g. you can observe how gravitational force is exerted by swinging a bucket containing water around on a rope) or by bringing many different pieces of evidence together (e.g. if, on earth, I drop a variety of objects, under a variety of conditions from a variety of places, they all fall downwards under the influence of gravity).

As science increasingly interprets the world beyond the range of our senses (e.g. electricity, quantum mechanics, particle physics), the previously general method of science has become strained by the demands of specific scientific purposes. For example, many biologists claim that the living world can only be interpreted by looking for a purpose or final cause of some sort. They believe that the distinctive adaptation of living things via the processes of evolution is a strong metaphor for the operation of some designing force (perhaps even with some ultimate goal), though this force is the Darwinian mechanism of natural selection rather than a being beyond nature (God). However, if evolution has a purpose we are left to wonder not only from where it stems (what it is caused by) but also in what is it contained (e.g. our genes)? It may be that in some cases the explanation falls short of the degree of belief required to uphold it.

> **?** Science says that my belief in its theory relies on the theory having a strong basis in observable fact. What observable facts does it offer to support the idea that species wish to, or have a need to, evolve?

Explanation

Explanations can be in answer to why (e.g. 'Why did I arrive late?' 'Because the electricity supply failed and the train broke down.'), they can be clarifications (e.g. 'I am right aren't I? This train is late isn't it?'), or in answer to requests for information about how (e.g. 'How does the fact that this train has broken down cause me to be late?' 'Because it has caused your journey time to be longer than if the train had not broken down.'). Science is mostly concerned with the 'why', as in 'Why did the train break down?'. Science is not satisfied with the answer, 'Because the electrical supply failed', considering it insufficient in itself, but wants to know why the connection can be made between the failure of the electricity supply and the train breaking down. To do this, science needs to build up observations over a period of time or develop a theory that can then be justified either by mathematical or experimental proof. We cannot get very far with explanation without using theories.

Theories

In science, theories are not just simple hypotheses (e.g. 'It is my theory that if we feed an electricity supply to the train it will run.'), but meant in the specialised sense of explaining something which cannot be observed by my senses (e.g. we know that the train needs an electrical supply but it is not apparent to our senses why this is so).

Theories are devised from observed information or are dependent on other theories so they have a restricted information base. A theory can never be conclusively established because all the supporting information for a theory is inductive which, unlike a deductive argument that is self-proving, is always subject to change in light of further investigation. So, not only do theories not have the support of deduction, they operate with information which is not only incomplete but often based on justifications which themselves are similarly based on theories.

For example:
> If the electricity supply fails, the train will break down. (i.e. the theory is that a certain observable consequence will be caused by a certain thing having happened).
> The train is broken down (i.e. the predicted, certain observable consequence has indeed occurred).

Therefore:
> The electricity supply must have failed (i.e. because the certain observable consequence has occurred, on the basis of the theory, it must have been caused by the certain thing having happened).

Not only is this a logical fallacy (affirming the consequent) that has produced an invalid result, but also the conclusion is drawn from the only theory available. There is no theory available here to explain the true reason for the train's breakdown, that is, that the driver has died at the controls. Even if science has knowledge of a theory to cover every eventuality, it cannot escape from this trap because the predictive ability of each theory rests on a general theory of regularity.

This means that we cannot expect science to produce certainty, but only, at best, a high degree of probability. Observable facts only go towards supporting or confirming the theory to some degree or another. Science cannot deduce the theory from the observed facts, so scientific theory can only provide an explanation for those observed facts.

> **?** Every time someone in England turns on an electric light bulb a pigeon dies somewhere in the world. Would the turning on of electric light bulbs be a reasonable explanation for the deaths of pigeons?

Verification of theories

Many theories we dismiss as false because we cannot confirm them (e.g. 'There is no such thing as telepathy', 'Magic is not real'). There are weaker and stronger cases of verification of theories. I might be able to verify (though not incontestably) that I am thinking the thoughts I am thinking, but I cannot verify that all true crows in the universe are black unless I have seen all the true crows in the universe and checked their colour. This is probably impossible because as every new moment in time occurs I need to re-check all the crows I previously checked to ensure they have not changed colour, and I also need to check all the new crows that have come into existence since the last moment I checked and so on. Finding one incidence of a non-black (and true) crow would falsify the theory.

However, science still tends to hold onto a theory even if there is the occasional deviation from it. Scientific theories require an enormous amount of empirical observation to establish them and usually more to falsify them. Because scientific claims interlock with many other empirical data, a single instance of deviation can usually be blamed on a part, but not the whole, of the theory. For example, the Law of the Conservation of Matter has long since been abandoned because of the discovery that matter is transformed into energy. Because, in part, many different sorts of energy can be postulated (e.g. chemical, kinetic, potential) to make the theory come out right in the end, the Law of the Conservation of Energy still holds. On the other hand, a theory such as the Theory of Universal Ether was finally abandoned after many attempts to prove it came out with only negative results.

Sticking with a known (and hard won) law is often preferable to its abandonment. The fact that many theories previously held by science have been overturned is, however, little comfort for the holders of any contemporary theory. Because scientific theories are not entailed but only suggested by their evidence, this leads to the problem of competing theories using the same body of evidence. This is particularly noticeable where statistical method is used and gives rise to the saying 'You can prove anything with statistics.'

> **?** Most scientific theories that were held before the nineteenth century have been overturned. What does this say about scientific theories?

Laws of nature

'Laws of the land' ('positive laws') are prescriptive imperatives, for example, 'Do this', 'Don't do that'. 'Natural laws' are law applied to our behaviour as human beings that, according to Plato (*c*.428–347 BC), appeal to an inner sense of right and wrong (e.g. it is wrong to murder another human being). 'Laws of nature' are applied to the structure of things and describe a universal state of affairs so regular in its repeatability that its occurrence is beyond doubt. Laws of nature are descriptive of what has been discovered. Human beings can prescribe how other human beings (or indeed other conscious beings) should act by imposing rules, but the uniformities of nature would continue to act as they do irrespective of any human prescription. A law of nature tells you how things do behave, not how they should behave.

There are several ways of defining a law of nature, though there is no consensus that all of them are necessary. Basically, a law of nature must be a universal statement of the form 'all A's are B's' or 'if something is A then it is (or has as a quality) B'. If only a percentage of A's are B's then it is a statistical law that, although better than nothing, always leaves open the question as to why the remaining percentage does not conform. In addition, a law of nature must be open ended in space and time. The statement 'If something is A then it is (or has as a quality) B' must apply to all occurrences of that 'something' wherever and whenever it occurs. Laws of nature must be capable of being expressed as hypothetical statements. For example, although it would be common that most true crows are black, we would not consider it a defining characteristic of being a true crow (we would probably still accept as a true crow a crow that was white). In this case we would not say that 'if there were a true crow (at anytime and anywhere) then it must be black', but we would tolerate the anomaly of the white crow by reclassifying the meaning of 'crow' and include in that classification the occasional true crow that was white. This is a case of simple reclassification of species and is common. However, we would feel more concerned about exceptions or the need to reclassify a statement such as 'providing an object with mass was within a gravitational field then it would always fall towards the centre of that field'.

The more general the statement the more likely it is to be accepted as a law of nature. There are low-level and high-level generalisations. A low-level generalisation such as finding some birds that had three legs would not really affect the rest of the universe, but finding exceptions to a high-level generalisation like the Law of Universal Gravitation would have immense consequences on the way we interpret the world. The General Theory of Relativity alters the meaning of this law but, because there is no experienced realm in which the exceptions that the theory proposes occur, the law remains intact.

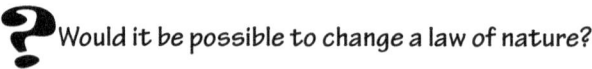 *Would it be possible to change a law of nature?*

Further questions
The questions here attack deeply ingrained beliefs about the state of affairs of the world. Question 6 seeks to undermine the commonly held idea that evolution implies some sort of intention on the part of the evolving species.

1. Explain the differences and similarities between the words:
   'assumption' and 'hypothesis'
   'cause' and 'motive'
   'idea' (in the scientific sense) and 'theory'
   'coincidence' and 'fate'

2. Is it possible to disobey a law of nature?

3. Would it be possible to discover a law of nature that is at the present time unknown?

4. If a law of nature (e.g. the Second Law of Thermodynamics which states that heat moves from a hot body towards a cooler one) did not apply from today onwards, how long would it be before it was considered a new law?

5. Could it be a law of nature that words beginning with 'A' do not begin with any letter from 'B' to 'Z'?

6. Say if you consider the following satisfactory or unsatisfactory and why.
   a. Animals breed because they wish to propagate their species.
   b. Flowers make themselves attractive to bees in order to spread their pollen.
   c. Life on earth has become diverse because of random mutation with no intention.

7. I have a theory that the Universal Law of Gravitation will go into reverse tomorrow and will stay that way until the end of the universe (or to infinity). Is my theory reasonable?

8. Repeated incidence (frequent or overlapping occurrences) that we do not understand we call 'coincidences'. Repeated incidence (frequent or overlapping occurrences) that we do understand we call 'laws of nature'. Does this mean that ultimately every coincidence is explainable? Carl Jung (1875–1961), for example, believed that all coincidences were explainable synchronous occurrences.

9. Weather prediction is an example of inductive reasoning. If global weather patterns change, would it be possible to predict the weather?

10. Is there any point in pursuing a theory that apparently makes no sense?

11. The General Theory of Relativity states that light bends in the presence of gravitational fields. Are there any reasons why this should not be a law of nature?

Notes

Question 1:

'assumption' – a view without any proof;

'hypothesis' – a proposition made as a starting point for further investigation that as yet does not have any proof;

'cause' – anything (physical or mental) that has an effect on something else;

'motive' – a fact or circumstance that causes a person to alter in a certain way;

'idea' (in the scientific sense) – a concept formed by mental effort;

'theory' – a supposition or system of ideas, based on a general principle, which explains something;

'coincidence' – a remarkable concurrence of events or circumstances without apparent causal connection;

'fate' – a power regarded from the present moment in time as predetermining events in a determined future and in retrospect as present occurrences which appear always to have been unavoidable.

Further reading

Anthony O'Hear, *An Introduction to the Philosophy of Science* (Oxford: Clarendon Press, 1989).

Roger Scruton, *Modern Philosophy: An Introduction and Survey* (London: Pimlico, 2004), Chapter 15.

12

Time

Is it reasonable to hope that at some time in the future we will be able to travel back in time?

Introduction

The philosophy of time is concerned with what time is (its nature) and not the ways we use for measuring it (its chronology).

Time is puzzling. Although we refer to it as a fourth dimension, it is very unlike the spatial dimensions of length, breadth and depth. Whereas our senses of sight and touch can check out spatial objects, time, although an unavoidable part of our experience, evades our ability to analyse. We can stand separate from spatial objects (though we still remain in space) in that we can think about spatial objects without being involved with them (because thinking does not take up any space). However, we cannot think about time without being part of the temporal process — there are no objects of time that we can stand apart from, and thinking always takes up time. Because we cannot separate ourselves from time, it defies objective scrutiny.

The nature of time

The commonest view of time is that it 'flows' like a river and the 'river of time' principle is firmly fixed in our minds. However, it is not clear whether we 'move through' this 'river' or whether it 'flows' past us. Whichever is the case, the analogy is weak because time does not seem, like a river, to be in any way substantive.

We tend to think that time is regular because, since the advent of industrial societies, we impose a regular system of measurement on it. But it is quite clear that our experience of time conflicts with this. When we are bored time passes slowly and when we are excited it passes quickly, when we are anticipating an exciting event (e.g. meeting a new friend) it passes slowly and when we are anticipating an unwanted event (e.g. the condemned prisoner on the night before his execution) it passes quickly.

> **?** What do I mean if I say, 'Today has passed slowly'?
> Is there any way in which I could claim that the fixed measure of time (the clock) was wrong?

Change

Without time it is impossible to imagine how change could happen. Without change happening it is difficult to imagine that we could establish in any way that time was passing. Something that is in state Y cannot be in a different state Z at the same time. It can only change into state Z if it occupies a different time to when it was in state Y.

There are two ways of viewing change. The first is the most conventional. An object or state of mind changes in some way (e.g. my smile changes to a frown, I once thought Louis XV was a good man and now I think he was bad) and that change is restricted to the object or to the owner of the state of mind. The second is less conventional and is called 'Cambridge change'. Cambridge change defines any change (no matter how apparently insignificant) as changing the state of the whole world. On this basis, if my smile changes to a frown the whole balance of smiles and frowns in the world changes (there is one less smile and one more frown). Or if I change my opinion about the character of Louis XV then Louis XV is himself changed (in that before my thought there was not the thought about him that I have now had), so the sum total of what constitutes 'Louis XV' has been altered. Whether he is alive or dead makes no difference to this.

> **?** Imagine witnessing the universe where all time had stopped (you are somehow outside this and immune from its effects). Describe what you see. Would the force of gravity still be in operation?

Time

Present

We regard ourselves as living 'in' the present; after all, this is where all of our experience is obtained. However, a present moment is difficult to define. Is the present: today, this minute, this second, or this instant? When we think like this we become confused about how 'big' a present moment is. If we look for the smallest instant we end up with merely an interface between future and past and this does not provide any present moment in which we can experience anything (and this seems absurd). If we imagine the point in time when we realise our experience of the present, we have to accept that the realisation must come *after* the experience itself (because of the lapse of time needed for the signal to be transmitted from our sensing apparatus via sense data to 'us'). Added to which, if the present instant is a discrete instance, then how do successive instants join one to another? If they do not join then it is difficult to see how something changes because change is a progressive occurrence that alters the state of something.

The only reasonable way to regard the present is as a specious present (the present of our experience). But, if we do this, because a specious present can have different 'lengths' according to how we experience it, we have to accept that the present is not objective and cannot be measured.

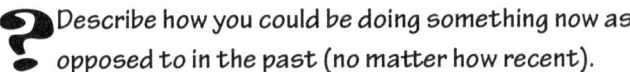 Describe how you could be doing something now as opposed to in the past (no matter how recent).

Past

All things that were once present become past. Once events pass into the past they become inaccessible and irretrievable. Our view of the past is that it has 'depth', in that things get further into the past. However, our experience is that sometimes we remember things that seem as if they were 'only yesterday' and without the supporting chronology by which we date things it is hard to know that 'older' past occurrences are somehow 'further away' from the present. We usually regard the past as a fixed collection of previous present events, like a container. But the past is intangible (it cannot be subjected to any objective analysis) and, unless we had memory of it, it is difficult to imagine how we could suppose that it was anything real. Indeed, it is hard to establish that past (even though a meaningful concept when used to reinforce the idea of a collection of previous present events) is anything more than a word we use to classify what we remember. Past as history is simply information collected about previous present occurrences that are available for us to inspect in the present.

> **? If no conscious thing could remember the past, are there any ways in which the past could be said to exist?**

Future

The future is the 'source' of the 'river of time'. Like the past it is intangible and inaccessible, but unlike the past (which seems fixed) events in the future, which have not yet happened, are undetermined until they do. In other words, tomorrow I may break my leg or I may not, it is not known until it happens. Some people imagine that it is possible to see into the future. If this is the case, the future is fixed and our lives are determined. A strong belief in this leads to a feeling that everything we do has already been fated in the future, that nothing is alterable, that it is all predetermined and that there is no personal freedom. An alternative view is that the future has no content at all; it is just the possibility that allows the next present to take place. As such, it is neutral to events that occur and merely provides the context in which the continuing specious present can happen.

It is hard to see how the future actually exists but, at the same time, if it did not, it is hard to imagine where the present 'comes from'.

> **? If the present is undeniably happening, where does it come from?**

The unreality of time

If the future seems little more than the potential for present events to happen, the present is so fleeting that it is past before we even have chance to know that we are experiencing it and the past seems nothing more than memory of previous presents, it is not surprising that many philosophers have considered time unreal.

According to Plato (c.428–347 BC), time is part of the deceiving world of appearance. According to Immanuel Kant (1724–1804), although much of our knowledge is derived from our experience, our experience of time may be of something that is created not by time but by our own minds. St Augustine (354–430) thought time impossible to deal with because even thinking about it brought on impenetrable problems.

J.McT.E. (John McTaggart Ellis (1868–1925)) was the strongest proponent of the unreality of time. He thought time unreal because its elements were logically self-contradictory. He divided time into two series: A (past, present and future), and B (earlier and later). He said that although our experience of time is in the B series (we only experience events as earlier or later), change, which is essential for time, can only happen in the A series (in that events were once future, then (changed) in the present then (changed) in the past). In other words, the B series is where we experience time but it relies on the A series. His denial of the reality of time is based on his conclusion that the A series is self-contradictory and so does not exist. Because the A series does not exist, our experience of time in the B series, although an experience of something, cannot be an experience of time.

McTaggart argued that the A series has separate phases of change (future, present and past) and these must remain separate in order for change to occur. But he pointed out that events can occupy two of these necessarily separate phases at the same time. For example, something that 'has been' is past in the present, and something that 'will be' is both present and future at the same time (and therefore future in the present). Because of this internal contradiction, he concluded that the B series could not be an experience of time (because the A series could not support it as it needs to if time is to be real) and if that were the case then time is not real.

However, even if we accept that time is unreal we are still left with defining whatever it is that seems like time, as well as trying to understand why we should experience something that is not time as if it were time. McTaggart describes reality as a complex timeless universe of immortal selves and our experience of time as a perceptual error occurring within the limits of our current perceptual abilities.

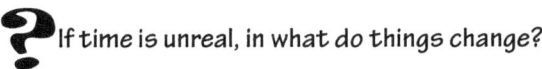 If time is unreal, in what do things change?

Time travel
Because of the apparently dimensional nature of time, it is intriguing to think that we can somehow travel in it. As far as we know no one in the

future has ever travelled back in time (at least not to any time that human beings have known about). Time travel demands that either future or past are real and that they can be inhabited by conscious beings that continue to experience their own present while we continue to experience ours. This implies that there is at least one more self-contained temporal dimension that runs alongside (or within) the other. Such a dimension must persist in parallel with ours and it must have such similarity to our own world that if we travel back (or forward) into it we can recognise it as our previous (or future) world. The present (or future) of this world would be in our past (or future), but our experience of it as time travellers would be synchronous with our own personal present. In other words, if we went back in time and spent a day in the past, we would still be a day older when we returned. Time travel does not imply that we could, for example, travel back in time and be someone else in a previous time, or be a younger version of our self.

> **?** Is it possible to travel backwards or forwards in time? Give reasons with examples to support your view.

Backwards causation

It seems unlikely that we can change the past; after all, we regard everything in the past as irretrievable and beyond further influence. However, there are ways in which the past can be affected according to how it is that we describe the nature of past. We may believe that the past (as history) contains certain facts at certain times that change into altered (new) facts at other times (e.g. we discover that Louis XV had red hair when we previously believed he had black hair). If the past is only conscious memory, then memories can be wrong (and can be discovered to be wrong therefore changing the previous belief) or people can be brainwashed or convinced of something different by strong argument. Also, based on Cambridge change, any thought that we have about any past event or thing changes that past event or thing.

> **?** Dr X claims that she can change the past by simply thinking about it. Is this a reasonable view to hold?

Light cones, event horizons and relativity

Since Albert Einstein's (1879–1955) work on Special and General Relativity, the formulation of quantum mechanics and the increased interest in, and knowledge about particle physics, our view of time has changed. Hermann Minkowski (1864–1909) coined the term 'space-time' with the intention of describing something which is neither spatial nor temporal. Space-time puts us (and everything else) into a specific zone of experience that is exclusively ours. On this account, we inhabit the waist of a 'light-cone' which joins the points of two opposing cones (of experience) which, although crossing over the cones of others in our immediate vicinity, become progressively distant from other light-cones as the model is expanded. On the universal scale, each of us is isolated in a particular frame of reference that is unlike the frame of reference of most of the rest of the universe. These ideas have led to the development of theories about black holes, wormholes and time-tunnelling with proponents such as Roger Penrose (1931–) and Stephen Hawking (1942–).

Can time have a beginning or an end?

It is a commonly held belief that time had a beginning or that it may have an end, but there is no firm evidence (empirical or mathematical) to back this up (although background radiation as the echo of the Big Bang is put forward as evidence that the universe began). It is possible to imagine that time may be infinite or finite in both directions — forward into the future, back into the past, or a mixture of either.

If the past is finite, then we have to wonder how it actually started because there would have been no time for it to start 'in'. If the past is infinite, then it would not be possible to have arrived at the present moment because there would be an infinite amount of past to cover before anything became present. If there is an infinite amount of future time, then all things will happen in every possible permutation and there will be an infinite number of occurrences of everything in every way. For example, there will be an infinite number of individuals like me with every possible slight variation. If the future is finite we are left wondering what will happen after time has ended (as we only know of things happening in time). In this case, all previous time and its contents would be meaningless or non-existent, and it is difficult to imagine in what this meaninglessness or non-existence might be happening.

> **?** If the future is infinite then this implies there will be an infinite number of 'me's with an infinite number of minor variations. Does this mean that 'I' would be immortal?

Further questions

The idea of time travel is tantalising and has much exposure in the science fiction of both films and books (e.g. *The Terminator* series, *The Curious Case of Benjamin Button*, *Star Trek*, H. G. Wells (1866–1946), *The Time Machine*). Most examples of time travel are fraught with problems. All the questions in this exercise concentrate on time travel and should not only highlight many of the difficulties associated with what time is or is not, but should allow you an opportunity to think at your full capacity.

1. If it were possible to travel back in time, then the future we inhabit (as our present) would be real to the past. If this were so, then there must be a future (which is equally real) 'beyond' our present. So, if anyone in the future had invented a way of travelling back in time, would we not know about it?

2. You know of a crime in the past, travel back in time and cause the crime never to have happened. When you return to your present, would you still have knowledge of the crime (and your prevention of it) even though you had caused it not to happen?

3. Is it possible for someone to travel into the future (say from today's date to AD 3000), have a child then bring that child back with them to the present?

4. Is it possible for someone from AD 3000 to travel back to a time before she was born?

5. Could someone from AD 3000 come back to today's date and invent a machine that destroys all human life in the year AD 2100?

6. Would it be possible for you to go back in time and, with your current knowledge, make sure that you won the lottery?

7. Describe the experience that would follow if time suddenly started to go backwards (that is, that the next moment was the previous moment and so on). If this happened, what would we be remembering (if anything)?

8. Instead of getting older, could I get younger? What would be the implications of this?

Further reading

Raymond Flood and Michael Lockwood (eds), *The Nature of Time* (Oxford: Basil Blackwell, 1988).

Gerald Rochelle, *Behind Time* (Aldershot: Ashgate, 1998).

Roger Scruton, *Modern Philosophy: An Introduction and Survey* (London: Pimlico, 2004), Chapter 25.

G. J. Whitrow, *The Natural Philosophy of Time* (Oxford: Clarendon Press, 1980).

G. J. Whitrow, *Time in History: Views of Time from Prehistory to the Present Day* (Oxford: Oxford University Press, 1988).

13

Human Rights

Why should any living thing have any moral right? After all, the act of living seems driven simply by a need to reproduce one's own kind, and this is a survival, not a moral imperative.

Introduction

Rights are considered essential to civilisation. They constitute a person's claim to the protection of social, legal or ethical interests necessary to uphold the person's dignity. Any theory of justice depends on the acknowledgement of rights. Natural (moral or inalienable) rights are those considered universally applicable to all (e.g. the right to life). Legal rights (embodied in state or international law) are generally the outcome of a struggle by those hoping to attain them.

Throughout their histories, all countries have progressively developed a system of rights both for the nation and for its citizens. The Magna Carta (Great Charter) (1215) obliged the then King of England (King John (1167–1216)) to abide by a list of laws and acknowledge certain rights. Over the following centuries, these came to be understood as human rights (e.g. the right of the church to be free of government interference, the right of individuals to own and inherit property and to be free of excessive taxes).

Philosophical debate in the three centuries preceding the second millennium developed a sophisticated view of natural rights unparalleled in previous times. John Locke (1632–1704) argued for the right of the human being to live in a state of nature, free from external authority, answerable only to God, and with an unalienable right to defend himself and his property against attack. Jean-Jacques Rousseau (1712–1778) argued for the collective citizenship to have control over its own destiny and was an inspiration for the French Revolution. His epigram, 'Man is born free; and everywhere he is in chains', became a rallying cry for many subsequent revolutionaries. John Stuart Mill (1806–1873) extended the utilitarianism of Jeremy Bentham (1748–1832) and advocated the personal freedom of the individual in his own home against any interference by the state or others (even if considered for his own mental or physical good) unless it was to prevent harm to others. Working in England and America, Thomas Paine (1737–1806) defended the rights of the citizen to welfare needs such as old-age pensions and education. Also in America, Henry David Thoreau (1817–1862) argued for the spiritual freedom derived from being with nature and put forward coherent reasons for disobeying unjust laws, indeed making it an imperative not to subscribe to immoral laws. The American Revolution against the British Empire in 1776 and the subsequent US Declaration of Independence drew on the many of these concepts of natural rights. The French Revolution of 1789 led to the Declaration of the Rights of Man and of the Citizen (1789), which incorporated (though probably as an exploitative tactic of the main mover of the French Revolution, Maximilien-Francois-Marie-Isidore de Robespierre (1758–1794)) Rousseau's central themes: equality, liberty and fraternity.

> ❓ 'We hold these truths to be self-evident; that all men are created equal, that they are endowed by their creator with certain unalienable rights, that among these are life, liberty and the pursuit of happiness'
> US Declaration of Independence (1776). Does this mean that we are entitled to do anything that makes us happy?

Thoreau's influence reached many who became engaged in non-violent resistance to what they considered unethical government action such as Leo Tolstoy (1828–1910), Mahatma (Mohandas Karamchand) Gandhi (1869–1948) and Martin Luther King, Jr (1929–1968). In England, the Poll Tax (Community Charge), introduced in 1990, was withdrawn in 1993 because of strong public feeling that led to demonstrations and many citizens refusing to pay. The original Poll Tax introduced in England in 1380 led to the Peasants' Revolt of 1381.

> **?** Are there any laws that, if I do not agree with them, I am entitled to disobey?

In nineteenth-century Europe issues such as slavery and serfdom, working conditions, low wages and child labour were all brought increasingly to public notice. In the US, government struggled for a solution to the problem of Native American Indians and slavery, the latter eventually leading to the American Civil War (1861–1865). At the same time, in Russia the serfs were freed in the Emancipation reform of 1861. However, neither the civil war in the US nor the freeing of serfs in Russia led to any immediate beneficial change in the circumstances of the underprivileged.

> **?** For most of human history, slavery has been an integral part of any modern society. Some of the greatest human achievements have been made by such societies. Is slavery wrong?

In the later nineteenth to mid twentieth centuries, there was an increase in groups representing anti-government feeling. This included terrorist groups as well as labour unions and movements for women's rights. For example, Gandhi's pacifist movement for national liberation brought independence and partition to India in 1947, the US Civil Rights Movement (1955–1968) underpinned the anti-Vietnam War protests of the 1960s. Amnesty International (1961–) demands that governments everywhere, regardless of ideology, treat their citizens in accordance with certain basic human principles.

United Nations agreements on human rights
Human rights, as we understand them today, support the idea that all human beings, irrespective of race, gender and class, should have equal civil, political and economic rights. Enshrined as a 'faith in fundamental rights' by the Charter of the United Nations (1945) and first internationally incorporated, using the term 'human rights', into the Universal Declaration of Human Rights (ratified 1948).

Universal Declaration of Human Rights (ratified 1948)
The Declaration declares:

- all human beings are born free and equal and entitled to freedoms irrespective of race, colour, sex, language, religion, political or other opinion, national or social origin, property, birth or other status;
- human freedoms shall include the right to life, liberty, security, freedom from slavery or servitude, torture, cruel or degrading treatment;
- all are equal before the law and entitled to its protection, not subject to arbitrary arrest, detention or exile, entitled to a fair hearing, entitled to be presumed innocent until proved guilty;
- everyone has a right to privacy, freedom of movements from one country to another, the right to seek asylum, to hold nationality;
- all have equal rights to marry freely;
- all have equal rights to own property;
- everyone has the right to freedom of thought, conscience, religion, opinion, expression, access to information (through any media and regardless of frontiers), peaceful assembly, right to take part in government, access to public service, universal and equal suffrage, the right to social security and development of the personality;
- all have the right to work, a free choice of employment, proper working conditions, equal pay for equal work, just and favourable remuneration, right to join a trades union, to rest and leisure, a reasonable standard of living, access to health care and, if a mother or child, special care and assistance;
- everyone has the right to free compulsory elementary education, and should expect further and higher education to be available and accessible on merit, parents have the right to choose education which shall develop and strengthen the human personality;
- everyone has the right to participate in cultural life and to copyright protection;
- all individuals have a duty to the law and to the freedoms of others, public order and general welfare.

> **?** How can we interpret the equal right to own property in a capitalist world where some can afford property and some cannot?

International Covenant on Civil and Political Rights (adopted 1966, in force 1976)
In 2011 there were 167 parties and 72 signatories to the covenant that includes the rights of a nation:
- to self-determination;
- to own, trade and dispose of its property freely;
- not be deprived of its means of subsistence.

> **?** If a nation trades in something a more powerful nation does not like, does the more powerful nation have a right to take action against it?

The covenant includes the right of an individual to:
- legal recourse when their rights have been violated, even if the violator was acting in an official capacity;
- life;
- liberty and freedom of movement;
- equality before the law;
- presumption of innocence until proven guilty;
- appeal a conviction;
- be recognised as a person before the law;
- privacy and protection of that privacy by law;
- freedom of thought, conscience, and religion;
- freedom of opinion and expression;
- freedom of assembly and association;
- appeal for commutation to a lesser penalty under the law;
- choose freely whom they will marry and to found a family;
- (as a child) be protected against discrimination based on race, sex, colour, national origin, or language;
- (as a nation) suspend some (but not all) of these rights in case of civil emergency only.

The covenant forbids:
- torture and inhuman or degrading treatment;
- slavery or involuntary servitude;
- arbitrary arrest and detention;
- debtors' prisons;
- propaganda advocating war;
- propaganda advocating hatred based on race, religion, national origin or language;
- the death penalty entirely for people under 18 years of age.

The covenant restricts:
- the death penalty to the most serious of crimes.

The covenant requires:
- that the duties and obligations of marriage and family be shared equally between partners.

 Is the death penalty ever justifiable?

International Covenant on Economic, Social and Cultural Rights (adopted 1966, in force 1976)

The covenant includes the right to:
- self-determination;
- wages sufficient to support a minimum standard of living;
- equal pay for equal work;
- equal opportunity for advancement;
- form trade unions;
- strike;
- paid or otherwise compensated maternity leave;
- free primary education;
- accessible education at all levels;
- copyright, patent, and trademark protection for intellectual property.

The covenant forbids:
- exploitation of children.

The covenant requires:
- all nations to cooperate to end world hunger.

> ❓ Would it ever be possible for 'all nations to cooperate to end world hunger'? What sort of ethical and practical obstacles may prevent this?

Geneva Conventions on the Treatment of the Victims of War (First, Wounded and Sick in the Field, 1864; Second, Mariners, 1906; Third, Prisoners of War, 1929; Fourth, Civilians, 1949)

The Geneva Conventions protect the rights of individuals, combatants, non-combatants, prisoners of war and enemy captives during war.

> ❓ A soldier, Jack, is engaged in a battle as part of a just war and is therefore entitled to kill or maim any of those who constitute the enemy. If one of the enemy, Jill, surrenders, and even though the battle continues and even though Jack's comrades are still killing and maiming Jill's comrades, Jack is no longer entitled to kill or maim Jill but must protect her under the rules of the UN Geneva Conventions. Because Jack is protecting Jill, one of Jack's comrades is killed by one of Jill's comrades. What are the moral implications of this?

Convention on the Prevention and Punishment of the Crime of Genocide (adopted 1948, in force 1951)

The convention bans the killing, or mental or physical harm or the intention to prevent births or removal of children of groups or members of groups because of their racial, ethnic, national or religious motives.

> ❓ A powerful country invades a less powerful country (and causes death and harm to the citizens including children) with the intention of changing a regime that it feels unsuitable. Does this contravene the UN Convention against Genocide?

Convention against Torture and Other Cruel, Inhuman or Degrading Treatment or Punishment (adopted 1984, in force 1987)

The convention makes torture and inhuman or degrading treatment illegal and unjustifiable no matter what the circumstances (e.g. state of emergency, threat, order from superior or the state) and forbids countries to deport a refugee to a country if there is reason to believe they may be tortured on their return.

> **?** Work out a definition of 'torture and inhuman or degrading treatment' then see how some of the most recent acts connected with the conflicts in Yugoslavia (1991–1999), (Afghanistan (2001–), Iraq (2003–2010), and Libya (2011) should be viewed in light of your definition.

Convention on the Elimination of all Forms of Discrimination against Women (adopted 1979, in force 1981)
The convention bans discrimination against women defining it as:

> ... any distinction, exclusion or restriction made on the basis of sex which has the effect or purpose of impairing or nullifying the recognition, enjoyment or exercise by women, irrespective of their marital status, on a basis of equality of men and women, of human rights and fundamental freedoms in the political, economic, social, cultural, civil or any other field...

and insists that adopting states abolish all discriminatory laws and protect women against discrimination by persons, organisations or enterprises.

> **?** Men do not take on the same responsibility as women for childbirth. Does this mean that men should not have the same rights as women?

Convention on the Rights of the Child (adopted 1989, in force 1990)
The convention bans discrimination against children (a person under 18 years of age) and provides special protection and rights appropriate to minors such as the right to:
- life, a name, a nationality, the preservation of his or her identity and the right to leave any country including their own;
- know and be cared for and have access to parents;
- freedom of thought, conscience, religion and expression;
- freedom of association, privacy and access to information;
- child care (if necessary), protection from abuse (physical or mental) and if a refugee, to humanitarian assistance, and social security;

- health treatment, standard of living, and if disabled, to conditions necessary to provide dignity and self-reliance;
- education and the practice of his or her own culture and language;
- engage in play and recreation;
- be protected from all forms of exploitation (economic, drug and sex);
- be presumed innocent until proven guilty, to legal assistance and to never have life imprisonment or capital punishment imposed on them;
- protection in times of war.

> **?** The legal age for moral responsibility in the UK is 10 years (lower than most other countries). A 17-year-old stabs and kills a mother and her 8-year-old son because of their race. The judge says that a life sentence cannot be imposed even though it was an unprovoked act of murder, as this would violate the 17-year-old child's human rights. Is this right?

Further questions

There has been a proliferation of human rights legislation since the early twentieth century. The assertion of these rights has become the subject of much civil legal action. Claiming rights and receiving financial compensation for rights infringement has become an acknowledged part of Western society. The questions here seek to explore the basis for some rights and how it is that we come to assume them as 'our rights'. It is important to distinguish between rights that are no more than laws connected with human entitlement (e.g. a right to education), and natural rights which are fundamental to human existence (e.g. freedom).

1. The Human Rights Act 1998 came into force on 2 October 2000 and incorporates into UK law certain rights and freedoms set out in the European Convention on Human Rights (1950, 1953, 1966), and largely in the UN Universal Declaration of Human Rights (1948), such as:
- right to life;

- protection from torture and inhuman or degrading treatment or punishment;
- protection from slavery and forced or compulsory labour;
- the right to liberty and security of person;
- the right to a fair trial;
- protection from retrospective criminal offences;
- the protection of private and family life;
- freedom of thought, conscience and religion;
- freedom of expression;
- freedom of association and assembly;
- the right to marry and found a family;
- freedom from discrimination;
- the right to property;
- the right to education;
- the right to free and fair elections;
- the abolition of the death penalty in peacetime.

Arrange these rights in a hierarchy of importance to the individual. Explain your reasoning.

2. How should we interpret a 'right'? For example does the 'right to education' mean a 'right' to education in any subject we choose which should be free and available for as long as we want it?

3. It is now the case in the UK that for certain crimes (e.g. sexual offences), the court is allowed to know of any previous criminal record of the defendant before the trial is completed. Does this contravene the entitlement under the Human Rights Act (2000) to protection from retrospective criminal offences?

4. Should any (or all) given human rights be lost if the individual does not fulfil any (or all) of his or her social responsibilities? For example, convicted wrongdoers may lose their liberty. Would this mean that someone who contravenes another's right to protection against discrimination should lose the right to be protected against discrimination?

5. During military conflict, innocent civilian life is lost (since the time of the Vietnam War euphemistically referred to as 'collateral damage' or 'friendly fire'). Does this contravene the basic 'right to life' of every human being? Should this ever be tolerated (i.e. are there any circumstances which make it acceptable)? Should those responsible be held to account?

6. Some rights are removed or curtailed if the individual does not accept social responsibility (e.g. an imprisoned wrongdoer loses the 'right to freedom of association and assembly') while others are preserved (e.g. the wrongdoer is entitled to a fair trial). Should a torturer have their right to be protected against torture preserved?

7. Preserving our rights to 'thought' and 'freedom of expression' should mean we could express any thoughts. Is this reasonable?

8. What is our right to think as we choose (a right seemingly impossible to remove)? How does this connect with any rights we might have to act as we choose?

9. The UN Convention on the Rights of the Child (1989) confers the rights of 'freedom of thought, conscience, religion and expression' as well as the right to 'engage in play and recreation'. Does there seem any conflict between these two rights?

10. On 20 October 2011, Muammar Gaddafi (1942–2011), for 42 years Libyan leader (Brotherly Leader and Guide of the Revolution of Libya), was shot and killed by members of the forces associated with the Libyan National Transitional Council. This killing met with general approval from Western governments. Does this raise any human rights issues?

Further reading

Hugh LaFollette (ed.), *Ethics in Practice: An Anthology* (Oxford: Blackwell, 2002).

John Stuart Mill, *On Liberty and Other Essays*, (ed.) John Gray, Oxford World Classics (Oxford: Oxford University Press, 1991).

14

Freedom and Determinism

If every cause has a preceding cause how is it possible for me to act freely? After all, everything I do will be caused by something else.

Introduction

Theories of free-will and determinism are concerned with interpreting human behaviour. It is commonly accepted that the notion of freedom is an essential feature of a full and meaningful life. Freedom means that we truly make free choices according to our will. Determinism holds that freedom is impossible: either our actions are governed by the will of God, or causal interconnectedness is so complex that any 'decision' we make is determined by various causes, or the future is somehow already decided and any act in the present can only be in accordance with what is (already) in the future, or that any so-called decision we make is presupposed by our genes, upbringing, childhood experiences or social conditioning. Based upon the principles of mechanics laid down by Isaac Newton (1642–1727), the French mathematician Pierre-Simon, marquis de Laplace (1749–1827) claimed that, in theory, given a complete knowledge of the universe at any time and of the laws of nature, the state of the universe at any other time could be known. In other words, if we know all the facts then there can be nothing left to chance.

> Is there a hierarchy of free-will? For example, do molecules of oxygen respond only to causes, animals to instinct and human beings to acts of will?

Types of cause

If a person's will is not subject to causes then it must be random or the subject of chance. However, we must wonder if an action which is subject only to chance is truly free anyway; after all, when a coin shows heads there is no alternative to what it shows. Perhaps freedom itself only makes sense when compared to lack of freedom. Our lives are guided by many emotions that do not necessarily fit a prescribed causal chain (e.g. gratitude, resentment, forgiveness, praise, blame, love, hate) so we could conclude that human (or emotional) freedom is different from scientific (or empirical) freedom.

Freedom and the individual

Determinism

Determinism can be positive or negative, rigid or non-rigid. Positive determinists, like David Hume (1711–1776), accept that there is a general human nature that we follow and that this does not hinder the development of the individual who, although remaining human and subject to human ways, can still be a special person in their own right. Negative determinists allow that I cannot choose to do some impossible thing (even though that thing is logically possible, e.g. swim underwater all day without breathing, which although empirically impossible is logically possible), but do not consider this inability a constraint on, or reduction in, my freedom.

Rigid determinism can come in one of two forms: religious and scientific. Calvinism, for example, takes a rigid, religious deterministic view. Calvinists hold that God's omniscience means that he knows every human action both past and future, and this means that all human actions are fixed (in God's mind). Because of this, humans do nothing freely. On this account, the ultimate destiny of the human soul is also known by God and is not connected to any actions of the individual. Less strict religions believe that free-will is God's gift and in its absence the idea of an ultimate destiny of the human soul (either in heaven or hell) is pointless. Laplace proposed a rigid, scientific determinism that held every action within the physical world (which includes human beings) is determined by the science of mechanics. The psychologist B. F. (Burrhus Frederic) Skinner (1904–1990) argued that all human behaviour is a result either of genetics or of social pressures and conditioning. His view scorned free-will as modern superstition.

> **?** To say that something was fate is to imply that something was meant to happen. To say that something is determined is to imply that we had no personal choice in its happening. Is there a difference?

Freedom

Metaphysical freedom holds that there is (to some degree or another) an absence of causal laws which govern our actions and that we (to some degree or another) have some sort of power to decide what will happen to us in the future.

P.F. (Peter Frederick) Strawson (1919–2006) says that free actions are the only actions for which the individual can be held morally responsible or, based upon which, we can properly feel resentment or gratitude. Common-sense morality allows that if we had no choice over what happened then we are not responsible for what happened. Incompatabilists believe that freedom and determinism are incompatible in that if determinism is true then no one can be held to moral account. If an incompatabilist believes that determinism is false (and that some actions are free), then he is a 'libertarian'. If he believes that determinism is true (and we have no choice and therefore no moral responsibility), then he is, for example like William James (1842–1910), a 'hard determinist'.

Compatabilists, on the other hand, believe that freedom and determinism are compatible. This argument, put forward by G.E. (George Edward) Moore (1873–1958), rests on the idea that freedom does not mean 'not determined' but is a choice made in the absence of coercion. If I choose on the basis that I would have done otherwise if I had chosen to, then I have made a free choice.

Both the incompatabilist and the compatabilist hold that there is essentially one correct view of freedom. Ted Honderich (1933–), however, argues that there are two types of freedom: one that is directly linked to causes (and therefore determined), and the other (personal feelings, aspirations) that is not so linked (and therefore free).

Quantum mechanics offers some support for incompatabilism with its interpretation of a randomised universe. But this sort of randomness is pure chance and such actions would, under most circumstances, not make us morally culpable (e.g. if I had cramp in my calf, grabbed my leg and inadvertently knocked over an expensive ornament I might claim at least reduced responsibility for the broken vase).

> ❓ A woman accused of murdering her husband says in her defence, 'I could not stop myself doing it.' The prosecutor says that the defendant had adequate time and opportunity to make a choice (she had lain in wait for her cheating husband for over an hour before bludgeoning him to death with a hammer). What do you think?

Predetermined future

Some regard the future to be predetermined (and not just possible but real). This has two distinct forms: fatalism and causal determinism. Fatalism states that there is no point in deliberating or taking any action because the future is prescribed; it will be the same no matter what we do. Causal determinism, on the other hand, proposes that the future may be determined only if we take some action or another.

> ❓ John is very ill. Jill thinks that he can only be saved if she calls the physician. John says this is pointless because he will either recover or not, whether the physician does or does not come. Who is right?

Freedom and the state

Liberty

In Ancient Greece, liberty meant being part of a participating democracy in which the individual was exposed fully (in both public and private life) to laws which he (only men could vote in Ancient Greece) had also taken part in formulating. To be free meant to abide by laws that were, as such, self-made. For such an individual the question 'Who should govern me?' could only be answered by 'Myself'.

Since Henri Benjamin Constant de Rébecque (1767–1830) and Jean-Jacques Rousseau (1712–1778), this style of participatory freedom has been replaced by individual freedom where, in a post-industrialised society, the individual's needs are considered best promoted through public welfare and representative democracy and his or her needs for freedom confined to the conduct of his or her own private life. So, whereas the Ancient Greek did not consider any part of life closed to public scrutiny, the modern individual believes in the right to say, do and act anything in the privacy of his or her own home providing this does not interfere with the similar rights of another. This is the 'rational self-interest' of the liberal individual, who asks not so much 'Who should govern me?', but 'How much government should there be over me?'.

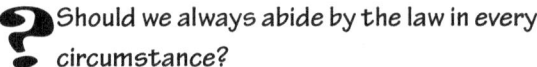

Should we always abide by the law in every circumstance?

Authority of the state

The authority of the state is an extension of the parent who knows best for its child. It occupies the position of the wisest. Members of such a state can never be repressed by the state (even though they might think they are), because the state knows always what is best for the individual's own good (and therefore always acts in the individual's best interest).

Our membership of the state may have come about by birth or choice but, as citizens, we are obliged to defer to the authority of the state. The state, in this way, always occupies the high ground, dictating to its subjects what is best for their physical, mental and ethical health. This can sometimes be seen as a 'nanny state' or a dictatorial state. However, any curtailment of freedom is still a restriction on the activities of the individual (e.g. even if it is said to be for national security, future good, state wealth). Indeed, while restrictions are in place, individuals will never express their desired freedoms and others will never have the opportunities to appreciate and understand them. In some ways, this is the conflict between a controlling totalitarian regime and a liberal regime with agreed human rights and the right of privacy. The liberal view is expressed most clearly by John Stuart Mill (1806–1873), who defends the individual's right to pursue his personal goals in his private domain believing that the state has no right to interfere (even if purportedly for the individual's own good) unless to prevent harm to others. Mill's defence of liberty upholds the rights of individuals to realise their own potential and, in so doing, express the potential of, and develop, the state. Western democracy, which supports this utilitarian view, is constantly accused of interfering too much with the privacy and rights of the individual. Threats from outside the state (e.g. terrorism) can also bring about a tightening of the state's authority over the conduct of the individual.

> **?** In order to prevent wrongdoers from inhabiting the streets at night, the state imposes a curfew from 9p.m. to 6a.m. Is this a reasonable use of the state's authority?

Political freedom
Any individual member of a state has a varying degree of political freedom. For a state to operate successfully a compromise has to be reached which balances the freedom of the individual with the necessary restrictions imposed by the state. Declared human rights are used to help reach this compromise (e.g. balancing such rights as freedom of expression with laws against sedition or unlawful public assembly).

One way of dealing with this is 'social contract theory'. Thomas Hobbes (1588–1679), whose own social environment led him to think in terms of 'perpetual war', believed that the human 'state of nature' should always be subject to the sovereign right of absolute power. John Locke (1632–1704) believed that our natural rights (to life, liberty and property) necessitated only a very limited power of government. Rousseau thought the contract should empower all individuals in the context of a 'general will'. By such a contract, the individual's natural liberty gives way to a 'civil' or 'moral' liberty.

> **?** Should I be able to do anything in the privacy of my own home or should the state have a say in what I do?

Various theories lay out how the individual (as a social being) should relate to the state. Mill worked out a utilitarian approach, which says we should be able to do anything we choose. Only if we cause harm to another citizen should the state take action. This not only applies to freedom of speech but also freedom of action, which means that we are entitled to cause ourselves as much harm as we choose. Opponents of this view say that if we cause ourselves harm then necessarily (and unavoidably) we cause others harm (e.g. by using the health service, putting others who come to our aid at risk). In addition, this can be seen as a negative approach that seeks simply the absence of restriction.

> **?** Is it wrong for someone to harm himself or herself and provide their own medical aftercare? Is it wrong for someone to harm himself or herself and expect the state to provide their medical aftercare?

Georg Wilhelm Friedrich Hegel (1770–1831) believed that individual freedom was not a matter of whim but should involve coherent, rational action that necessitates involvement in the duties of society and state.

> **?** I am conscripted into an army to fight against another nation. I do not claim any conscientious objection (even though I have reservations about the justness of the cause). Have I acted freely?

Karl Heinrich Marx (1818–1883) put forward the influential idea that only if individuals were involved in the collectively controlled economy of the state could they be truly free.

> **?** John and Mary work on a state-owned collective farm run by the local community. They are very poor and, because of lack of investment, the farm is run down. Although they wish to leave to find a better life, they do not have enough money to travel to another country. In what ways are they free because they take part in a collectively controlled economy?

Free speech

Free speech (which applies to both verbal and non-verbal forms of communication) is generally accepted as the foremost civil liberty. Free speech is considered a necessary condition both for a healthy individual and for a healthy state. Free speech maybe legitimately curtailed, for example, because there is no time for discussion or because of the laws of libel, slander or incitement. However, although time constraints may seem acceptable (there is always another time), prohibition because what is said or written harms another is deemed by some to be nonsense. Harm can be caused to individuals who feel hurt or maligned (e.g. racial or religious insults), or to vulnerable members of a society (e.g. children exposed to pornographic material). Harm can also be seen in light of its potential to affect the well-being or standing of the individual (e.g. exposing embarrassing aspects of a celebrity's personal life). Freedom of speech, therefore, can be regulated or curtailed by what is considered its 'worth' (as harm) to another. In litigious democracies, the harmful worth of what is said is more often than not (though there are notable exceptions, particularly in ethnic cases) conferred more commonly on the wealthy or privileged (e.g. politicians, the famous).

> **?** Words are an expression of our thoughts. To say we have no right to say something (in particular) implies that we have no right to think that thing. Are there things we should be allowed to think that we should not be allowed to say?

Further questions

Freedom and determinism are central matters of concern in philosophy. 'Freedom of the individual' is not the same as the sort of freedom that can be granted as a right, dealt with here as 'freedom and the state' (e.g. the freedom to drive at 17 years of age). 'Freedom to act as an individual' comes with choice, and this rests upon the questions of whether or not the future is fixed, whether causes bring about effects, or whether powerful (or divine) forces somehow control us. 'Freedom to act as granted by the state' is invariably controlled by some legislative process (and therefore subject to change in the human world). A determined universe (almost certainly) means we have no choice, and no choice usually means a severe reduction (if not extinguishment) in individual meaning or purpose.

1. If I trip over an uneven paving slab, it is common sense to assert that the paving slab being uneven was caused by circumstances beyond my control. However, was I in control of all the causes that led to me tripping over the uneven paving slab?

2. I can turn left or right at a road junction. If I have no particular place to go and decide to go left, was that a free choice?

3. Someone claims in his defence that he is a wrongdoer because his parents and their parents before them were wrongdoers. It is, he says, 'in his genes'. Is this defence in any way reasonable?

4. The law considers some actions committed when the offender had a 'diminished responsibility'. This would normally imply some sort of psychological or mental condition. Could some people who commit crimes plead a diminished responsibility because they had obviously not been able to fully grasp the importance or wrong of their illegal action (i.e. they would not have committed the crime had they had a serious concern about its wrongful nature)?

5. Aristotle (384–322 BC) said that the future was determined because something either would or would not happen. This means that you either will or will not break your leg tomorrow; in either case, the future is determined. Does this make sense?

6. Do I have a duty to the state to report wrongdoing? If I report wrongdoing, have I acted as a free 'individual' or as a 'component of the state'?

7. A film star has had an unflattering photograph taken of her on the beach. Should the other members of society see the photograph (after all, if they did not follow details of her life, go to see her films and so on, she would not be famous), or should the film star be protected from publication because she would be mentally 'harmed' by others seeing the unflattering image?

8. Should our ultimate aim as individuals be freedom *from* the state or freedom *within* the state? Are these two senses of freedom compatible?

Further reading

Hugh LaFollette (ed.), *Ethics in Practice: An Anthology* (Oxford: Blackwell, 2002).

John Stuart Mill, *On Liberty and Other Essays*, (ed.) John Gray, Oxford World Classics (Oxford: Oxford University Press, 1991)

15
Politics, Political Equality and the State of the World

Politicians control representative democracies. In order to be voted into power, democratic politicians must be popular (as opposed to expert). Their expertise at running the country is not necessarily known until they take power. Is this right?

Introduction

Politics is about being involved in decisions connected to distribution of materials and the rights and liberties that people should enjoy in any state. Politics is about power. Such power is very great and, according to John Locke (1632–1704), was fundamentally the right of making laws that carried the death penalty for transgression. Power is about control, and political power is about control of the state and all its members. Most individuals find it difficult being controlled by others unless there is a clearly defined exchange of individual gain for lessened individual freedom (in this way it is similar to ethical conflict). Individuals move from their given individual state of nature because membership of the state provides them with protection from threats both within their society and beyond it. The state also provides an infrastructure for trade normally beyond the grasp of the individual. In these ways, both the social and economic safety of the individual is satisfied. This 'social constraint' is the basis for all Western democracies.

Equality means people in similar moral situations should be treated similarly. But what counts as a similar moral situation and what as similar treatment is contentious. Some states may strive to provide basic political and legal rights but, because it is clear that complete equality amongst people is impossible, states (at best) try to reduce or ameliorate inequality.

Contemporary human society has probably a greater sense of concern about the state of the world than has ever previously been had. This derives from increased wealth in the West and an increasing globalisation and interconnectedness (of trade, information, opportunity and so on). Increased consumer demands (which lead to higher production and greater natural destruction), noticeable imbalance between the richer and poorer nations (which leads to poorer nations demanding an industrialised route to economic prosperity which the richer nations have, to an extent, passed through), new wealthy economies driving and supporting consumer demand, and the adverse effects that human industry and behaviour have on the natural world and ecology in general all add to this.

Ethical concepts
Political philosophy looks at the nature and conduct of government ('political ethics') as well as the social organisation that it influences (the 'descriptive-explanatory' (fact-based) view). Ethical concepts include ideas on individual autonomy and self-determination as well as theories of justice, democracy, rights and political obligations.

Political ideas
Plato (*c*.428–347 BC) was the first political philosopher, concentrating much of his effort on the relationship of justice with the individual and the state. He sets individual justice above all else, believing it leads to reason and so eventually the just state. His just, utopian state, Kallipolis, is highly ordered by class and law (e.g. involving eugenics, state education, no personal property) and tightly controlled by those specially trained for the role (the Guardians).

> ❓ Would a democracy be better run by a specially trained class of politicians as opposed to those who sought election because of their own political motives?

Aristotle (384–322 BC) believed, like Plato, that the state was more important than the individual, though Aristotle (concerned more with classifying the world) takes a more descriptive-explanatory view than Plato. Aristotle believed that individuals trained to pursue happiness would bring about the perfect state (according to Aristotle, the most virtuous pursuit of the individual). Aristotle's ideal state tolerates slavery, un-emancipated women and strict class divisions.

St Augustine (354–430) and St Thomas Aquinas (1224/5–1274) both emphasised the relation between religious and political authority. Aquinas proposes that the proper function of secular government is to work towards obtaining religious goals.

Thomas Hobbes (1588–1679) proposed a modern view of government supported by many non-governmental organisations (NGOs). Hobbes' government is highly authoritative, subordinating its citizens in exchange for providing their security. If the sovereign power fails in its obligation to protect the citizens then their responsibility to abide by the law disappears.

John Locke (1632–1704) believed that a secular government was necessary in order to protect the individual's property, and that such a government was essential if individuals were to realise their own personal freedom.

> **?** If the state provides insufficient police to keep order in the streets, should the citizens take policing into their own hands?

Jean-Jacques Rousseau (1712–1788), proposed a social contract which attempts to reconcile the two competing forces of individual autonomy and authority of the state by making the individual morally obliged to obey the law. Rousseau proposed that the individual should give preference to the rule of the majority (the 'general will') over their own individual wishes about the common good. This means that the individual must sometimes accept that they are in a minority. According to Rousseau, all citizens must abide, by virtue of their social contract, with the general will and must involve themselves directly with the democratic process (not 'taking part' via a representative democracy).

John Stuart Mill (1806–1873) takes an 'anti-state' view which combines the ethical and the descriptive-explanatory views in a form which, like that of Rousseau, attempts to blend the needs of both the individual and (to a lesser extent) the state. Mill's main reason for allowing the state to coerce its population is in order to protect one individual from harming another (i.e. the 'harm principle'). Such harm must be evidenced by actual violation of one person's right by another. Mill makes interesting exclusions from state coercion, for example, the very young, the very old, or societies or groups that have themselves become 'old'. Mill does not sanction controlling the person for 'his own good'. Mill's utilitarianism (i.e. the principle of achieving the greatest happiness) promotes the individual's right to freedom of thought, speech, individuality and rejection of religious authority. Mill advocates selecting political leaders with exceptional skills and morality. His liberal individualism does not support the rule of the majority; instead, it promotes a system that is able to represent the wishes of minorities. Mill believed that extra votes should be given to those with superior intelligence.

Karl Heinrich Marx (1818–1883), via his historical materialism, describes society as consisting in an economic base, or infrastructure, with a non-economic or ideological superstructure. Marx and Friedrich Engels (1820–1895) argue that class conflict (between the bourgeoisie and the proletariat) is depicted in all post-feudal society. This they believed (by their time) had focused into a conflict between wage earners and capital from which, after an eventual struggle, capitalism would be overthrown. Marx and Engels afford more emphasis on the study of history and economics than they do on ethical values.

For most of the twentieth century, two main political movements stood in opposition, liberal free-market-supporting capitalism (in one form or another) and Marxism (in one form or another). As the century progressed, and with the end of the Cold War (c. 1946–1991) and the collapse of the Soviet Union, together with a decline in living standards in parts of the Western world, the contrast between the two has become blurred. Since the 1970s, the People's Republic of China (PRC) has reformed its industrial and agricultural base to create by 2010 the third richest country in the world behind the US and the European Union (EU).

John Rawls (1921–2002) proposes that individuals should make decisions ignorant of the plight of those whom their decisions affect. Robert Nozick (1938–2002) advocates a more conventional conservative state with clearly defined, yet minimal control. The recent thinking of Charles Taylor (1931–), Michael Sandel (1953–) and Alasdair C. MacIntyre

(1929–) stresses the importance of community over the individual ('communitarianism'). Other forces for reassessment of political systems have come from feminism, minority groups, the less developed world, undemocratic countries, and from philosophers such as H. L. A. (Herbert Lionel Adolphus) Hart (1907–1992) and Ronald Dworkin (1931–), who put legal interests central to their political thinking.

Politics in practice
Voting
Democratic systems operate on a system of regular (and fairly frequent) opportunities for individuals to make known their opinion about who should be in power (voting). Voters' decisions about who to vote for are based upon the public declarations of intent of different political parties or factions (e.g. manifestos). In the act of voting, we are demonstrating in an official way not only our equal feeling of human dignity but also our autonomous power of self-direction. Although this act is emotionally symbolic (no one person truly believes his or her one vote will actually make any difference), it is also important for psychological well-being.

> **?** Currently, in the UK, more eligible voters do not vote than do vote for any particular party. Does this mean that the greatest democratic mandate is for no government?

In a totalitarian state, individuals are not given a choice of who should be in power (e.g. the country could be run by a dictator installed and supported by the military) and, if they are, they can only cast their vote for one candidate or candidates who represent the same party.

> **?** A democratic system encourages change in government whereas (unchallenged) dictatorial power may persist over long periods. Does this mean that a country is more likely to benefit from a dictator because there is more opportunity to put his or her wishes into practice than the ever-changing governments of a democracy?

Control of information
While members of a political party are in power, they also have power to influence the way information is presented (e.g. it is commonly understood that no 'sane' government would ever hold a referendum it believed it could lose). In moderate political environments, there are only minor differences between political aims, but as this gap widens (the distance between right and left opens) the more reason (and opportunity) there is for political propaganda. In democracies, associations between political groups and news organisation can sometimes be problematic.

> **?** If the state controls the information I receive then there is no point in me voting because I think only what the government want me to think (and they want me to think that they are the best). Does this make sense?

Capitalism
Capitalism (as a market-based, commodity-producing economic system controlled by capital) allows individuals to employ the nation's wealth for their own benefit. Communism as Marxism-Leninism (originally designed as an economic system by Marx), allows only the state to employ the nation's wealth and shares back equally the benefits that accrue. In the second half of the twentieth century there was a global power struggle between these two forces. By the beginning of the twenty-first century most national Marxism-Leninism had fallen back under the dominance of capitalism (being replaced by it in the case of Russia, or co-opted into it in the case of the PRC). Only the Democratic People's Republic of Korea and the Republic of Cuba can claim a strict adherence to Marxism-Leninism. In a capitalist West the welfare of individuals rests upon the performance of corporations — if they fail then individuals suffer. The most recent phase of capitalism is the neoliberal movement that supports capital markets operating in a global free trading and non-regulated environment. It has its roots in the work of Adam Smith (1723–1790), John Maynard Keynes (1883–1946) and Milton Friedman (1912–2006). Neoliberalism has found recent political expression, starting in the 1980s under the premierships of Baroness Margaret Hilda Thatcher (1925–) in the UK, Ronald Wilson Reagan (1911–2004) in the US and Augusto Jose Ramon Pinochet

Ugarte (1915–2006) in Chile. Western political support was strengthened by the industrialisation and global market spread of the PRC and the Asian countries. The recipe still holds sway in the largely unfettered free trading global environment which exists today, and has so far weathered a strong threat to its continuance in the form of the banking crisis and credit crunch which triggered a world recession in 2007 (recovery from which in 2012 remains slow and faltering).

> **?** If all the wealth of a nation were shared back equally to individual members, some people would be worse off than they would like. If each individual is allowed to own whatever wealth they can get, this leads to greed and inequality. Which is right?

The state of the world

The environmental movement has its roots in the West in the second half of the nineteenth century as preservationists such as John Muir (1838–1914) and Henry David Thoreau (1817–1862), conservationists such as Gifford Pinchot (1865–1946) and those concerned with disease and water pollution brought increasing awareness of the state of the world to the public. During the Cold War years of the twentieth century, environmental issues became increasingly linked with politics. In the twenty-first century, the environmental debate encompasses all features of nature from the earth itself, to its atmosphere and all life forms that it supports.

Living species

All environmental ethics support a positive view towards co-existence with, and responsibility for, other living things. Peter Singer (1946–) proposes a utilitarian theory to support equality of consideration for all life forms. The approach he advocates is one of empathising with the situation of other life forms: that is, trying to understand what it is to be like them. Tom Regan (1938–) promotes our responsibility to other life forms without imposing any reciprocal responsibilities upon them. Holmes Rolston III (1932–) argues that we should adopt a respect for the species itself and not the individual species member. He believes the dynamic form of the species is more important than the short-lived form of the individual.

> If forced to choose, should we be saving individual whales or the environment in which their species exist?

There are concerns about the human species overcoming other species (e.g. causing the extinction of other species because of its own greed) as well as devastating its own environment (e.g. destroying vast areas of rain forest in the Amazon Basin). The fear is that humans will ultimately destroy the environment they rely on and will therefore cause their own extinction. The United Nations Convention on Biological Diversity (originated at the first Earth Summit in Rio de Janeiro in 1992, in force in 1993, adopted in Nagoya, Japan in 2010) highlights the fact that as well as destroying other species there are increasing concerns about the way some members of humankind relate to and respect the cultural integrity of others. This concern is manifested in the movement to preserve cultural diversity in the face of globalisation, formulated in the Cartagena Protocol on Biosafety (adopted 2000, in force 2003). In 2010 the United Nations declared 2011–2020 the United Nations Decade of Biodiversity.

> Are there any reasons why a language with less than 50 speakers should be preserved?

Greenhouse gases, global warming and climate change
The supposition that it is the emission of greenhouse gases (CO_2) from industrial activities that is causing the climate to change for the worse, puts pressure on the industrialised nations (in particular the PRC, the US and Europe) to reduce such emissions. The Kyoto Protocol (the United Nations Framework Convention on Climate Change, originated at the first Earth Summit in Rio de Janeiro in 1992, adopted in Kyoto in 1997, in force 2005) acknowledges that 'change in the earth's climate and its adverse effects are a common concern to humankind'. The ratifying nations agree to work towards a reduction in greenhouse gasses by implementing legislation directed mainly towards reducing CO_2 emissions.

> In 2007 the PRC, the US and EU together produced 56.25% of the world's greenhouse gasses (the US

producing almost 20% yet only accounting for just over 4% of the world's population). Should this be tolerated by other nations of the world?

The United Nations adopted an agreement (Cancun, 2010) to curb climate change and set up a 'green climate fund' to help developing nations take part.

> **?** Suppressing the industrial development of less-developed countries will reduce benefits to their populations already had by the developed Western world. Is this reasonable when, even though the weight of political and much scientific opinion supports it, it is not certain that short-term human production of greenhouse gasses is directly linked to a normally long-term pattern of climate change? Even if the case for human influenced climate change is certain, would it be right to disbenefit others who have not yet had the chances that industrialisation has brought to the developed world?

Disposal of rubbish

All species create waste products. Humans create inorganic waste that is a product, not of their own bodies, but of their own technology and material consumption. This non-organic waste causes problems that have variously lasting effects (e.g. some things will degrade in only a few years, some radioactive waste will still, as far as we know, be unsafe in thousands of years). Modern civilisations are therefore faced with how to balance providing the benefits of modern technology for their citizens against how many ecological problems that provision will cause both now and in the future.

> **?** Is it right that any human generation should leave waste products for future generations to deal with?

Further questions

This chapter covers a broad range of topics which, although interrelated, can also be dealt with separately. In order to analyse these matters successfully, they need to be stood back from so that an objective view can be had. Individual party politics, our own status and wealth, and our own desire or otherwise to work with the environment need to be identified and set aside.

1. Explain the similarities and differences between:
    'power' and 'authority'
    'programme', 'plan' and 'policy'
    'concern', 'care' and 'consideration'

2. If you were going to design a nation state, what sort of political system would you put in place and why? In particular, consider how the leaders would gain power, how resources would be utilised, and how the rights of the individuals in this society would be established and upheld.

3. Every economic and social system that has ever existed has ultimately run its course. From this we should suppose that capitalism will, at some time, end. If it does, what do you think would replace it? Would it be better? Who would benefit most and who would lose most?

4. Robert believes in equal opportunity for all. Robert failed his school exams and is currently unemployed. Robert thinks that he should be the chief executive of a large corporation because that would make him equal to other chief executives. Should Robert be given the opportunity to be a chief executive by law?

5. Rachel would like to be a world-class long distance runner. She has trained hard since a child, has the physical and psychological attributes required of a top-class athlete, and is fully committed. Unfortunately, Rachel and her parents are very poor and she cannot afford to travel to the important eliminations and heats. Rebecca is not such a good athlete as Rachel, is not particularly committed and lacks much of the natural toughness required at the top class of her event. However, Rebecca's parents are very rich and support her in every way, and Rebecca herself is very beautiful and has become a favourite of the newspaper photographers. Rebecca has been chosen to be part of the national team and Rachel has not. How can this be squared with the idea of individual equality?

6. Would you be prepared to be worse off in order for everyone to be equal? Would you be prepared to be worse off in order for a few people to be slightly better off?

7. If the richer nations have grown rich because of their industrial activity, should they reduce their activity and let the poorer, non-industrialised nations catch up by the same unrestrained activity that they themselves benefited from? On the other hand, should they expect poorer nations to stay poor as part of their sharing of the overall responsibility to ease the polluting pressure on the world?

8. In a representative democracy elections are fought together with the full weight of the available 'publicity machine' (newspapers, radio, television, internet). Does this mean that anyone ever has a 'free vote'?

9. Should CO_2 emissions be fixed on a global *per capita* basis? This could mean countries like the US and UK having severe cuts in their emissions and less developed countries being able to increase their emissions. Alternatively, it could mean that countries like the US and UK could buy up surplus *per capita* emission entitlements from poorer countries to boost their own entitlement. Would this be a reasonable system?

10. If each living thing is striving to attain its own good (a Kantian argument from the moral worth of means), what right do we have to stop it attaining that good?

Notes

Question 1:

'power' – the ability to do or act, a body or government vested with authority;

'authority' – a body having power with the right to enforce obedience;

'programme' – a definite plan of future events;

'plan' – a detailed method by which a thing is to be done;

'policy' – a course or principle of actions adopted or proposed by a government or other controlling body;

'concern' – to have an interest in things which affect another;

'care' – to protect or have charge over another;

'consideration' – thoughtfully take into account matters when deciding or judging something.

Further reading

Hugh LaFollette (ed.), *Ethics in Practice: An Anthology* (Oxford: Blackwell, 2002).

Ronald Grimsley, *The Philosophy of Rousseau* (London: Oxford University Press, 1973).

Edith Hamilton and Huntington Cairns (eds), *The Collected Dialogues of Plato including the Letters* (Princeton: Princeton University Press, 1961).

John Stuart Mill, *On Liberty and Other Essays*, (ed.) John Gray, Oxford World Classics (Oxford: Oxford University Press, 1991).

Thomas Nagel, 'What is it Like to be a Bat?', in *Mortal Questions* (Cambridge: Cambridge University Press, 1979), pp. 165–80.

Jonathan Wolff, *An Introduction to Political Philosophy* (Oxford: Oxford University Press, 2006).

16

War

What would make anyone want to go to war?

Introduction

War pervades human history; except for disease, there is nothing so closely associated with human suffering. Yet, as a thing in itself, war is mysterious. It is hard to conceive of individuals of any nation ever wishing to go to war with the population of another nation, and it is impossible to imagine that any sane individual would want to destroy the population and assets of another country with the ultimate aim of seizing its territory or changing its political processes. Even so, individuals do go to war. The motivations for war must therefore be so powerful as to galvanise people in ways that go against their natural temperament, intuition or common sense. It is therefore likely that human beings are only motivated to war by the wishes of the state (or those that control the state) and not from their own free-will.

> **?** Under what circumstances would you be prepared to go to war? Under what circumstances would you not be prepared to go to war?

Human motivations

Common human motivations (e.g. greed, desire for territory, desire for excitement and adventure), although all capable of generating intense human feeling are unlikely to be shared by all members of the society in such a way that they (of their own volition) would start a war. Religion has more potential to do this (e.g. the Crusades, territorial Judaism) but it is rarely the case that all members of a society share the same religion. However, secular ideologies (e.g. communism, capitalism, imperialism, fascism) in this context, work much like religions. For a nation to go to war it is more likely to be because of a desire (rightly or wrongly) of a few individuals who, by propagandising the cause (truthfully or otherwise), rouse members of a society to act together.

> **?** What do you think individual citizens had to gain from the following conflicts (remember every war has at least two sides): World War I, World War II, Vietnam War, Gulf War, conflict in Iraq, conflict in Afghanistan, conflict in Libya? Do you consider any of these gains to be rightly desired?

What is a war?
War is a conflict among political groups involving hostilities of considerable duration and magnitude. It is where the state in this context employs its armed forces to confront (by attack or defence) the armed forces of another state. War is generally conducted in accordance with recognised customs and 'laws'. By common consent, a war is 'just' if it is an act of self-defence. The principles of 'just war' (i.e. must be conducted by the state for a just purpose) have their roots in the work of St Augustine (354–430) and later St Thomas Aquinas (1224/5–1274). The terms of just war govern whether it is right to use armed force in the first place (*jus ad bellum*), what is acceptable when war is being waged (*jus in bello*), and what should dictate the end of war, peace agreements and the treatment or prosecution of war criminals (*jus post bellum*).

> **?** The same principles of 'just war' were used to justify the Spanish and Portuguese invasion of South America in the fifteenth and sixteenth centuries, and the war against Nazi Germany between 1939 and 1945. Does this seem reasonable?

War can be sanctioned as just, even if not in self-defence but in some recognised, worthwhile cause (usually a 'humanitarian' cause), if there is consensus from a recognised group (e.g. consensus for action from the United Nations Security Council made up of five permanent veto-holding members, the US, UK, France, Russia and the PRC, and ten non-permanent members). It is more difficult to accept the idea of 'just cause' for the waging of war against a state that poses no immediate threat or which simply represents a regime considered 'unsuitable' (e.g. a regime which is not democratic).

> Is the 'war against terrorism' truly a war?

Killing

Modern warfare utilises much technology (indeed war is, and always has been, a major innovator of technology) and this can mask the fact that war is about killing. It is unlikely (if not impossible) that a war could be fought without killing (although there is an increasing acceptance of 'cyberwarfare' involving one nation penetrating the computers of another for economic, political or security reasons). Taking the lives of others is at the root of warfare and any considerations about war must keep this fact central. There are different forms of killing in war: self-defence, in cold blood, face to face, impersonal, killing of someone good or someone evil, killing of a member of a professional army, killing a willing conscript, killing an unwilling conscript, killing an innocent civilian, assassination. In addition, it can involve the killing of one or two (e.g. in personal conflict) or many (e.g. a nuclear bombardment). Each of these types of killing has a different character and attracts various levels of human approval or condemnation.

> Can you think of any circumstance in which someone would be justified in killing another person? If so (on the basis that there are always two sides in war) would this still hold if the person being killed were your own child (or parent)?

The ethics of going to war

Some would say that war is abhorrent to human nature (and implicitly wrong) and cannot therefore be governed by any ethical principles. To create a code of conduct for war is like creating a code of conduct for murder. However, this is denying a form of human conduct that is recurrently present and proposing that ethical principles can only operate in 'good' (i.e. ethically sound) conditions. The rights of individuals involved in conflicts have been incorporated into various formal codes (e.g. the Geneva Conventions for the Protection of Prisoners of War).

> **?** In World War I (1914–1918), conscripted soldiers were shot for desertion or for failing to go 'over the top' when ordered to do so. Was this right?

The act of war

War is an act of the state and the use of force must be sanctioned by the state. There must be just cause: that is, there must be fault on the other side that justifies taking action. The state must go to war with the right intention: that is, to prevent an evil or obtain a good.

Just cause

Historically, just cause was seen as the most important moral criterion for war. As moral relativism has spread in recent times (e.g. the polarisation of moral values guiding the Western world and the world of Islam), just cause has been downgraded in its use for wars between nation states. For example, it was seen as appropriate by the US and UK to attack Iraq in 2003 because the regime of Saddam Hussein (1937–2006) was considered 'inappropriate'. It has, though, remained the main moral measure for wars of humanitarian intervention (i.e. in order to save the lives of civilians who are starving, threatened by disease or at risk from internal state strife). Justification in order to prevent civilian casualties, however, can sometimes easily be connected to the cause for removing a regime or its leader (e.g. the NATO attack on Libyan government forces and the desire to remove Muammar Gaddafi (1942–2011) in 2011).

> **?** Individuals in the UK are not allowed to use disproportionate force to protect their property, others or themselves. Neither are they allowed to attack others who they think may attack them at a future time. Should this rule govern nations as well?

Even though there seems a sufficiently just cause for war, it may not be sufficient to cause a state to go to war. For example, a country may be invaded by another but, because it is poorly armed and outnumbered, does not consider itself able to go to war to defend its territory. If a just war is waged this does not release those taking part from the moral constraints implicit to the conduct of war (e.g. it would be inappropriate for an army to commit acts of torture against its enemy even though its enemy commits acts of torture against it).

> **?** *Why does it always appear that the enemy's justification for war is weaker than our own?*

During a war

Rules of war demand that force is used in proportion. It would be a disproportionate response to bomb a city with a population of three million people because one of your own soldiers had been killed. The question of proportionality is difficult because opposing forces rarely use the same weaponry or technique and would not commonly be at the same level of technical competence. For example, it is hard to know what is an appropriate, conventional military response to a terrorist attack by a suicide bomber.

> **?** *Should all deaths in war be considered equally significant or are some deaths more important than others (e.g. the deaths of your own troops, or the deaths of children)?*

Pacifism

Pacifism rejects war in its entirety as morally obscene and something brutish (like capital punishment) that belongs to a more primitive age. Pacifists think that conflicts between nations should be settled by international gatherings (e.g. the United Nations, international courts). Pacifism can be usefully sub-divided. Absolutists, like Mahatma (Mohandas Karamchand) Gandhi (1869–1948) (who practised non-violent civil disobedience — *satyāgraha* or 'zest for truth') and the later Leo Tolstoy (1828–1910) both held all violence (including war) to be wrong. Modern-war pacifists who, while accepting primitive historical conflicts to have been justified (where there were no viable alternatives), find modern warfare so objectionable that is must be rejected. Positive pacifists, for example the Society of Friends (Quakers), work actively to promote peace. Bertrand Russell

(1872–1970) (himself imprisoned during World War I for his anti-war stance) was, in his support of the Campaign for Nuclear Disarmament (CND), a leading example of positive pacifism in the twentieth century.

> **?** Is it morally possible to hold the view that killing is wrong under certain circumstances and not wrong under other, different, circumstances?

Pacifism is easy to understand in its 'reactionary' sense (e.g. as a response to a particular conflict or proposed conflict), but not so easy to interpret where a broad conflict does not exist. For example, should a government enforce non-violence and by so doing contradict its own standpoint? In addition, if the state is empowered to use force on the individual's behalf, then we might conclude that the individual (upon whose behalf the state is using force) should be allowed to defend himself with force. If the state is powerless to act in the enforcement of rules then society will disintegrate into tyranny and anarchy.

> **?** If a state declares itself a pacifist state (and totally disarms) then it is not in a position to fulfil the primary obligation of the state to protect its people. Does this mean that state pacifism is impossible?

Self-defence

We do not live in a pacifist-based world and it is assumed morally acceptable that the individual has the right to self-defence. The individual has a right to life, to bodily integrity and to enjoy what he or she owns undisturbed (a natural philosophy supported especially by John Locke (1632–1704) and Jean-Jacques Rousseau (1712–1788)). This finds expression in the United States Constitution (1789) and the European Conventions on Human Rights (drafted in 1950, in force 1953 and incorporated into UK law in 1998). The implication of these rights is that no other person has a right to interfere with an individual's right to: respect, life, freedom from torture and servitude, liberty, a fair trial, privacy, conscience and religion, expression, association, marriage, freedom from discrimination and abuse of rights. Self-defence may be applied to a state or an individual.

Usually the state looks after the individual's rights to be protected from an aggressor. However, in the absence of the state's power (e.g. there is not a policeman to hand), the individual expects to be able to defend himself. The state uses its own military or civil power to protect its borders, assets, population and way of life. The principle of self-defence is directed at the maintenance of peace. Defence should not usurp the laws of the state nor threaten civil or international order. Self-defence should not be considered a gift of the state but a gift of nature that is supported by the state.

> **?** Should a weak nation have the right to defend itself against a powerful nation? If you think it does, then how could such a defence be mounted? If you think it does not, then what moral reasons can you offer for this?

There are four basic principles of self-defence in respect of war. When using lethal self-defence, the intention must be self-protection and not to kill for any other reason (e.g. it must not be an act of revenge). There must be a true aggressor (i.e. there must be an actual act of violence and not merely the threat of future violence). The aggression must be unjust and not, for example, an aggressive act of morally acceptable 'policing'. The force used to repel the attack of the aggressor must be moderate and proportional to the type of attack sustained and the difficulty involved in repelling it.

> **?** Could attacking a state that is considered may have the ability to cause great harm in the future (e.g. because it may be able to create nuclear weapons) be considered an act of self-defence? Would such an attack ever be morally acceptable?

The right of self-defence is commonly understood to extend to protecting a third party (e.g. a member of a family under threat by an aggressor, a weak nation needing the protection of a more powerful one), but if this is the case, the four rules of self-defence must still be met. In such cases, any action is only permissible and not necessarily obligatory. It is generally accepted that the right of self-defence can be invoked for an attack on someone's life more than merely his property. This also applies to an attack on the nation's citizens as opposed to its infrastructure.

Waging the just war

If the principles of self-defence are met then a just war can be waged. War involves killing innocent people and others who may well consider themselves acting in self-defence. Those who fight in wars are somehow (e.g. according to George Orwell (1903–1950)) absolved from the moral responsibilities of this killing. Tolstoy says that conscience lies dormant for the period of the war — a kind of 'moral anaesthesia' pervades. The modern-war pacifist says that by using modern technology and acting from a great distance in complete safety, the soldier's conscience is numbed into failing to realise that lives are actually being lost. This is also the case for the general public who can find it difficult to link actual death with often highly controlled war news coverage, some of which resembles video game imagery. Euphemistic terms have evolved over history to describe acts of war (e.g. 'conflict' instead of 'war', 'holy war' as a way of justifying undertaking war, itself a term replaced in the twenty-first century by 'war against terrorism'), but it has been during the twentieth century that most euphemisms have been created. Civilian death is referred to as 'collateral damage', military occupation as 'peace-keeping', killing those on your own side as death by 'friendly fire', bombing is a 'surgical strike', a bomb with relatively low radioactive fallout is referred to as 'clean', weapons in the US Strategic Defence System (commonly called the 'Star Wars' system) are referred to as 'assets', assets do not fire weapons they 'deliver' them, and those who may be killed by them (the so-called 'soft-skinned targets') are simply 'casualties'. The just cause for war (and the starting of war) has been subject to much euphemistic treatment: 'pre-emptive strike', 'preventive strike', 'protective reaction', 'anticipatory attack' and (in the case of the Iraq War (2003–2010)) 'pre-emptive self-defence' have all been used by nations to back up a case for war. Enemy fighters who lack the substantial recognition of a state are referred to as 'insurgents' or 'terrorists'. Those that fight against an unfavoured state are called 'rebels' or 'freedom fighters'.

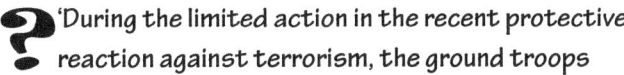

'During the limited action in the recent protective reaction against terrorism, the ground troops *called up air support who carried out a surgical strike. Collateral damage was kept to a minimum with the loss of only a few to friendly fire (a problem of incontinent ordnance) with overall casualties at a minimum.' Try to interpret this imaginary press release.*

Terrorism

Whereas civil disobedience is non-violent illegal protest against the state, terrorism is violent protest against the state, another state, organisation, religion or institution. In its most common form it is the use of terror or unpredictable violence and, although used since ancient Greek and Roman times, is these days usually identified with the operation of individuals or groups who attempt to overthrow or destabilise existing political or other establishment institutions.

Conflict is not necessarily driven by greed or grievance. Religious commitment focuses individual desires in a way that can lead to a desire for violent overthrow of 'opposing' forces. This is strengthened when the individual terrorist believes that self-sacrifice will lead to glory or immortality.

> **?** *Does the fact that a terrorist willingly sacrifices his life for his cause mean that his cause is more worthwhile than an opposing cause for which the defenders are not positively willing to bring about their own deaths?*

An absolutist rejects violence (and its outcomes, e.g. killing) as a thing in itself. A consequentialist asks whether violent protest is ever justified by virtue of the ends it may attain (e.g. the overthrow by the population of its hated dictator) or the speed at which those ends may be met (e.g. many more lives would be saved if a hated regime is ended quickly). Any consequentialist justification must be measured against the corrupting effects of violence (i.e. violent acts accustom the society to violent acts who therefore tolerate more violent acts and so on). It is hard to justify terrorism in the twenty-first century by virtue of its gains. Most terrorist activity has resulted in worsened situations (e.g. Hamas, *Harakat al-Muqāwamah al-Islāmiyyah*, the 'Islamic Resistance Movement' in Gaza, now faces a more ruthless Israel), for example, counter terrorism and its consequent violence (e.g. extreme Protestant groups in Northern Ireland formed to defend against the IRA), a surge of state violence (the US and UK attack on Iraq in 2003 as a result of heightened fear of terrorism from Al Quaeda after the attack on the New York Twin Towers on 11 September 2001 ('9/11')), state-sponsored sanctions (e.g. UN sanctions against Iran (2006–) and occupation (e.g. Afghanistan occupied by US and UK forces in 2001).

There is a point at which the terrorism is so institutionalised that it can be considered state terrorism (terrorism sponsored or conducted by the state has a history stretching back to the ancient Greeks). For example, it is difficult to distinguish between the acts of terror committed by Israel against the Palestinians and the acts of terror committed by the Palestinians against Israel. Where there are differences they are connected to the use of an established army as opposed to 'members of a group' (e.g. the established Israeli army as opposed to Hamas terrorists in Gaza), the use of modern weaponry as opposed to suicide or *ad hoc* bombing (e.g. the advanced technology of the drone aircraft as opposed to the roadside bomb), or are simply a matter of viewpoint (i.e. a subjective as opposed to an objective morality).

> **?** Is it right for the state to commit acts of violence (e.g. the assassination of a hated dictator of a foreign state) that would usually be considered murder, assassination or a violent act of terrorism?

Treatment of the enemy and negative categorisation
The Geneva Convention 1949 regulates the treatment of individuals, combatants (and non-combatants), prisoners of war and enemy captives during war. The enemy is by its nature considered a moral opposition (and therefore deemed to hold different moral views). This process of negative categorisation can cause the enemy to be seen as morally inferior and therefore not deserving of the same humanitarian treatment expected for the personnel of the 'morally superior' side. During World War II, Germany considered the Western Allies (more or less) morally equal and treated them accordingly. Military tribunal tried acts of rape, looting and murder perpetrated by German military personnel against Western

Allied powers and the perpetrators were punished accordingly. In the East, however, because the Germans considered the Russians sub-human, such acts not only went unpunished, they were positively encouraged. Similarly, whereas in general Western Allied prisoners of war were treated humanely and most survived the war, there were exceptions. Of the estimated 5,700,000 Russian prisoners captured by the Germans 3,300,000 died from immediate execution, starvation or ill treatment.

In 2002, the US established a centre at the US Naval base in Guantanamo Bay, Cuba, for the detention of prisoners taken by the US mostly in Afghanistan and Iraq. Detainees were kept in circumstances considered outside the rules of the Geneva Convention 1949 because they did not match the Geneva Convention's definition of 'combatant' forces (e.g. because of lack of uniform, state military control). In 2006, the US accepted Article 3 of the Geneva Convention 1949 (armed conflict between forces within the boundaries of one nation). Those held since 2008 have been classified as 'enemy combatants'. Detainees have been regularly subjected to a form of torture known as 'water boarding'. In January 2012, 171 detainees remain in Guantanamo Bay.

> **?** Is it right for a nation to alter the status of prisoners of war according to how 'evil' that state considers the enemy's cause?

Nuclear war
Although many nuclear weapons have been designed, tested and produced, they have only been used twice, both times at the end of World War II when on 6 August 1945 the US dropped an atomic bomb on Hiroshima, Japan and then on the 9 August on Nagasaki, Japan. In Hiroshima between 90,000 and 166,000 mostly civilian casualties were killed in the immediate effect and in Nagasaki between 60,000 and 80,000. More suffered and died in the following years. Between 1946 and 1991, a Cold War of ideological distance and suspicion grew and was maintained between the Soviet Union of Russia (and its satellite nations) and the West (mainly the US). This led to a proliferation of nuclear weapons in both number and sophistication. During this period the UK, France, the Soviet Union, the PRC, India, Pakistan, Israel, North Korea and South Africa all gained

nuclear armaments. Since the end of the Cold War, there have been efforts to reduce the number of nuclear arms with arms reduction and non-proliferation treaties and a determination on the part of the countries that have nuclear arsenals to prevent other countries from obtaining them.

> **?** Is it a greater wrong to kill a large number of people with one nuclear bomb than to kill the same number of people with many conventional bombs?

Globalisation

Since the end of the Cold War, and the breakup of the Soviet Union as the opposing super-power to the US, the US has (as the world's only remaining super-power) increasingly taken on the role of 'policing' the world. This has led to a largely uncontested view that the system of Western democracy should be a model for all nations throughout the world. Because of this, 'policing' (e.g. on humanitarian grounds, or led or sanctioned by the United Nations) has come to include the intention of installing democracy in nations where the US consider appropriate political systems do not exist. The uprising against established dictators in some Arab states (Arab Spring 2010–2011) and the Western support given to the rebel forces in Libya consolidates this view.

> **?** The intention to change the regime in Iraq by force in 2003 could be termed a 'war against a disagreeable regime'. Is there anything morally wrong with this?

Further questions

As well as commentary on conflicts throughout the twentieth century, this chapter contains debate on the recent wars in Afghanistan (2001–) and Iraq (2003–2010) and the modern-day nature of terrorism. It must be born in mind that these conflicts have a long history (e.g. problems laid down by British imperialism), spawn further difficulties (e.g. in Pakistan) and, like the cause of anti-US terrorism, are not fully resolved. Since the US/UK invasion of Iraq, some of the basic principles of war have become confused. The definitions of just cause, self-defence, the classification of what a war is, as well as the treatment of prisoners of war, have been altered to suit changed political motivations. Any up-to-date news reportage can be useful here. Ask yourself straightforward questions such as: 'Was this just cause?', 'Was this an act of self-defence?'.

Question 1 is an invitation to 'guess' the worth in lives of the conflicts mentioned. The actual figures are given in the 'Notes'. Questions 2, 3 and 4 ask you to put yourself in the place of someone involved in war or possible war. Question 5 challenges the conflict between ethical purpose and rules that govern war. Questions 6 and 7 look at the status of terrorists in respect of the ethics of war as well as in respect of their enemies. Questions 8 and 9 challenge the notion of killing quantitatively and at a distance.

1. If war is about killing (inasmuch as the 'winning side' usually suffers less loss), how many people (distinguish between military and civilian) do you think it was or would be 'worth' killing for the following?

World War I (1914–1918)
World War II (1939–1945)
Korean War (1950–1953)
Vietnam War (1955–1975)
(Persian) Gulf War (1990–1991)
Conflict in Afghanistan (2001–)
Conflict in Iraq (2003–2010)
Conflict in Libya (2011)

Explain your reasoning.

2. Would you go to war for the state if you were the only one that would go? Would you not go to war for the state if you were the only one that would not go? Explain the logic behind your answers.

3. Would you go to war for the state and put your own life at risk?

4. Would you go to war for the state and put the lives of your family and friends at risk?

5. Is it morally defensible to have 'rules of war'?

6. Terrorism does not operate within the generally accepted rules of war. Does this mean that terrorists should be punished not only as the enemies of the state but also as breakers of the rules of war?

7. In July 2003 the sons of Saddam Hussein, Uday (1964–2003) and Qusay (1966–2003), were killed by US troops. The US had offered a reward for their capture 'alive or dead'. There was apparently no attempt by the US troops involved in the action to capture the men alive so that they could be brought to trial. What rights were violated here and could this violation be justified?

8. Are there degrees of wrong involved in killing? For example, is killing one person less bad than killing one thousand, or is killing six people but also killing yourself (e.g. a suicide bomber) not as bad as orchestrating (or even simply inspiring) the killing of many people but not actually doing it yourself (e.g. Osama bin Laden (1957–2011) and the destruction of the New York Twin Towers)?

9. Was Osama bin Laden 'brought to justice' or unlawfully killed by US Special Forces on 2 May 2011?

10. The act of war usually takes place between state-supported forces and combat between them leads to death and injury. Is it right that the state should use unmanned drone aircraft and pinpoint individuals to be killed by remote fire? How does this differ from murder?

11. Some countries that have nuclear weapons have submarines continually patrolling the oceans ready at any time to launch a devastating nuclear attack. If such an attack occurred, who would be responsible? For example, would it be the launch operator on the submarine, the politician who gave the order, the company that manufactured the weapons, the members of the state that sanctioned the political act?

12. In human history there have been far more human beings killed by other human beings as morally right killing sanctioned by the state (in wars) than when it has been outlawed in society as morally wrong murder. Because of this, do you think that it seems more reasonable to assume that the killing of human beings by human beings is the more natural state?

Notes
War casualties
World War I (1914–1918)
Of 65,038,810 personnel mobilised on all sides 8,528,831 were killed, 21,189,154 wounded and 7,750,919 lost as prisoners or missing (a total of 37,468,904 military casualties).

World War II (1939–1945)
The Allied forces lost 14,141,544 military personnel killed, 4,443,544, wounded, 899,219 lost as prisoners or missing. In addition, there were

15,133,673 civilian deaths (including 3,200,000 Jews). The Axis powers (Germany, Italy and Japan) lost 5,634,232 military personnel killed, 9,116,000 wounded, 4,830,000 as prisoners or missing. In addition, there were 2,806,941 civilian deaths. The Soviet Union suffered approximately 10,000,000 military deaths and approximately 14,500,00 civilian deaths. To these figures can be added approximately 2,200,000 Chinese military personnel killed in regional conflicts together with up to 22,000,000 civilians, a further 1,200 French killed in resistance and North African fighting, 115,187 US military personnel killed from 'non-battle' causes, and 5,638 killed who were members of the Allied Merchant Marine.

Korean War (1950–1953)

An estimated 4,000,000 deaths including civilians.

Vietnam War (1955–1975)

An estimated 47,000 US military personnel killed in combat, 11,000 killed from other causes and 303,000 wounded. The Army of the Republic of Vietnam (ARVN) lost an estimated 185,000 to 225,000 killed and between 500,000 and 575,000 wounded. North Vietnam and the Viet Cong lost an estimated 900,000 killed with an unknown number wounded. Approximately 1,000,000 North and South Vietnamese civilians were killed.

(Persian) Gulf War (1990–1991)

An estimated 8,000 to 100,000 Iraqi troops were killed against an estimated 300 US/UK deaths.

Conflict in Afghanistan (2001–)

Between 2001 and 30 November 2011, there were 1,761 US military deaths, 390 UK deaths and 593 deaths from other coalition forces. There are no reliable figures for civilians, but they could be between 7,276 and 8,826 deaths due to the actions of insurgents and between 6,215 and 9,007 due to US-led military action. Between 3,200 and 20,000 civilians were killed in the initial invasion.

Conflict in Iraq (2003–2010)

On 1 May 2003, US President Bush declared the hostilities between the US/UK and Iraq over. Casualties to this date were: 163 US and 14

UK military personnel killed, 80 US and 29 UK civilian or non-combat personnel killed, 2,320 (approximately) Iraq military killed and 6,076 to 7,787 (plus) Iraq civilians killed. Numbers of casualties on all sides have continued to rise since 1 May 2003. By March 2011, US military fatalities in Iraq were 4,441, UK fatalities were 179, other forces 139. The number of Iraq security and military forces killed in the same period was 9,902. The estimated number of civilians killed over the period ranges from 92,000 to over 1,000,000.

Conflict in Libya (2011)
In October 2011, the Libyan National Transitional Council estimated the numbers killed at 25,000, with a further 50,000 injured.

Further reading

A. J. Coates, *The Ethics of War* (Manchester: Manchester University Press, 1997).

David Fisher, *Morality and War: Can War be Just in the Twenty-First Century?* (Oxford: Oxford University Press, 2011).

Thomas Nagel, *Mortal Questions* (Cambridge: Cambridge University Press, 1979).

17

Punishment

Why do we punish those found guilty of committing crimes?

Introduction

Because punishments are typically not unlike the crimes that the punished wrongdoer has committed (fines are like theft, imprisonment is like kidnapping, capital punishment is like murder), and because they are enforced or inflicted by the state, they need justification. This is so particularly in a democratic society where quite clearly they conflict (to some degree or another) with human rights and liberty. John Stuart Mill (1806–1873) argued that everyone should be free to conduct their own 'experiments of living' as long as they did not harm anyone else. Although in theory this view supports human individuality, in practice it can be an opportunity for the strongest and most ruthless to exploit the weakest and those at risk. With this in mind, governments curb our freedoms using laws and impose punishments for their transgression.

The central problems of punishment are its meaning and its justification. Punishment usually involves the following necessary ingredients:

- it must involve pain or some other unpleasant consequences;
- it must be because of breaking the law;
- it must only be done to the wrongdoer;
- it must be intentionally administered (by others);
- it must be within the constraints of the state legal system.

❓ Friedrich Wilhelm Nietzsche (1844–1900) says that culturally the 'meaning' of punishment is to awaken the feeling of guilt in the guilty but, he thinks, this is not true, for punishment actually hardens the wrongdoer's attitude and alienates them further. Do you agree?

Determinism

Some people believe that every human action has a cause beyond the control of the individual. If this were so then every criminal act would also have a cause (e.g. genes, the environment, upbringing). In this case, the determinist would argue, although there are 'wrongdoers' they are themselves not responsible for their actions because they do not make (uncaused) free choices. However, the determinist would still see the need for corrective action and would support help for the wrongdoer or even the capital sentence (though not as a method of punishment but as a way of ridding society of a problem).

> **?** If you steal something that you want, and have a gene that predisposes you to steal things you want, are you responsible for your actions? Should you be punished for your crime or not? Are there any limits to being able to move the 'blame' to a cause separate to our selves?

Justifications for punishment

Punishment can be justified in four main ways. The first, retribution, is a moral argument. The other three — as a deterrence, in order to protect the society and in order to reform the wrongdoer — are all utilitarian and stem back to the thinking of Jeremy Bentham (1748–1832) and John Stuart Mill.

Retributivism

Retributivist theory is traceable back to the Old Testament and the *lex talionis* ('an eye for an eye'). The modern case for this view is put by John Langshaw Austin (1911–1960), who says that simply, retributivism means that the wrongdoer deserves the punishment regardless of any beneficial consequences the punishment may have. In other words, those that break the law deserve to suffer — they must pay back society for their wrongdoing by their own suffering. The punishment is given on an increasing scale according to the increasing severity of the crime. When applied as *lex talionis* (also referred to as *jus talionis*, 'the right of retaliation', by Immanuel Kant (1724–1804)) the punishment should be directly equivalent to the crime (e.g. murder should be punished by death). However, usually, when retributivism is applied, it is modified by exception (e.g. a wrongdoer who is mentally ill), mitigation (taking into account the wrongdoer's circumstances) and by standardised punishments being used where it would be ridiculous or socially unacceptable to apply directly equivalent punishments (e.g. blackmail, rape). Retributivism is based on the human instinct of revenge and is considered by some to be too basic for a civilised society. Retributivism does not take into account the effects of punishment on the wrongdoer and, as such, ignores the consequentialist moral purpose. Retributivism is 'backward-looking' (reviewing the crime which has happened) and, even though there is increasing interest in the plight of the victim, concentrates on the wrongdoer not the 'wrong-done'.

> **?** It is appropriate to consider the rights of the victim. Would it be appropriate for victims to punish directly those who had committed criminal acts against them?

Deterrence

Deterrence is a strictly consequentialist (utilitarian) view justifying punishment on the basis of its ability to discourage wrongdoing in the case of both the wrongdoer and others who know of the punishment. The modern case for this is put strongly by the philosopher and lawyer H. L. A. (Herbert Lionel Adolphus) Hart (1907–1992). Deterrence is not concerned with reforming the wrongdoer; rather it is using the punished wrongdoer as an example to the rest of society. Deterrence punishment is prone to the criticism that it works whether or not the victim of the punishment is guilty or innocent (so some of the legal safeguards to protect the accused are not so important). On the other hand, it is criticised for not being truly deterrent, the argument being that certain crimes would be committed irrespective of the punishment (e.g. the crimes of a psychopathic murderer) or that certain punishments (e.g. small fines, particularly for those who can easily afford them) do not deter anyway. These arguments are difficult to prove statistically and so remain politically and socially contentious.

Punishing the wrongdoer as a deterrent to others can be seen as using the wrongdoer as a means to an end unconnected with the original crime.

For example, punishing a rioter harshly to deter others from rioting could be seen as immoral. The law that the rioter contravened does not include extra punishment in order to act for the state in preventing others from committing the same crime.

> **?** It is argued that punishment does not deter criminals from acting criminally. If the punishment for any crime were capital, would this be a deterrent?

Protection of society
Punishment based on the idea of protection of society is based on the consequentialist view that society is safer if certain (more often, violent or sexually perverted) wrongdoers are kept securely out of the way. It is a view proposed by Bentham. This method, however, often protects society from wrongdoers who pose no further threat. For example, even though it would be a good idea to imprison a serial and persistent rapist, it would serve no purpose to imprison someone who committed a one-off crime under specific and unrepeatable circumstances (e.g. the passionate murder of a particular violent spouse). Also, unless imprisonment is for life, released prisoners can return to society better equipped to do harm (and to evade further detection), so the protection effect is reversed.

> **?** In order to protect society, crimes should be divided between those committed by persistent criminals and those that are one off (not taking into account the severity of the crime). Persistent criminals should be imprisoned for the rest of their lives and those convicted of one-off crimes should be fined. What do you think?

Reform
The argument for reform is based on the consequentialist view that a reformed wrongdoer will not commit further crimes, so protecting the public and allowing the reformed criminal to make a future positive contribution to society. However, it is hard to discriminate between wrongdoers who need reforming and those who do not, and wrongdoers who will respond positively to reforming treatment and those who will not.

For example, a persistent thief might not respond to reforming treatment, whereas a one-off wrongdoer may not need reforming. In practice, reform usually forms part of a punishment system that blends it with both deterrent and protection elements to satisfy consequentialist moral principles (i.e. even though the punishment is severe, the state as punisher has a strong moral justification because of the reforming element). Reforming punishment is not necessarily given on an increasing scale according to the severity of the crime, although, because of length of prison sentences etc., those convicted of the worst crimes can benefit from increased reforming facilities. Philosophically, the problem is that reform is reform and punishment is punishment — the two are logically distinct.

> **?** What makes it right that convicted criminals should be encouraged to study or learn trades while in prison when such programmes are costly and not afforded to members of society who have not broken the law and continue to contribute to society's wealth?

A society with no punishment
Plato (*c*.428–347 BC) argued that if members of society were sufficiently well educated (and that those with noticed predispositions to criminality should be purposefully re-educated) then there would be no need for punishment. Anyone who could not abide by society's laws should be banished (deported) from society.

Civil disobedience
Civil disobedience is a justification, on moral grounds, for breaking the law. Some argue that the law should never be broken and any dissatisfaction with it should be channelled through legal means, others believe that they have a moral right to disobey laws that they hold to be unjust.

There are many examples of the success of civil disobedience, and many individuals in history who have employed it. Bertrand Russell (1872–1970) was imprisoned for six months in 1916 for his anti-war stance. Many Americans were imprisoned for their stand against conscription to the Vietnam War (1955–1975) that, in some part due to this, eventually lost public support. The British suffragette movement, although not entirely responsible for women's suffrage, brought about much support for the movement that eventually achieved emancipation for women over 30 years of age in 1918. Mohandas Karamchand (Mahatma) Gandhi (1869–1948) and Martin Luther King, Jr (1929–1968) both advocated civil disobedience; Gandhi playing a leading role in achieving Indian independence from the British Empire, King helping to bring about civil rights for black Americans in the southern states of the US.

Civil disobedience requires a public act. It is not sufficient to break the law (on moral or whatever grounds) and keep it a private matter. The intention of civil disobedience is to draw attention to some matter of public concern, not to undermine the law of the state itself. Henry David Thoreau (1817–1862) suggested a private form of civil disobedience amounting to personal freedom based upon a high level of ignoring the state. Acts of civil disobedience are generally peaceful. Acts of terrorism differ not so much by the moral imperative inherent to the cause but in the manner in which civil disobedience is approached (civil disobedience is usually a pacifist act, terrorism usually involves violence). Criticism of civil disobedience is usually either on the basis that it is undemocratic or that it starts a 'slippery slope' to lawlessness.

In a democracy, breaking laws made by elected representatives (particularly when the lawbreakers are small in number) goes against the principle of representative democracy. Most members of society disagree with some aspect of the law yet abide by it as part of their contract as a member of that society. However, as the intention of civil disobedience is made public, it is often used to highlight 'bad' law and press for change. Some believe that no lawbreaking should be tolerated, no matter how strong the moral principle involved and no matter how 'bad' the law in question may seem; the laws of the state are sacrosanct and if the state tolerates any unlawful questioning of them it will eventually lead to anarchy. Against this, those who act with civil disobedience would claim it is the very reputation of the law that they uphold by suffering publicly under the laws of the state in order to make their moral case.

> **?** What laws would you seriously consider breaking because you did not agree with them? What would be the outcome of your action?

Capital punishment

The subject of capital punishment is a contentious issue. It is forbidden in the UK since 1965 (except for treason and piracy with violence abolished in 1998), throughout the EU and much of the civilised world (with the notable exception of the PRC, India and the US). It is a form of 'state murder' where the state is given authority to take the lives of criminals who commit (usually, though not always throughout history) the worst of crimes. Taking a supportive view in this debate does not oblige the supporter to the *lex talionis* — the principle of 'an eye for an eye' — indeed St Thomas Aquinas (1224/5–1274) supported it for the sake of the welfare of the whole community.

Supporting capital punishment can be seen from the points of view of justice or utility. The argument from justice says that people deserve to be punished for criminal wrongdoing and in the case of the worst crimes (e.g. murder) the severest punishment should be prescribed (e.g. capital punishment). The argument from utility can take one of four forms: it is a deterrent (the criminal will not repeat the crime and others will be put off committing a similar crime), it is less cruel than life imprisonment, it satisfies the family and friends of the victim, and it satisfies public outrage.

There are a number of reasons for holding a view against capital punishment. Wrongly convicted (innocent) persons will sometimes be executed. Capital punishment is uncivilised (e.g. if torture is considered uncivilised, then why not 'state murder'). The balance of bad effects on the criminal awaiting punishment is worse than the effects on the victim or his or her family and friends, therefore execution is not justified on retributivist grounds (Fyodor (Mikhaylovich) Dostoevsky (1821–1881) and Albert Camus (1913–1960) both argue this). Lastly, if people do not act freely (because the world and all its causes are determined) such punishment is never justified. Arthur Koestler (1905–1983) and Clarence Darrow (1857–1938) both uphold this view, in addition Darrow maintains the argument holds for all punishment.

Statistically, capital punishment does not reveal itself as a deterrent (indeed, the opposite, as it can inflame some individuals to kill) and, because of the fallibility of the judicial system, is generally accepted inadmissible in civilised society.

? Are there any circumstances in which a criminal should be forced to surrender his or her life to state-regulated capital punishment?

Further questions
The polarisation of views about capital punishment can sometimes obscure the need to analyse the reasons that we have for punishing wrongdoing in general. Thinking about types and lengths of sentence is useful to get a grip on this subject. The conflict between human rights and capital punishment is worth exploring, as are the economic constraints placed on modern Western prison systems.

Civil disobedience is included here and, although not a system of punishment is an area where otherwise law-abiding citizens fall foul of the legal and punitive system. Thoughts on civil disobedience would appropriately be allied with Chapter 14. 'Freedom and Determinism'.

1. Are there any circumstances in which someone known to be innocent should be punished?

2. Are there any circumstances in which a person should be executed without trial?

3. Should a premeditated murder carried out by someone for money be punished in the same way as a murder committed by someone who had themselves suffered at the hands of their victim?

4. A man has committed a series of child murders, destroying the potential of many young children and causing untold misery to their surviving parents. Should this man be punished for his crime in a way that makes him endure some of the suffering that he has caused his victims?

5. If the only punishment for any crime was life imprisonment, would this act as a deterrent to would-be criminals?

6. Is there any moral justification for imposing harsher sentences on criminal in order to prevent others committing similar crimes?

7. To deter would always be better than to punish, and deterrents protect society more effectively. If criminality can be genetically screened for at birth, should individuals who reveal 'criminal genes' be removed in order to protect society?

8. In order to protect our society from crime, those that commit crimes should be permanently removed from society. Would this be a reasonable method for dealing with crime?

9. Dr Jones, a skilled surgeon with an international reputation, has killed several of his grateful patients in order to inherent their wealth. He was tried and imprisoned. After he had been in prison for three years, he worked out a novel surgical technique that could save thousands of lives. He says that if he is released he will share his knowledge with the world and work for the rest of his life carrying out the life-saving operations free of charge. What should be done with Dr Jones?

10. Is permanent deportation a more appropriate method of punishment than imprisonment?

11. If a law is a 'bad law', how should we seek to change it? Should we break the law in order to do so?

12. Is anything so wrong as to justify the removal of our fundamental being — our life?

13. When someone is hanged, an executioner has to release the trap door. When someone is electrocuted, an executioner has to throw the switch. When someone is killed by lethal injection, an executioner has to administer the drug. In these cases, are the executioners also murderers?

Further reading

R. A. Duff, *Trials and Punishment* (Cambridge: Cambridge University Press, 1986).

Ted Honderich, *Punishment: The Supposed Justifications* (Cambridge: Cambridge University Press, 1989).

Hugh LaFollette (ed.), *Ethics in Practice: An Anthology* (Oxford: Blackwell, 2002).

18

Abortion

What it is that constitutes being alive as a human being?

Introduction

Abortion is concerned with the removal of an unborn foetus from its mother, which will mean that the foetus will not continue to live. It can be natural (a miscarriage or spontaneous abortion) or it can be induced deliberately. Since the late 1960s abortion has been made legal on request in many countries, though it still remains illegal with exceptions (e.g. for rape) in others, and is illegal with no exceptions in a few (some Central and South American countries, Malta and Vatican City). However, unlike some human matters that have been legislated against (e.g. slavery), abortion (like racism) remains socially contentious. It is unclear if legislation on abortion has followed moral right and it is therefore unclear whether the law represents moral right.

It is legal in the UK to induce an abortion if two physicians agree that (if the pregnancy is less than 24 weeks) having the child would result in more mental or physical harm to the mother than having the child, or (at any time during pregnancy) if the abortion is necessary to save the mother's life or prevent her suffering permanent mental or physical harm, or if there is a high risk that the child will be seriously mentally or physically handicapped. Abortions can be performed on any pregnant woman but, if she is under 16 years of age and cannot prove she understands what is involved, she must have her parents' consent. Any physician who declares a moral objection to induced abortion need not help in the performance or arrangement of abortion. No consent from the father is needed for an abortion.

> **Is there a point at which human life begins? If so, try to decide what it is.**

The views: pro-life and pro-abortion

However, this legal settlement of the matter has not brought about a social consensus. Indeed pro-life and pro-abortion views are completely polarised, and pro-life anti-abortionists continue a bitter fight against those who uphold the right (or sense) of abortion. Such are the passions raised by this subject that, at the end of the twentieth century in the US, laws were passed to protect the rights of the defenders of abortion. Because the legalisation of something does not necessarily convince people that it is morally right (e.g. slavery, child labour, racism have all been legal at one time or another), there is a large body of opinion about this issue which disagrees with the law.

Pro-abortionists may base their view on its general (legal) permissibility or its cost, health or emotional benefits (broadly social, physiological and psychological reasons). For example, early abortion is less physically risky than problems in later pregnancy, unwanted children should not be born, a woman should not have a child just to give it away, the belief that the health (mental or physical) of the rest of the woman's family should not be jeopardised by an unwanted pregnancy, abortion should always be available for the victims of rape or incest, the very young or the old. However, much of the ethical debate revolves around rebuttal of the pro-life (anti-abortionist) stand and arguing that a new individual does not exist until it is born (this can include prematurely) and can sustain a life physically independent of its mother. In addition, there is the human rights issue that supports the woman's right to choose whether she should continue with her pregnancy.

Pro-abortionists may also consider it right within the law inasmuch as the aborted foetus is not considered an independent human life (a person). Pro-life (anti-abortionists) may feel it wrong because it involves the deliberate taking of a human life (no matter what its stage of development) and that no cost, health or emotional benefit is sufficient to condone breaking this central human standpoint. For example, the procedure may injure a woman's ability to conceive in the future, the procedure may adversely affect the woman's mental health, or even that abortion reduces the supply of children for adoption. However, the ethical considerations are based upon a belief that human life is sacred and that it begins from the moment of conception. This means that abortion, at the very least, involves a diminished sense of respect for human life, and at worst is a form of killing. In taking this view, anti-abortionists must accept that since the 1960s, what for them is legally condoned human murder, has been carried out on an unprecedented scale throughout the world.

> **?** Is scale important in ethical judgements? Should we be appalled by large-scale abortion for no reason other than birth control in a way that we would not feel appalled about an isolated instance? For example, in the US, where more than one in three women will have an abortion by the time they are 45, over 90% of all abortions are for reasons of birth control.

If abortion is 'wrong', the wrongness involved is occurring on a vast scale. In the US between 1973 (when legalisation made abortion legal throughout the entire nine months of pregnancy and for any reason) and 2007, there were over 48 million abortions (the yearly average between 1998 and 2007 being in excess of 850,000). Almost half of these were women over 25, two-thirds of who were white. Over 90% of these abortions were done as some form of birth control, 1% performed because of rape or incest, 3% because of foetal abnormalities and 3% because of the mother's health problems. Of the approximately 46 million abortions carried out each year worldwide (that is about one for every three live births), three-quarters (78%) of these occur in the developed countries where approximately 26 million are obtained legally. Worldwide, the lifetime average is for one abortion per woman.

Terms
Those who hold different views on abortion can use different terms for the same thing. We must be guarded about the emotional connotation of terms chosen to appeal to the proponents of each particular view, for example, 'unborn child', 'embryo' or 'product of pregnancy'. 'Foetus' (Latin for 'offspring'), which is both accurate and adequate, is used here.

The anti-abortionist argument
The basic anti-abortionist (absolutist) argument runs like this. The protection of innocent human life is central to human morality. If the foetus is an innocent human life, and if it is wrong to deliberately kill (or even cause pain to) an innocent human life, then it must be wrong to deliberately kill (or even cause pain to) a foetus.

The basic argument is commonly dealt with under convenient headings.

Visible and separate
The anti-abortionist claims that there is a right to life if the foetus becomes visible or separate. The pro-abortionist argues that a foetus who has become visible using X-ray and ultrasound would seem (on this argument) to have a right to life that is unavailable to one who has not been the subject of X-ray or ultrasound. Further, the anti-abortionist would suggest that if separation is an issue, we would have to accept that a child still connected to its mother by an umbilical cord could be killed whereas one separated could not.

> **?** A pregnant woman is about to have an ultrasound scan to determine the condition of the foetus. There are concerns of adverse genetic predispositions being passed on by the mother. The machine breaks down and there is no replacement available, nor will there be until the legal time for abortion has passed. Does the foetus have a right to life? Decide on a course of action.

Viable
The anti-abortionist claims that there is a right to life once the foetus becomes viable (that is, the foetus has the capacity to survive outside the womb). The US Supreme Court ruled, in the case of Roe v Wade (1973), that the state has a 'compelling interest' in the life of a foetus once it becomes viable and has 'the capacity of meaningful life outside the mother's womb'. The pro-abortionist argues that 'meaningful life' is difficult to interpret, but the implication is that there is a point, 'viability', when the foetus is no longer dependent upon the mother. However, even though the

foetus is separate and 'viable', it is very much dependent upon another for a long time and would not survive without that care.

> **?** Modern technology makes it possible to keep a foetus alive at about 18 weeks. Does this then mean that the right to life changes with changes in technology?

Looks like a human

Some anti-abortionists claim that because a foetus looks like a human it should have the same rights as a human. More exactly, even though it does not look like an adult or mature human, it does look like what it is, that is, a human in an early (pre-adult or mature) stage of its existence. The pro-abortionist claims here that, in the early stages in particular, a foetus does not look like a human (it is, after all, to begin with, a clump of cells) and the attribute of 'human-ness' can only be given to something with more coherently testable human traits.

> **?** What is it to 'look like a human'? How does deformity or amputation of limbs affect this?

Pain

The anti-abortionist claims that the foetus feels pain (though this claim is not a major issue in the debate). It is generally accepted that the foetus cannot feel pain until the 25th week of development. Awareness of pain alone is not considered sufficient to qualify as sentience. If pain were deemed sufficient for conscious susceptibility to sensation then the pro-abortionist should accept that the post-25-week-old foetus should at least be anaesthetised before it is aborted on the basis that it is wrong to inflict pain on another (sentient) human being.

> **?** Does the absence of pain give us the right to inflict normally painful processes on another? For example, is there a difference between torturing someone who can feel pain, someone who cannot (for physiological reasons) feel pain, someone who is anaesthetised against pain, or someone who has been psychologically trained to withstand pain?

The pro-abortionist argument
The basic pro-abortionist objections to the anti-abortionist argument revolve around two fundamental elements: 'When does the life of a human being start?' and 'Is it permissible to kill another human being?'

When does the life of a human being start?
Are we certain when the life of a human being starts? The basic anti-abortion argument relies on classifying the foetus as a human being and in so doing implies a continuity of that human existence from the moment when the sperm and egg combine to form a new cell, to the moment of birth and beyond. At any point, we are (says the argument) dealing with a human being with a right to life. According to the argument, because there is a strict numerical identity between zygote, embryo, foetus, child and adult, this makes it metaphysically impossible to establish any point before which the foetus is not a human being.

Objection 1 — brain activity
To be a human implies that we have a functioning brain. The foetus displays no brain activity for the first six weeks of its existence; therefore, during this time it cannot be a human being.

However, we must consider whether being human does in fact imply having a functioning brain. It is possible to function as a human being with a damaged or reduced brain function. 'Brain death' (more exactly 'brainstem death', the functioning absence of which would almost certainly amount to a form of 'death') is considered the medical criterion for human death. However, many human physiological functions (e.g. heartbeat, blood pressure, hormone circulation) persist after brainstem death in just the same way that they persist in the foetus before the onset of brain activity. Brainstem death may well mean 'irreversible unconsciousness', but the foetus has a developing brain and its human existence cannot be determined easily by this seemingly convenient analogy.

> **?** A terminally ill and incurable patient is progressively losing brain function. Each new loss of function requires a technological aid to replace it in order to keep the patient alive. In the end, the loss of functions will

outstrip the available technology and the patient will die. Before this situation is reached the natural brain function has sunk below the level at which a foetus can be legally aborted. Would it be right to kill the dying patient at this point?

Objection 2 — vagueness of continuous change
It is all very well to talk of the numerically continuous existence of one thing whose nature changes, but can we say, in all honesty, that a single-celled zygote is also the human being that it will ultimately become?

This objection, the so-called 'sorites paradox' (or 'paradox from vagueness' from the Greek *soreites* meaning 'heaped up'), relies on our inability to establish any tangible difference in immediately preceding and succeeding phases in a continual process which ultimately reveals a form distinct from its form earlier in the process. In other words, when does an acorn become an oak tree? At what point am I overweight? When do a number of grains of sand become a heap? Because there is no solution to these problems, raising them merely raises the problem in itself as opposed to any object vulnerable to that problem in particular. In the same way, it is difficult to prise apart the point at which the sperm and egg unite and so distinguish between human and pre (non)-human.

> **?** Is there such a thing as a continuous process (such as the change from non-human to human) or can all apparently continuous processes be broken down into discrete and separate phases?

Objection 3 — potential
Some say that the sperm and the egg separately are human life in that they contain life's potential.

But many things contain the potential for being something else but they can in no way be called something else (e.g. the acorn and the oak). We do not generally regard something for what it will be (because we do not know what it will be). However, we do educate children in the hope that it will improve their futures, and we invest in something (e.g. a house) in the hope that it will potentially be worth more to us (e.g. even if only in reduction of indebtedness) in the years to come.

> ❓ Two foetuses have been fertilised in the same mother and are compared at a stage when they can both legally be aborted. One has a congenital proneness to a number of serious diseases, any of which will mean (within the limitations of medical science at the time) a life of disability and reliance on state or family care. The other has all the genetic attributes of beauty and physical and mental excellence. The mother only wants one child. What should she do?

Objection 4 — fission and totipotency
In about the second week of the development of the foetus, the so-called 'primitive streak' appears and establishes a bilateral symmetry of a multi-layered organism. Before this, the spherical cell formation is capable of fission, that is, sub-division in such a way that the divided cells can form an entire individual (most commonly twins). Up to the eight-cell stage (two to three days), each cell (if removed) is capable of forming a separate individual (each of which can also potentially twin) — it is 'totipotent'. This means that the forming of the individual need not be the moment when the existence of the foetus begins (i.e. at fertilisation), but could be, instead, the forming of a twin or the start of a divided cell. This process also means the 'death' of the 'parent' cell, but whether this is a 'death' about which we should feel grief is unlikely as is the claim to proper 'parentage' of the original.

> ❓ Cells, as part of their natural process, divide. Is this the birth of a new living thing?

Objection 5 — cloning and parthenogenesis
The main technique for cloning sexually reproducing organisms involves removing the female genetic material (the nucleus) of the ovum and replacing it with another nucleus that is either a sperm or some body cell. The resulting organism will be a 'twin' of the donor (and need not be male). Carp, mice, sheep, monkeys, cats, dogs, cattle, horses, water buffaloes and camels have been successfully cloned. In 2009, a Pyrenean Ibex was the first extinct animal (extinct since 2000) to be cloned, though it survived for only seven minutes.

Parthenogenesis involves the development of an embryo from an unfertilised egg (this is the normal method of reproduction in some animals such as water fleas or aphids). Applying this view to human beings, we could view the egg itself (unfertilised) or, in the case of cloning, the cells (e.g. bones or skin) themselves, as human beings and be forced to revise our view that the point of fertilisation may be the starting point of life. This would be a difficult view to hold, though, for if we pulled a hair from our head we would be responsible for killing a 'human being'. More sensible would be to recognise the point of cloning or initial (parthenogenic) development to be the point at which (even though not fertilised) the nature of the cell is changed.

> **?** A cell may eventually develop into something we recognise, but as a cell is it more a chemical thing than a living thing?

Is it ethically permissible to kill another human being?
Feminism
The 'pro-choice' lobby (part of the movement for legal and social equality for women that began in the 1960s) supports abortion, arguing that women have the right to choose what happens to their bodies. The denial of abortion, they argue, denounces this right and instead (by implication at least) supports the rights of the foetus, the father or society. The right to choose how our bodies are used, in this case whether or not they should be 'used' for a pregnancy, is at the root of this 'human rights' argument. Opponents would argue that the mother's human right (if used) goes against the unborn child's right to life. It is, therefore, implicit in the pro-choice argument that the foetus is not considered to have an independent human life (and therefore human rights) until it is born.

But can we consider a foetus part of the woman's body? It is not, after all, a body part in the normal sense but a (potential) child who is nourished and sustained by the mother. In addition, the mother, in this case, is subordinating the rights of a (potential) child to her own and in so doing considering her human rights in favour of another's.

> **?** A pregnant mother finds out that her foetus has a genetic predisposition to something that she dislikes. She decides it is right to legally abort. This dislike could be as trivial as a predisposition to eating meat when the mother is a vegetarian or as serious as the future child having a deformity which, though not life-threatening, is objectionable to the mother. Should the mother abort?

Abortion based on the circumstances of the pregnancy
It is commonly thought that some foetuses should be more rightly aborted than others (e.g. products of rape, pregnancy where it is later discovered the father has AIDS).

However, the anti-abortionist would hold that no matter what the circumstances that bring the pregnancy about, it is still wrong to 'kill' the foetus in order to protect the right of one's own bodily integrity. And if it is indeed killing, what has the foetus done to deserve this fate, for surely undeserved killing can never be condoned?

> **?** No human at any stage of its development should be killed unless it is at fault. A foetal product of rape carries no personal blame (and so is not at 'fault'), therefore it is wrong to abort the foetal product of rape. Analyse this argument.

Objection on the principle of double effect
Physicians are obliged to save life wherever possible. If the saving of a mother's life demands the sacrifice of the foetus then the implicit judgement is that somehow the life of the foetus is less worthwhile, less human, less worthy of social or medical protection than the mother's (and can therefore be sacrificed).

> **?** If a pregnant woman's life can only be saved by aborting the foetus, is it right to do this? If a foetus' life can only be saved by killing the mother (or even letting her die), is it right to do this?

The 'backstreet' objection

Making abortion illegal, the anti-abortionist says, will not stem the demand for it, nor will it prevent those sufficiently motivated from obtaining termination of their pregnancy. If abortion cannot be controlled within the law then illegal abortionists will exploit the desperation of others to their own physical and emotional cost. However, laws do not necessarily (though they can) follow the demands of society (e.g. legalisation or criminalisation of some drug use, enforcement of anti-drinking prohibition in 1920s US) and ethical responsibilities are not usually in response to the social fact of prevalence (e.g. because crime is widespread it would not be considered morally right to condone it).

> **?** Banning all abortion would lead to an increase in backstreet abortion and the consequently increased mortality of pregnant mothers. Is this a reason to justify killing foetuses by legalising abortion?

The 'every child should be wanted' objection

It is commonly accepted that every child should be wanted. However, the important principles of parenting are that the child should be loved, nurtured and kept free from pain, and an unwanted child could still be afforded these rights. It does not follow that a wanted child should be kept alive whereas an unwanted child should be killed.

> **?** 'Wanted' and 'unwanted' are psychological values held by a parent. 'Wantedness' may indeed affect the child, but should it affect the right of the child to live? For example, many unwanted children grow up into happy successful adults who themselves are loving parents of others.

Further questions

Abortion is a contentious issue. It is about the continued existence (or not) of a most fragile life form — an unborn child. Any association (or not) we have had with it also affects the views we hold. Supporters of the opposing views defend their arguments with great commitment. Such things must be kept in mind when considering this topic. If there are doubts in your mind about how objective you can be, then concentrating on the point at which human life begins can be fruitful without being so contentious.

Questions 1 to 4 are of a general nature, questions 5 to 8 focus more closely on the pro and anti-abortionist arguments.

1. Should taking responsibility for your own action (i.e. it is your own fault so you should bear the consequences) be a reason for having to continue with a pregnancy?

2. A 19-year-old woman is involved in a road accident and falls into a coma. When she recovers consciousness (seven months after the accident), she is found to be seven months pregnant. She admits that on the night of the accident she was raped. She does not want the child. Even though the time for legal abortion has passed, should she be offered an abortion?

3. A woman becomes pregnant with triplets using IVF (in-vitro fertilisation). At 20 weeks, she discovers that the laboratory dealing with the IVF process mixed up the sperm cells used. One of the foetuses is of another race, one has a predisposition for a life-threatening and incurable disease, and one was fertilised by the sperm of her husband who has since left her and who she detests (because of his violent mistreatment of her). She would still like children. What, if anything, should she do?

4. Is abortion a religious, ethical or medical matter?

5. A foetus may be viable after about 18 weeks (by which is meant it may survive but only with help from others). A small child would find it difficult to survive without help from others. Is the small child more viable than the 18-week-old foetus?

6. All living things should be protected. It does not matter what stage of maturity that living thing is in. Is this a convincing argument against abortion?

7. A time traveller returns from the future to witness the abortion of a foetus at 20 weeks. The father is claiming that the foetus has great potential as a human being and should not be aborted. The pregnant woman, his wife, claims her own rights to have the child aborted and the abortion is carried out. When the time traveller returns to his own time, he puts the details of the aborted foetus into his 'alternative-world' computer program and finds that if the foetus had been allowed to go to full term, and develop as a human being, its life would have saved millions of lives in the century ahead. Can we properly ignore the unknown potential of a foetus irrespective of its stage of development?

8. A famous violinist has a fatal kidney disease and your blood is of the right type to save him. A group of his supporters plug you into him (after drugging you) so that your blood can cleanse his and he can be saved. The process will last nine months, after which his own kidneys will be able to take on the job themselves. Is it right that your body should be used in this way? (Judith Jarvis Thomson (1929–)).

9. The decision to have an abortion may rarely seem clear cut, e.g. J. J. Thomson's basic analogy in question 8 is similar to a case of rape (in that it is a violation of your rights). But what if you had offered your services by mistake, or you thought you were giving blood as a short one-off donation, or perhaps you agreed at first but then changed your mind, or you agreed to start with but a close family member is taken ill and you then decide to call the agreement off?

10. The case of the Russian conjoined twins Masha and Dasha Krivoshlyapova (1950–2003) raises difficult questions about what constitutes a life. Masha and Dasha each had two arms but shared three legs (two good ones, the left controlled by one and the right by the other, and a vestigial third), they shared some internal organs (though not all), their pelvic bones joined and their spines met at the coccyx. Their circulatory system was interconnected, though their nervous systems were not. Since their spinal cords did not connect, they had separate senses of touch. They would become ill separately and sleep separately. They each had their own stomach and separate upper intestines which joined to form a single lower intestine and rectum. They had four kidneys, one bladder and a single set of reproductive organs. They had distinct personalities and both were psychologically maladjusted.

    a. We refer to two individuals whose embryonic development has taken place at the same time in the same mother as 'twins'. If the birth does not bring about two separate individuals, we usually consider the birth to have brought about one child (who may or may not have certain physical defects). Is it proper to consider conjoined 'twins' as true twins or are they one individual with a certain physical deformity? At what point does an individual with a certain physical deformity become a 'twin'?

b. What is an independent, self-supporting life? Is someone who is dependent on regular kidney dialysis an independent, self-supporting life?

Further reading

Hugh LaFollette (ed.), *Ethics in Practice: An Anthology* (Oxford: Blackwell, 2002).

Peter Singer, *Practical Ethics* (Cambridge: Cambridge University Press, 1993).

Judith Jarvis Thomson, 'A Defence of Abortion', in Peter Singer (ed.), *Applied Ethics* (Oxford: Oxford University Press, 1986), pp. 37–56.

19

Euthanasia

We consider ourselves to have the natural right to life. Are there any reasons why this should not include the natural right to death?

Introduction

The principle of protecting innocent human life is central to human morality; the view that it is preferable consciously and deliberately to end human life goes against this central belief.

> **?** Someone, obviously injured beyond any chance of help, begs to be 'put out of her misery'. You are in a position to end her life. What should you do?

The term 'euthanasia' (from Greek *euthanasia*, 'good death') originally had two distinct meanings: 'active', involving the painless putting to death of someone suffering acutely from a terminal condition, and 'passive', involving not preventing the death of someone suffering from a terminal condition. These days the concept of the 'terminal condition' has been mostly dropped. If a person requests their life be terminated it is called voluntary euthanasia (VE) or assisted suicide. If a person is mentally incapable of making a decision and euthanasia takes place, it is called non-voluntary euthanasia (NVE). The modern debate mostly centres on voluntary euthanasia that involves the active help of another person (voluntary assisted euthanasia (VAE)), and in particular, where a physician gives the assistance.

> **?** Everyone can tolerate a different level of pain. Can you work out what 'acutely suffering' might mean?

The controversy about VE revolves around the opposing Christian or Kantian duty-based view and the utilitarian (consequentialist view). The duty-based view says it is morally wrong to take any life (including your own). The utilitarian view says that if the killing brings about the greatest possible good (e.g. by eliminating pain) then killing is the correct course. In the case of VAE, medical ethics prohibit 'mercy killing' because a physician's first obligation is to preserve life (according to the second part of the Hippocratic oath a physician pledges only to provide beneficial treatments and to refrain from causing harm or hurt). Arguments in support of any form of euthanasia generally base that support on the belief that the relief of unbearable (physical or mental) suffering supersedes all other needs.

> **?** Relieving pain is a good. Causing death is a harm. Is it possible to imagine a situation where there is more good brought about by the relief of pain than there is harm brought about death?

The Christian view
Euthanasia appears to conflict with the Mosaic commandment 'You shall not murder'. However, the central theme of Christianity, 'Love one's neighbour', may direct someone to end unbearable pain (by killing) as an act of love.

> **?** John and Jill, both committed Christians, have been devoted partners for 60 years. Jill has an incurable illness that is progressively reducing her ability to move her body and consequently she has increasingly less control over her own functions. Her mind is still fully alert but the distress caused to her by the disease is causing her severe depression. She believes in a life after death and asks John to help her die. What are your thoughts on this?

The Kantian duty-based view
Immanuel Kant (1724–1804) believed that we should treat people as ends in themselves and not means to ends. In other words, we should respect their individual humanity, not what their existence might otherwise

lead to. In order to fulfil this obligation, Kant's duty-based ethical theory involves a categorical imperative (a formal moral law based on reason) that, in turn, would oblige us never to kill. However, in conflict with this, we may be similarly obliged (in respecting the humanity of another) to assist someone's own suicide if that person believed that suicide was what he or she truly wanted.

> **?** A physician feels duty bound to regard her patient's care as more important than any other consideration. After long and serious consideration, her patient (who is reliant upon medical care to survive), decides he wants to die and asks his physician to turn off the life support machine that keeps him alive. What should the physician do?

The utilitarian view
John Stuart Mill (1806–1873) worked out an ethical theory based on the consequences of action, not upon obligation to duties. This utilitarianism means calculating the potential effects of all the various courses available then, as a result of adding up all the possible happiness and unhappiness for everyone involved, taking the course that should bring about the greatest overall happiness.

> **?** Elizabeth is dying from a terminal disease. Her suffering is very great but she wants to live out every moment of her life no matter how painful it may be. Elizabeth's family (six children, eleven grown-up grandchildren and sixteen great grandchildren) are all very distressed and many of them are ill with anxiety and depression because of the situation. They all agree that Elizabeth should be given something to speed her death. Is there anything right about this idea?

The right to die
Since 1941 physician-assisted and non-physician-assisted suicide has been legal in Switzerland. Physician-assisted suicide has been legal in Oregon in

the US since 1997. In 2002 voluntary euthanasia and physician-assisted suicide became lawful in the Netherlands, allowing those with hopeless and unbearable suffering to seek help to die. In the same year, Belgium passed a law permitting suicide without defining the method. There is no other country in the world that enshrines the right to die in law. Legal attitudes in other countries range from tolerance to intolerance.

Euthanasia and purity of motive
Physicians are pledged to the Hippocratic oath, but there are still unscrupulous physicians (e.g. Dr Harold Shipman (1946–2004), convicted in England of 15 murders in 2001 though thought to have killed at least 215 people). If VAE were legal, some argue, it would be easy for an unscrupulous physician to kill a patient for motives that were not necessarily directed towards the best interests of the patient. In addition, if VE or VAE were legal, then involuntary euthanasia is (seen by some) as an unwanted step closer. It is the start of a slippery slope. If there is a right to take life initially, in the restricted sense of VAE, this might progressively alter as those who wished to die made increasingly specific demands. Soon, opponents of euthanasia might argue, we would be facing the moral dilemmas (as is the contemporary case with genetic manipulation and human reproduction) associated with social engineering and eugenic control. Adolf Hitler's (1889–1945) extermination scheme (after the War called 'Action T4') was initially based on an involuntary euthanasia programme.

> ❓ A young mother says she would like to use genetic engineering together with IVF to enable her to produce twins so that, six months after their birth, she could choose which one she would like to keep. She argues that allowing one to die is not wrong because without the genetic manipulation she would only have had one child anyway. What do you think?

Medical science
Ladan and Laleh Bijani (1974–2003) the Iranian twins joined by the skull, wished to be separated even though there had never been a successful separation of adult conjoined twins. The operation in July 2003 lasted over

50 hours and although eventually the twins were separated they both died without recovering consciousness. Ladan and Laleh accepted both the difficulties of the separation and the poor chances of success.

In some ways, their case is similar to a terminally ill patient wishing for VAE in that in both cases there is a wish to have an intolerable situation curtailed. That for the subject of VAE the alleviation of suffering means certain death, whereas for Ladan and Laleh it meant only possible death is a matter of degree — the decision is basically (logically) the same.

> **?** How can we view the grading of risk in the matter of our own life? The law says it is wrong to willingly take our own life (or for someone to assist us in taking our own life). The law says it is not wrong to allow ourselves to be the subject of a risky medical operation if the risk is justified by the severity of our condition. Would a terminally ill patient who wanted to die be justified in demanding an operation that could not cure the condition and would lead to certain death? Would a physician be acting in accordance with the Hippocratic oath to undertake such an operation?

The law

Conjoined twins are also called 'Siamese twins' after the twins Eng and Chang Bunker (1811–1874) who were born in Thailand (then Siam) and remained joined for the rest of their full lives. There is precedence for separating conjoined twins where both are considered to have an equal chance of survival (Giuseppina and Santina Foglia born in Turin, Italy, 1959, and Mpho and Mphonyana Mathibela born in South Africa, 1986), and for not separating conjoined twins where separation is considered impossible (Masha and Dasha Krivoshlyapova born in Russia in 1950 who, after years of institutional abuse, grew up still conjoined though both psychologically maladjusted).

Conjoined twins Mary and Jodie Attard were born in the UK in October 2000. The nature of their joining meant that Mary's heart-lung function was incapable of maintaining her own life and she was dependent upon Jodie to keep her alive. If they remained joined then they would both die in the short term. If they were surgically parted then Jodie's life could be saved but, in doing this, Mary would die. In other words, Mary was incapable of leading a self-supporting life and could only live for a short time with the support of Jodie. Jodie could lead an independent self-supporting life but would die if left joined to Mary. For religious reasons, the parents requested that there should be no medical intervention.

The legal ruling over the case of Mary and Jodie was that they should be separated. This meant that instead of medicine being responsible for the saving or maintenance of life, it would, when it separated the children, be responsible for condemning the one to die. The case meant that the rule of law took precedence over the ethics of medicine. Mary died during the operation in November 2000 and Jodie survived.

> **?** In the case of Mary and Jodie, the law instructed the physicians to carry out a procedure that contravened the physicians' fundamental obligation to work towards saving or protecting the life of another. Should such obligations be absolute or subject to specific alteration (as in this case)?

Further questions

Euthanasia is a contemporary social concern with an active minority seeking help for assisted suicide outside their own country or pleading their cases in the courts. The matter is by no means resolved. Indeed, it could be considered a moral issue in the early stages. Because it deals with death and, as euthanasia, provides only one chance for the individual to take action, it is difficult to untangle it from the implicit sadness and misfortune that attends it.

Some of the questions here depict examples of situations people have been faced with; some propose situations they might be faced with.

1. Imagine your friend has a terminal illness. She is in great pain and has been told that she will die in the next day or so. She asks you to pass her a drink that you know contains a sufficient amount of barbiturate to end her life. What would you do and why? Explain the moral basis for your action.
2. Conjoined twins Mary and Jodie were born in the UK in 2000. The

nature of their joining meant that Mary's heart-lung function was incapable of maintaining her own life and she was dependent upon Jodie to keep her alive. If they remained joined then they would both die in the short term. If they were surgically parted then Jodie's life could be saved but in doing this, Mary would die. For religious reasons the parents requested that there should be no medical intervention. The law courts ruled that they should be separated.

    a. To what extent should the parents' wishes influence what happens in such a case?
    b. Should any person ever be sacrificed for another?

3. John's father is due a large inheritance on 23 January. John's father has always made it clear that he would like to be helped to die if ever he should find himself terminally ill and in great pain. John has always said he would help him with this. John's father is terminally ill and can stand the pain no longer. On 20 January, he asks his son to help him take his own life and, as he puts it, 'give me a happy release'. If John's father dies before 23 January, he will not receive the inheritance and John will not inherit from him. John tells his father that he will not help him until 24 January. What are your thoughts on this?

4. Mary is suffering from a terminal illness, is in great pain and distress and has made plain her wish to die. Mary's husband, who is fit and well, cannot bear the idea of Mary taking her own life and would suffer years of mental torment if she did. Mary's solicitor, who refused to help Mary make a 'living will' (an advance directive by means of which she wanted to express her wish to die if she ever found herself in the circumstances she is now in), has informed the police of her possible intention. The police have told Mary that she will be breaking the law if she carries out her wish (as would anyone who assists her). Mary believes it is her basic human right to live her life freely and as she wishes (and that includes dying if she wishes). Try to come to a decision about this on utilitarian grounds.

5. The leader of a state, John X, who is considered a threat to world order, is terminally ill. The leaders of opposing states offer to pay John X's physician to prescribe a fatal dose of barbiturates. What should the physician do?

6. In a battle, part of a state-sanctioned just war, an officer calls for a volunteer for a mission that will lead to the volunteer's certain death. Is it right to allow someone to volunteer for such a mission or is this aiding a suicide?

7. Richard has been accused of large-scale fraud and is facing ruin. When he discovers he is going to die from a painful disease, he contemplates suicide. He asks his friend to help him die, knowing that in truth his main motive is to avoid the shame of his wrongdoing. What are the moral implications of this?

Further reading

Hugh LaFollette (ed.), *Ethics in Practice: An Anthology* (Oxford: Blackwell, 2002).

20
Animal Rights

Should some of the ethical standards that we believe rightly applied to human beings (e.g. 'do not kill', 'do not cause undue suffering') also be applied to all forms of animal life, some forms of animal life or only to human beings?

Introduction

The movement which these days is called the 'movement for animal rights' or the 'animal liberation movement' grew out of various laws passed in Western Europe during the nineteenth century to protect the welfare of animals (e.g. pit ponies). It stems from the revolutionary thinking of Jeremy Bentham (1748–1832), who advocated that we should include the interests of animals in our ethical thinking. Prior to Bentham, with the exception of St Thomas Aquinas (1224/5–1274), and Immanuel Kant (1724–1804) who thought that being kind to animals would foster our own innate kindness, there was no philosophical consideration for animals in themselves. God declared in Genesis 1 that humankind had dominion over animals and although it says later that oxen should be rested on the Sabbath, St Paul (c.5–c.67) said this was only to benefit humans. St Augustine (354–430) pointed out that Jesus sacrificed the Gadarene swine to show that we have no duties to animals. René Descartes (1596–1650) considered animals merely mechanisms with no feelings.

The modern view arose in the 1970s. Peter Singer (1946–) argued that 'speciesism' (a term coined by Richard D. Ryder in 1970) was no different from racism or sexism and that animals should be extended the same basic principles of equality as we extend to humans. His argument is directed against factory farming and animal experimentation and concludes that vegetarianism (as an alternative to the pleasures of eating meat when its production also produces suffering) is the only ethically acceptable diet. His test for the justification of experimenting on an animal is whether we would do the same to an orphaned human child with a comparable mental level to the animal. Only if our answer is 'yes' could we claim to be non-speciesist. Tom Regan (1938–) claims that all mammals (above a certain age) are 'subjects-of-a-life' and therefore entitled to certain basic rights. A broad debate has stemmed from this and a strong social movement has evolved. The animal rights movement is involved in such areas as animal experimentation, vegetarianism, hunting, zoos, circuses, the keeping of pets, animal habitat and the broader ecology.

> **?** The modern animal rights movement has only existed since the early 1970s. For the whole of human history before that, animals were not regarded in any way as having rights in themselves. If the animal rights movement is right about its attitude to animals then nearly all humans who lived before about 1970 were wrong. What do you make of this?

What is a right?
A right is a moral, legal or social entitlement to protection afforded to the individual in his or her pursuit of good. Central individual rights are the natural rights to life, the respectful treatment of that life and the right to be allowed to fulfil the nature of that life undisturbed. Without these basic rights, no other rights can meaningfully flow.

Rights and responsibilities
Rights imply responsibilities. Those whose actions are prompted by immoral purposes lose their rights. Such acts of responsibility are commonly regarded as human activities. Sometimes humans apply the implicit human attributes of responsibility to animals (e.g. to try, to understand, to wish), but such application does not necessarily imbue the non-human species with those attributes. Generally speaking, to claim rights the individual must know that he or she is pursuing good and must have free-will in pursuit of that (good) purpose. In other words, the individual must be a person. Unless the individual can (to some degree) fulfil these conditions, it is inappropriate to accord rights to that individual.

> **?** If I say, 'My canary understands everything I say', do I mean my canary actually understands everything I say?

Understanding the outcomes of our actions
Knowing that we are pursuing good requires knowledge of what Aristotle (384–322 BC) called the final cause, that is, the object in our mind that we believe will be the final outcome of our actions.

> **?** When a beef cow is led into a slaughterhouse and sees other cows ahead being killed, does that cow 'know' it is going to be killed?

We do not know why we do everything we do. In order to claim rights we have to be able to say we know the final cause of at least some of the things we do: in other words, that we are pursuing our ends with conscious intention.

> **?** Can you think of any examples of any animals being aware of a (moral) final cause of their actions?

Moral choice
The idea of free-will and rights assumes that we are in a position to make free choices (i.e. that we are not in a completely determined world). If the individual pursues a goal, then that individual must have been aware of that goal when they set their actions in train (e.g. if I want to take a bus, then I must first of all find a bus going to my destination). All living things move towards goals (e.g. for food, to reproduce), but it cannot be said that all living things make choices about what in particular are their goals or how they should realise them. In order to act morally the individual must be making a moral choice, that is, individuals must distinguish between the ultimate right or wrong of their actions. Only by reducing the apparent freedom of the individual to an increasingly determined world can this sort of choice be seen as driven by, for example, genetic makeup, environment, upbringing or instinct.

> **?** Is it conceivable that a dog, because he has become dissatisfied with the food he is being fed, waits for his owner to return so he can bite her? Could you modify the scenario to reveal some free moral choice on the part of the dog?

Are animals entitled to rights?

To establish whether or not animals are entitled to rights, they (as individuals) can be tested against certain characteristics commonly attributed to persons. However, it must be born in mind that a human would pass all these tests because the testing method is a human-centred, human-benchmarked one.

The test of consciousness

Human beings consider themselves conscious animals of the highest order. The problem for animal rights here (in that the claim for rights is accessible only if the test is passed) is connected to our evaluation of the consciousness of animals (e.g. we do not claim the same rights for vegetables which we generally consider to be without consciousness). Using this test places great demands on our objectivity, as there is always a danger of anthropomorphising our view of animals (i.e. using words and thinking in ways which apply properly to human beings but only metaphorically to animals). We find it very difficult not to impose our own conscious-derived terms (e.g. like, hate, know) on animals (e.g. 'She likes that toy', 'She hates other dogs', 'She always knows what I mean').

We can define consciousness as the awareness of feelings or experiences when our environment (including our own body) constitutes 'such and such' (e.g. be aware of pain because I put my hand on something hot, enjoy the warmth of the sun). Only an extreme mentalist would accord consciousness to every living thing, and most rule out consciousness to living things which science declares cannot feel pain or pleasure. Commonly, the smaller the thing is the less we are inclined to believe it has consciousness, though we must be guarded against 'sizism' in this context. Science conventionally tests for consciousness based on behaviour, but this is fraught with the problems of anthropomorphism and presuppositions of certain sorts of behaviour that prove our case (e.g. my pet comes to me because she enjoys being stroked).

Many animals congregate in large social groups (e.g. ants, termites, bees, schooling fish, flocks of birds, humans). Such behaviour is often deemed evidence of a conscious will to cooperate. However, such behaviour may be for different reasons (e.g. protection, pooling of resources, mutual responsibility or care of the young) and does not necessarily support actively conscious behaviour (e.g. it may be genetic, in response to threat, a reaction to weather).

> **?** Some animals pair for life (e.g. swans, wolves, condors, French angel fish). Does this mean that such animals have the same conscious feelings for one another as humans who follow the same social pattern?

The test of pain

It is clear that some animals are sensitive to pain, but it is not so clear whether those sensations amount to anything more than physiological responses that we, as humans, interpret in the same ways that we understand our own responses to pain. In other words, an animal may experience the sensation of pain but may not have any emotional response to that sensation. We tend to evaluate patterns of animal behaviour (e.g. an animal cries out if injured, shrinks back from the source of the pain, attends to the wound, whimpers and so on) as close enough to our own responses for us safely to draw the conclusion that those responses derive from some sensation, more or less similar to the sensation we would have if we were subjected to a similar pain. After all, we only 'know' (assume) other humans experience pains (or any sensations) in the way we do by a similar form of analogy. Generally, we differentiate certain classes of creatures from others using this form of arbitration. The result is that whereas we include chimpanzees in the class of animals who feel similar sensations to ourselves (e.g. because we can see they seem to), we exclude oysters (e.g. because we cannot see they seem to).

> **?** A man kicks a dog and it yelps. Do we know the dog is feeling pain in the same way that we do, or are we imposing our own feelings upon a situation where no such feelings exist?

The idea that pleasure or pain can provide evidence of consciousness is problematic. Pleasure means that a life can go well, pain that it can go badly. On this basis, not just animals are conscious. If a plant does not receive water then its life will go badly (it will die). Because of this, it germinates in appropriate environments, develops root or leaf systems in order to derive maximum amounts of water uptake, develops systems to reduce respiration and so on However, few accept that a plant is conscious in the same way that a 'thing that attracts rights' is conscious.

> **?** Describe how an animal can appear unhappy. Analyse the humanising words that you may have used (or may have wanted to use) in order to do this.

Being 'subject-of-a-life'

Regan defined consciousness in a way that includes more than just sentient awareness of an environment coupled with a pleasure-pain system that fits in with a life orientated to good or ill. He thinks that (as well as the pleasure-pain system) to be 'subject-of-a-life' an individual must have beliefs, desires, perceptions, memories, a sense of its own future, welfare interests, preferences, an ability to initiate actions in its own interest and a continued identity which is independent of others or the interests of others. For Regan, all mammals fulfil these criteria. That birds, fish and other non-mammals fail to fulfil these criteria does not mean that they should be killed for sport or other non-food reason.

> **?** If I drop a live lobster into boiling water, its life will have gone badly. Is this reason enough to preserve its right to life irrespective of whether I believe it has, for example, a sense of its own future?

Language

For Ludwig Josef Johann Wittgenstein (1889–1951), language is central to our own self-understanding and an understanding of the world. In other words, we think in language. If animals use coherent language (and therefore think about themselves and the world), then we would find it almost impossible (because of this similarity to ourselves) to deny them basic, individual rights.

Jane Morris Goodall (1934–) revealed that chimpanzees not only make tools (using twigs to prize out insects much like the New Caledonia crow and some finches on the Galapagos Islands) but also exist in complex and highly developed social groups. She believes that a chimpanzee Washoe (1965–2007) (and others) have genuinely learned language (in the form of American Sign Language). This claim for Washoe (and others) is strongly disputed by those who assert that the chimpanzees have not learned the language but merely make gestures in response to various cues, or indeed make random gestures that are seen as comparable to certain signs by wishful-thinking observers.

> **?** No ape has a brain structure that seems sufficient to support language ability. No ape has vocal chords that would enable it to speak. No ape has been shown initiating a conversation (with either its sign trainer or any other person). Does this mean that no ape has language?

However, there is not necessarily a link between language and rights. Humans who do not have language have human rights in the same way that humans who have highly developed language do not have enhanced human rights. Discovering language in an animal species other than humans would not automatically mean us bestowing rights on them (even though we may acknowledge that they had inherent rights not previously acknowledged). Such a discovery would more properly mean that we had a deeper (psychological or scientific) understanding of that particular species.

> **?** If it were found that oysters had a fully developed language, would this mean that they would be entitled full rights as individuals?

Self-consciousness

Self-consciousness is an important aspect of Regan's proposal of 'subject-of-a-life'. However, just as language need not automatically bestow individual rights, neither would self-consciousness. For example, someone in a coma does not have self-consciousness but retains individual rights. An ant may not have self-consciousness but this does not necessarily mean that the ant does not have a right to life. It is difficult to imagine any animal other than a human being truly self-consciousness (i.e. having a developed sense of self, an ability to think about its own thoughts, an ability to reflect upon its own mistakes or an aptitude to alter its conduct in response to ideas it has about possible future outcomes). Some pro-abortionists claim that the foetus does not have a right to life because it only has a potential for future self-consciousness. In the same way, the ant may well develop self-consciousness in the future (no matter how unlikely this may seem, and no matter how distant that future time), whereas the comatose human (with probably little future potential) does not have to prove any such future case to be entitled to individual rights.

> **?** A chimpanzee is placed in front of a mirror and given a comb. It grooms itself and pulls faces at its own reflection. Is this self-awareness proof of consciousness?

Pursuing goals and desires

All living things pursue goals of a simple sort, for example, to reproduce themselves, to move towards the light or to find food. The pursuance of goals that would attract rights, however, must be more than this. Some of the higher primates demonstrate an apparent ability to deceive by guile. However, we may be seeing such deceit as somehow different (and similar to human deceit) from deceit practised by other animals (e.g. a spider's web, animals who camouflage themselves) when in fact it is merely a higher primate case of a trait that is rife throughout the animal kingdom (in particular for the acquisition of food).

> **?** A venomous snake, camouflaged against its background, kills and eats a lizard that is also camouflaged but unable to disguise its body heat from which the snake detects its presence. Are there any individual rights involved here?

Acting in self-defence

It is sometimes argued that animals that act in their own self-defence must not only be self-conscious (they are concerned about protecting themselves) but must also be aware of their own future. The example of animals 'filled with fear' in an abattoir is sometimes given to support this claim. However, many humans are incapable of properly defending themselves (e.g. the very young, the very old, those with particular physical or mental disabilities), and they are not excluded from having individual rights. Whole races have shown themselves short of cunning and the ability to protect themselves, and, although they may have been conquered or wiped out by natural forces, no one would argue that they should not have an entitlement to individual rights.

> **?** A hedgehog, when physically threatened, rolls up into a ball. Does any part of this action mean that the hedgehog should attract any form of individual rights?

Rights-based views
Those who believe in animal rights from an ethical point of view, think it wrong to kill animals for food because those animals have an individual right to life. This view also necessitates vegetarianism. The individual animals that have a right to life, of course, include the prey of the individual animals that are carnivorous. This prey (before it is consumed) may also feed on others and so on. On the rights-based view, all of these animals have the same individual rights and these should be protected (even though in a carnivorous food chain there is a continual downward violation of those rights if they exist). The rights-based vegetarian can eliminate meat that he or she may otherwise eat (by not eating it), but (in order to be ethically consistent) should also have the same concern (expectation) for all other animals down the food chain.

> **?** Any food we eat contains bacteria that are at risk if we consume them. Should we avoid all food on ethical grounds?

To convert the world to include rights for all animals would mean a regulated and policed world in which all carnivorous animals were fed a nutritional vegetarian diet. This would lead to species that could not tolerate such a diet becoming extinct, huge pressure on natural food resources and a mechanism for policing (and punishment) the size and scope of which the world has never seen. In defence of the rights-based view, we could say that animals are driven by instinct to eat what they eat and so do not have free-will to choose what they eat. However, if animals do not have free-will then one of the strongest connections to the entitlement to individual rights is broken. It may also be argued that animals do not have duties to each other (and so eat each other). Again, inherent absence of duties like this (as opposed to known irresponsible action) does not remove entitlement to individual rights.

> **?** Is it sensible that I should entitle a shark to individual rights (and therefore do not eat it) if that shark (in 'ignorance' of its duties) continues to eat smaller fish to which I also entitle individual rights?

A consequentialist view

Consequentialists, such as Singer, take an ethical view of vegetarianism, believing it wrong to eat animals who have suffered either in the way they were bred (e.g. intensive farming, force feeding) or the way they were killed (e.g. with cruelty or without proper consideration for their welfare). Singer accepts that if animals are raised well and killed painlessly there is nothing ethically wrong in eating them, particularly on the utilitarian grounds that the pleasure derived (to the human) is greater than the suffering caused (to the animal).

> **?** If a consequentialist vegetarian believes it is impossible to protect the individual rights of animals all the way down the food chain, can they support a belief that it is worth protecting the rights of the animals that humans feed on?

An ethical progress view

Upholders of animal rights believe the view to be a natural part of ethical progress. Just as we used to discriminate against slaves, or other races, or because of gender or sexual inclination, and do no longer, so we should work towards eliminating discrimination against animals. It seems reasonable to recognise duties in respect of animals (because we use them as a resource) in the same way we recognise duties concerning the natural environment as a whole (e.g. reducing emissions of greenhouse gases, disposing of waste properly). Animals are of great benefit to humankind (e.g.

as food, as material, as companions) and without them human life would be poorer. In order to maintain the environment that encourages the richness that animals bring, we should nurture and respect those animals (i.e. reduce their suffering if possible).

> **?** A consequentialist like Singer believes that it would be appropriate to experiment on animals if, at the same time, we were prepared to experiment on human beings of the same mental capacity (e.g. the profoundly mentally disabled). Such human experimentation could be very beneficial to humankind in that it would yield results for medical research more quickly and more certainly than non-human testing methods. What do you think?

Hierarchy of desires

Singer believes that animals are 'replaceable'. As long as they are kept in good conditions there is no reason why we should not use them for our own purposes. This he extends to a utilitarianism of preference whereby the preference of humans (e.g. to hunt animals or eat meat) should be considered more important than the desires of animals not to suffer.

> **?** As a preference utilitarian who takes a consequentialist view of animal rights, how would you weigh up the rights of all those involved in hunting animals and killing them for sport and what would be your conclusion? Would this be different from your own opinion?

Companion animals — the keeping of pets

Animals have been domesticated or kept in domestic environments either for work or as companions throughout time. Companion animals have been kept or tolerated for religious reasons (e.g. cats in ancient Egypt, cows in India), as tokens of power (e.g. cats kept by witches), used as aids for the disabled (e.g. where guide dogs for the blind also serve as work animals) or purely as pets (dogs being the most widespread animal used for this purpose). Many humans find the companionship of an animal pet a great benefit (i.e. it is company, something to touch, something to care for and relate to) but the question still remains as to whether or not it is in keeping with what we consider basic individual rights to keep animals in captivity like this.

> **?** Would it be morally right to keep another human as a pet? Is it morally right to keep an animal as a pet? Do any differences here point to differences in the way we view individual rights?

Further questions

As a movement with a philosophical foundation, the movement for animal rights is probably the most recent. Attitudes about the preservation of animal rights, however, can produce strong human emotion and action taken in support of these views can lead to polarisation of opinion.

1. Are rights something bestowed by others or are rights inherent to an individual?

2. Should the formulation of rights bestowed by others (e.g. I stop the killing of foxes by hunting and therefore grant certain foxes a right to life) derive from a moral investigation of the bestower's morality or a classification of the individual onto whom the rights are bestowed? For example, if I grant an animal a certain right, it is because I have decided on the basis of my own moral purpose; that I believe the animal deserves the right I grant, is only part of what causes my decision (e.g. I may abhor all killing).

3. Are only some animals entitled not to be killed?

4. I think my dog has rights because he 'knows' what I am thinking, 'understands' my instructions and 'acts for my good' by protecting my house. Is this true or am I anthropomorphising?

5. I like my cat and she likes me. Does this make sense?

6. When a lobster is dropped into boiling water (to prepare it to be eaten), the air expelled from within its shell causes a high-pitched noise. Would you drop a live lobster into boiling water? Has your answer anything to do with the noise it would make if you did this?

7. In what ways can an animal be said to have beliefs? Are they in any way similar to the sorts of beliefs held by humans?

8. Can you think anything without using language to think about it? What is it that you can think about in this way?

9. 'Look, now she is refusing to do it just because she is being stubborn.' Is this human's remark about her pet coherent?

10. You are trapped alone on an island and are unsure about whether or not the only source of food (berries high in trees) is safe to eat. You will starve to death if the berries are inedible. Would you consider it right to test out the berries on the local rabbits (which you know are themselves poisonous as a result of toxins released onto the island by previous chemical warfare experiments) before you try them yourself? What is your reasoning? Would your views be the same if the only other animals on the island were ants, not rabbits?

11. Animals kept as pets have sometimes been bred for the purpose (e.g. dogs). Is such breeding an injustice to the rights of the animal (and to the natural evolution of its genes) from which today's pets have been born?

12. Humans have a special relationship with animal pets that is sometimes of great value to humans. Does keeping a pet animal (and therefore servicing that human need) interfere with that animal's rights?

13. Do 'cyberpets' have rights?

Notes

Question 1 ~ 'Anthropomorphising' means the attribution of a human form or personality to an animal (or god or thing). Analysing how easily we do this (e.g. it is done sometimes in order to feel a 'closeness' with animals or nature) is necessary to best understand our attitude towards animal rights.

For Question 3 listing the results is useful. For Question 4 it is a good idea to list animal beliefs and human beliefs in two separate columns.

Further reading

Tom Regan, *The Case for Animal Rights: Updated with a New Preface* (Berkeley, CA: University of California Press, 2004).

Tom Regan and Peter Singer (eds.), *Animal Rights and Human Obligation* (Englewood Cliffs, NJ: Prentice-Hall, 1989).

Peter Singer, *Practical Ethics* (Cambridge: Cambridge University Press, 1993).

21

Genetics

If new scientific discoveries lead to new technical abilities, and technical abilities enhance the quality of life for humans, should there be any moral limitations on scientific progress?

Introduction

Evolution theory depends on attributes that lead to success being passed from one generation to another. Genes are the organic mediums that transmit these attributes. Genes are composed of deoxyribonucleic acid and are the smallest units of hereditary material. Genes are attached to chromosomes that form long strands. Different forms of genes (called 'alleles') combine in different dominant and recessive relationships to define the particular gene type.

In the 1860s Gregor Mendel (1822–1884) demonstrated (in his study of inheritance by controlled plant breeding experiments with peas) that genes pass on characteristics in a random fashion. These 'germinal units', as Mendel called them, were first called 'genes' by Wilhelm Ludvig Johannsen (1857–1927) in 1909. By the middle of the twentieth century, chromosomes (the existence of which had been discovered by Wilhelm Friedrich Benedikt Hofmeister (1824–1877) in 1848) were understood to be the carriers of hereditary information and responsible for the determination of the characteristics of organisms. It was known that they were composed of protein and an acid, deoxyribonucleic acid (DNA), but no one knew what DNA looked like, how it was arranged in the chromosome, how it duplicated itself during cell division and how it directed protein synthesis. In 1953, Francis Harry Compton Crick (1916–2004) and James Dewey Watson (1928–) showed that the DNA portion of the chromosome was made up of two chains coiled around one another to form a double helix.

Genetics

> **?** Are our minds independent of the influence of genes? After all, even if mind is not physical this physical nature must affect the characteristics of any particular mind because of its interaction with the body.

The genetic population

A 'genetic population' (or 'Mendelian population') is a community of a sexually reproducing species (usually smaller than the entire species) in which the individuals share a common gene pool (i.e. the sum total of all the genes in that community). Each member of such a community must have an equal chance of mating with another member of the community. Adaptive modification of the gene pool (by mutation) results in natural evolution of the community.

> **?** Being part of a gene pool means we have a responsibility to protect it (it is, after all, our 'genetic future'). As individual humans, should we regard our genetic pool as the whole human race, our own racial type, our family, those with whom we would like to reproduce or those with whom we share a religious or political belief?

Natural changes in the gene pool

In nature, genetic characteristics are passed on to offspring and will differ according to the dominance or recessiveness of certain genes, or to mutation in genes which may be beneficial (e.g. resistance to antibiotics in certain bacteria, or to pesticides in some plants), threatening to the survival of the organism (e.g. cystic fibrosis in human beings), or both (e.g. sickle-cell anaemia which also has a side effect of giving some immunity to malaria).

> **?** In nature, the males of many species go to a lot of trouble to attract females (e.g. competitive displays, plumage, shows of courage, nest building). This means that, for example, those males with the best plumage may get the greatest opportunity to reproduce their genes. Is this bias (in this case towards finer plumage) an appropriate influence on the species gene

pool? After all, it probably (in itself) serves no beneficial evolutionary role.

Forced changes in the gene pool
It has long been known that it is possible to modify the character of both animals and plants by selective breeding, a rather hit-or-miss method which has been greatly improved by the use of artificial insemination. Chickens, pigs, cows and turkeys along with potatoes, cereals and brassicas all have wild ancestors that were less useful or productive.

> **?** There are many species bred by humans that could no longer survive in the wild (e.g. many, if not all breeds of dogs). Is there any utilitarian or duty-based moral defence for this?

The human genome
The human genome is the entire array of gene-bearing DNA sequences contained in a human cell. In other words, it is what dictates the physical nature of the human individual. The position of each part of the over three billion DNA base pairs of chromosomes contained in the human genome is now known. This has potential implications for medicine (e.g. seeking out proneness to certain diseases) and for society (i.e. knowing what genes cause proneness to what diseases means that human offspring can be engineered to avoid such diseases or proneness).

> **?** Should knowledge about the human genetic makeup be used to shape the nature of human beings? Is this knowledge different from any previous scientific discovery that has benefited (and therefore changed) humankind?

Genetic engineering
During the second half of the twentieth century there were advances both in the understanding of the nature of genes as well as in the technical ability to manipulate them. It is now possible to manipulate the characteristics of individuals by 'genetic engineering', a term used to encompass the activities of genetic engineers whose scientific expertise is coupled with the

funding and profit-driven resources of multinational businesses. Genetic engineering is, in essence, cutting out chromosomes in one organism (or using synthetically produced chromosomes) and splicing them into the chromosomes of another. This activity includes gene manipulation, gene cloning, gene therapy and genetic modification. Genetic engineering leads to the mass production of protein-based chemicals that would otherwise be scarce. This means that whoever creates these chemicals can command a high price for them.

> **?** Should the direction and pace of scientific progress (which includes medical progress) be dictated by funding which is profit driven?

Gene cloning

Gene cloning is the process of making large quantities of DNA once it has been isolated from the chromosome. Because it is possible to insert a DNA fragment into another organism and so produce a clone of the original, cloning allows for unlimited copies of a gene to be produced. Viruses can be used to transmit a gene from one organism to another.

Because cloning replicates genetically identical organisms from a single parent, it can be used for the rapid multiplication of plant species with desirable genetic characteristics. Cloning of plants is used to propagate plants for commercial needs, to aid recovery of threatened species and to benefit food and resource production (e.g. genetically modified soya and rapid-growing wood pulp trees). Cloning can also be used to replicate living things.

Although there was some early cloning work carried out on frogs at Cambridge in the 1970s, it was not until the publication in 1997 of the work at the Roslin Institute in Edinburgh led by Ian Wilmut (1944–) that cloning whole animals became a reality. Dolly the sheep (1996–2003), named after the singer-songwriter Dolly Parton, was cloned from one cell taken from the udder of a six-year-old ewe. Cloning like this means that any living thing can be replicated from the original tissue with identical DNA to that original. Many experiments in cloning an ever-wider range of species have now taken place. Human cloning leading to identical twins as part of the natural reproductive process is commonplace; cloning of medicinal (stem) cells or body parts remains contentious. Cloned proteins have become the subject of patents owned by pharmaceutical companies and medical treatment based upon these proteins is therefore subject to the regulation of supply imposed by the companies.

> **?** Is there something abnormal about cloning an organism or is it simply using scientific understanding to speed up a normal process?

Stem-cell harvesting

Although stem cells can be harvested from adult cells, it is also possible to grow an embryo to an early stage and harvest the stem cells. Stem cells can be used for the benefit of genetically related individuals in a variety of medically therapeutic treatments. Harvesting the stem cells kills the embryo though non-fatal harvesting is subject to further research. Since the beginning of the twenty-first century, stem-cell research into an increasing range of cell types has been progressively approved in many parts of the world (initially the Scandinavian countries, the UK, South Africa and the US).

> **?** Should any of these theoretical possibilities be put into practice? What are the moral implications?
>   a. It is possible to grow a kidney from harvested stem cells that will save the life of a genetically related child.
>   b. It is possible to harvest stem cells that will immunise a genetically related child from a rare, non-life-threatening disease.
>   c. It is possible to harvest stem cells to help develop the lung capacity needed for top-class athletic competition in a genetically related child, the daughter of parents keen to have a child who is an athletic champion.

Genetic modification

Genetically modified animals

In 1993, sheep with human genes were created which could produce human proteins in their milk for the production of the blood-clotting agent ('Factor VIII') used by haemophiliacs. In 1996, a genetically modified mosquito was produced which did not carry the encephalitis virus.

In 1996, Rosie the cow (and her eight sisters) was born with the genetically modified ability to produce the protein alphalactalbumin in her milk (a rich source of amino acids for new-born children). Since then goats, pigs, cattle and primates have been bred with genetic modifications, some of which are trademarked (e.g. 'Enviropig'). There is no reason why, for example, pigs with human genes will not be born to provide a supply of cells or organs for donation to humans.

> **?** What rights do genetically modified animals have? For example does a 'spare part' pig have a right to a normal life as a pig or is its function only to provide spare parts for human beings?

Genetically modified human beings

We should only consider some living thing to be altered genetically if its fundamental characteristics have been changed by some external, unnatural means. This excludes medical help to conceive children using IVF (in-vitro fertilisation); and although this may be considered a way of getting around genetic deficiencies and bringing a life into existence by artificial means, it does not alter the genetic characteristics of a living thing. However, if when using this method, parents opt for the removal of a gene that may carry a threatening disease, then this is a genetic alteration. Technical skills with IVF, coupled with growing skills at genetic modification, make the joint use of these processes increasingly possible.

> **?** Two members of an ethical committee cannot agree: one believes that adjustments to an embryo are acceptable if it is to remove the threat of a future disease, the other believes that any such alteration is wrong, thinking that life is full of risks and we should all face whatever nature has in store for us. What do you think?

Genetically modified plants

Because of the direct relationship between plants and human beings (we all consume food), there is wide public concern about genetically modified plants (GM plants) and, subsequently, genetically modified food (GM food). Much of this concern centres around the possible effects of eating food the effects of which on both human health and the environment is not yet known.

The first genetically modified plant was a tobacco resistant to herbicides, grown in France in 1986. In 1994, the Flavr Savr tomato with a longer shelf life was approved in the US, and in 1995 (amid concerns that its use could lead to resistant strains of harmful insects), the Bt Potato with its own insecticide was approved ('Bt' stands for 'bacillus thuringiensis', a bacterium with pesticidal qualities). Amid growing public concern, some counties (particularly in Europe) have tightened up their regulations controlling the import of GM foods. There have been no known incidents of harm caused to humans by GM foods. In 2011, 11 different GM crops are approved in 25 countries worldwide.

> **?** What are the differences between GM plants and plants that have been naturally bred for their suitability? Are we entitled to have a particular view about GM plants based on these differences?

Genetically modified plants are the product of much expensive research and are, as such, part of a larger framework of capitalism currently dominating the Western world (e.g. patents for the Flavr Savr tomato and the Bt Potato are corporately owned). Some argue that any benefits to the poorer world (e.g. in increased food production) will be at the expense of poorer nations who will become increasingly indebted to the richer nations. For example, in 2009, of the 1.8 million deaths worldwide from AIDS, 1.3 million of them occurred in sub-Saharan Africa. Much suffering could be reduced if the worst affected African nations could afford the readily available but expensive drugs that are controlled by the richer nations of the advanced world. The problems caused by the opposing forces of benefits and costs apply with equal force to the production and distribution of carefully patented and controlled GM food.

> **?** Should all genetic resources and information be shared for the benefit of humankind?

Eugenics

Eugenics is the theory that the human race can be improved by the controlled selective breeding of individuals with desirable characteristics. Eugenics has a long tradition. For example, in history, upper class and aristocratic marriages have been as much about the breeding of progeny as about alliances and the acquisition of land. Plato (c.428–347 BC), as well as advocating the killing of the disabled new born, suggested a system of breeding festivals for the gifted and state-controlled nurseries for the offspring. Aristotle (384–322 BC) proposed abortion by choice and, like Plato, humane killing of the mentally and physically handicapped. The term 'eugenics' was coined in 1883 by Charles Darwin's (1809–1882) first cousin Francis Galton (1822–1911). Galton put forward the idea of marriage between men of genius and women of wealth. He endowed a research post in eugenics at University College London, the most famous holder of which was probably Karl Pearson (1857–1936) whose extreme ideas (based around applying statistical method to Darwinian theory) lent much weight to the racial views of ancestral inheritance in Europe and the US in the first half of the twentieth century. There was much false scientific information given in support of eugenics during this period. By the 1930s, most states in the US practised sexual sterilisation aimed at eliminating the mentally retarded, epileptics and sexual deviants. At the same time there was a growing belief in Aryan superiority in Nazi Germany and a partially carried out plan to eradicate unwanted members of society ('Action T4'). In 1995, the Chinese government passed a law requiring those who intend marriage to undergo screening for 'inappropriate' genes. If such genes are found then the couples must agree to sterilisation or long-term contraception.

> *'Surely,' said John, 'genetic screening is a good idea. It would save money on health care too!' What do you think of John's view?*

Gene therapy

Eugenic possibilities are greatly increased since the advent of genetic engineering where individual parents are now in a position to select children who are not prone to certain inherited diseases or (more contentiously) have, or do not have, certain physical or mental traits. This is called 'gene therapy' and is a tool of the medical geneticist. The application of gene therapy in the case of, say, selecting against the gene for cystic fibrosis or suppressing cancer-producing cells, is, on the face of it, more or less clear. However, selecting for accepted good looks or athletic prowess might be considered questionable; it would be being done to satisfy the parents not necessarily the child, and such treatment would probably only be available to the wealthy. Such treatment remains ethically contentious but its use in curative and corrective medicine continues. The ultimate direction and application of gene therapy is not known.

> **?** Do you consider it ethically proper to eliminate any undesirable traits from a human population by selective breeding? If so, which traits and why?

The use of knowledge

It is not in keeping with human knowledge that something is known but not utilised. Many modern consumer items, for example, stem from discoveries being applied rather than consumer demand for a discovery to be made. The question then arises as to what is considered appropriate use of this knowledge and what is considered inappropriate. If different aspects of cloning, genetic engineering or gene therapy are considered appropriate, then decisions about how the benefits should be shared out (e.g. by ability to pay, by justified need, on utilitarian grounds) and who should regulate them (e.g. physicians, the law, politicians) need to be made. Even if there is a general principle that applies to a practical problem, there will almost certainly be exceptional cases that need to be decided on their individual merits.

> **?** Two good parents lose their daughter in a tragic accident. They already have two sons and want to have another child but feel it must be a 'replacement' daughter. They have asked their physician to support IVF treatment with gene manipulation that will lead to the birth of a girl. What needs to be considered in trying to make a decision as to whether or not this should be allowed? When these factors are weighed, what should be the decision and why?

Genetic screening

The practice of medicine favours prevention over cure. To prevent genetic makeup leading to problems it is necessary by genetic screening to determine genetic makeup either before conception (screening of the parents) or during the foetal stage (screening of the embryo). Genetic screening can be regarded as an early stage of genetic selection (and therefore eugenic selection). Since 1997 in the US, all parents have been offered a test to see if they are carrying the recessive gene for cystic fibrosis (the most common inherited disease in the US). If they test positive, and conception has occurred, they are offered the alternative of an abortion. With increased understanding of the human genome, screening will ultimately become possible for a wide variety of disorders and predispositions (e.g. cancer, Alzheimer's disease).

> **?** If it were possible to screen for all diseases that would lead to premature death, would it be right to terminate every foetus whose chromosomal make up put them at such risk?

Genetic forensics

In genetic forensics, DNA profiling matches samples of DNA from crime scenes with those of suspects. There are a number of large DNA databases in the world, the largest being the US's FBI CODIS (Combined DNA Index System). The UK's National DNA Database collects DNA samples from crime scenes and suspects. DNA profiling is also used in civil cases (such as cases of contested paternity) and in advancing the sciences (in particular, archaeology).

> **?** Should a DNA database include every member of the state?

Further questions

Although genetic concerns have accelerated as technological advances have been made, the ethics of genetic manipulation — vaunted by Aldous (Leonard) Huxley's (1894–1963), *Brave New World* (1932) — can be traced back to at least the Ancient Greeks and the pro-eugenic attitudes of

Plato and Aristotle. Genetic engineering is both contentious and changing. Different people and different nations hold different views. It is a problem in no way solved and needs dealing with as such — an ongoing mixture of newly arising issues which provide the ground for active and meaningful philosophical debate.

Science's ability to 'change nature' is sometimes seen as a corruption of nature (e.g. leading to the expression 'Frankenstein foods' for GM foods). It is important to look at this critically, balancing the benefits of living in a scientific society against our view of what is 'natural'.

Questions 3 to 9 concern the sorts of issues that are currently being discussed by those both supportive and fearful of the consequences of scientific work with genes.

1. The owners of a new drug that could save the lives of millions of people hold back the supply of the product for commercial reasons. Without the commercial involvement, the drug would never have been discovered in the first place. What are the ethical implications?

2. Would you consider 'temperament' to be an attribute of mind? If it is, then it may be reasonable to suppose that attributes of mind are genetic. After all, the modern cow has been bred with a temperament conducive to being milked which the original species of wild cows do not have.

3. What is your ethical response to the idea of cloning the following?
   a. An athlete who can run twice as fast as any other human being.
   b. A surgeon whose hand/eye skills are twice as advanced as any other human being.
   c. A person who has a brain capable of remembering all known facts.

4. Using genetic profiling on the remains of a body 1,000 years old, you have discovered that you are related to a rich and powerful family. Should your claim for part of their wealth and power be upheld?

5. Using genetic engineering, human cells can be incorporated into an animal's genome (e.g. for medical research). Is there a level of alteration at which this transgenic animal should be entitled to human rights?

6. Most (probably all) of the non-animal food we eat is a result of selective breeding of originally wild plants. These new species have had an effect on all other species by cross-pollination. Is there any difference between this and the production of GM plants? Describe any differences in detail.

7. Parents (both athletes) would like a child with great athletic potential. Expensive genetic manipulation is offered to them that will produce this. Do you think this right or wrong in any way?

8. Is it appropriate to use genetic information to investigate the activities of criminals but inappropriate to use genetic information to work out insurance premiums (e.g. the risks involved in life assurance for those with gene susceptibility to, say, Huntington's disease)?

9. Is it wrong to choose the sex or character of our children?

10. Because of the costs involved in the genetic engineering of human embryos, it is likely that certain sections of society will not be able to afford the costs. If this leads to a social and genetic underclass, does this make human genetic engineering wrong?

Further reading

Steve Jones, *The Language of Genes: Solving the Mysteries of Our Genetic Past, Present and Future* (London: Anchor, 1994).

22

Life, Death, Immortality and Reincarnation

Is there a difference between 'not being' after our life and 'not being' before our life?

Introduction

'What is it to be alive?' 'What is death and should I fear it?' 'Is there a life after death?' 'Could I return in another body after I die?' 'What is the meaning of life anyway?' All these are everyday questions with obvious philosophical importance. Reflecting on these things is what makes being human special. According to Socrates (470–399 BC), the good life is the examined life and the unexamined life is not worth living.

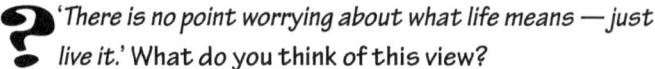
'There is no point worrying about what life means — just live it.' **What do you think of this view?**

Life

According to Henri Bergson (1859–1941), life is different from all other forms of matter — it is creative in a way that inanimate life is not. Human life implies vitality, the urge to accomplish or initiate. Life, as a thing in itself, is represented by a complex organic structure able to utilise energy, maintain itself and reproduce. Science has not located any vitalising ingredient that we could call 'life'. Some structures seem to be neither organic nor non-organic (e.g. viruses), and this fits in with evolutionary theory that advocates variously evolving species at different phases of their evolution.

Is there a vital spark of life?

Human life as opposed to other animal life

Aristotle (384–322 BC) believed (as did St Thomas Aquinas (1224/5–1274) and Immanuel Kant (1724–1804)) that we are distinct from animals because we have a mental life that is rational.

There are commonly held assumptions that distinguish human from other animal life. Animals may desire but they do not choose. Animals have consciousness but not self-consciousness. Animals do not make judgements about the long-term future based on the past. Animals recognise each other but do not relate as persons (e.g. with some moral sense of justice, liberty). Animals do not generally have the same rights as humans (nor do they have the same duties of responsibility). Animals lack imagination (e.g. they cannot speculate about possible outcomes). Animals have a limited repertoire of feelings. Animals do not have a sense of humour. Animals do not have speech (though they may vocalise).

> ❓ If a human being's brain were successfully transplanted into a dog, what sort of four-legged form of life would we be dealing with? If a dog's brain were successfully transplanted into a human, what sort of two-legged form of life would we be dealing with?

'My' self

The problem of personal identity, first proposed in a modern sense by John Locke (1632–1704), is a difficult and puzzling one. Locke thought that continuity of consciousness (i.e. knowing our own part in the present and projecting it into the future) guaranteed our personal identity.

> ❓ John is 80 years old and remembers when he was 40 years old. When he was 40 years old, he could remember himself as a child. Now that John is 80 years old he can no longer remember himself as a child. Is the 80-year-old John the same person as the child?

Bishop Joseph Butler (1692–1752) said that Locke's claim that our identity is guaranteed by a chain of memories was circular. He said that only true memory claims could guarantee identity but, because we needed a 'self', an 'identifier', in order to identify these claims, and this was what we were trying to prove in the first place, this so-called guarantee gets us nowhere.

Bernard Williams (1929–2003) says that continuity of existence rests on continuity of body. Sydney Shoemaker (1931–) says that the concept of bodily continuity is of itself no guarantee of continued identity.

> **?** (Using Shoemaker's thought experiment) John and Jane's brains are removed. John's brain is put into Jane's body and Jane's brain is put into John's. How do we now regard Jane (as the body) and John (as the body)?

Ludwig Josef Johann Wittgenstein (1889–1951) denied that there was truly anyone of whom we could ask the question, 'Who is that person?'. But still it remains that, even if Wittgenstein is right, there is importance in the question 'Who am I?'

> **?** Before John's brain was transplanted into Jane's body and Jane's brain was transplanted into John's body, they were told that after the operation John's body would suffer a lifetime of torture and Jane's body a lifetime of pleasure. Should John feel anxious?

Derek Parfit (1942–) says that personal identity cannot be guaranteed by continuity of consciousness and that all that 'I' should wish for is that some of me should continue.

> **?** Would I be more satisfied if my brain continued to live after the rest of me died than if my left arm continued to live after the rest of me died? What are the reasons for your answer?

Death

Death is the final and irreversible end of life, or, more exactly, it is the condition our body is in after our life has ended. However, this is not the same as saying that I am dead because my body is dead. If, for example, my life consists in my physical and mental existence, do both my body and my mind have to be dead before my life can be considered ended? Or, could I be considered dead if I were permanently unconscious (with no apparent mental activity) even though my body remained alive?

> **?** If I am pronounced dead, frozen for 1,000 years then brought back to life, would I have always been alive?

Fear of death

Thomas Nagel (1937–) says that anticipation that death leads to nothingness is an unavoidably disconcerting feeling. Nevertheless, this is not a universal feeling. Many have argued that the fear of death is irrational. In ancient times, Socrates took the view that if 'I' could not experience anything after death then 'I' have nothing to fear. Epicurus (c.341–270 BC) said that death and us could 'never meet'; because where I am, death is not, and where death is, I am not, our fear is, he thought, truly irrational. Wittgenstein believed that anticipation of death was part of being alive and that death itself could not be an experience (because all experience is confined to life). The Roman Stoics, believing in physical and mental self-control, faced their own death with undiluted calm.

However, generally speaking, we fear the loss of our life more than anything else. We might fear loss of wealth, for example, because of the fear of the consequences of poverty, but we fear loss of our life because in losing our life we lose all potential. Fear of death is often the irrational fear of what it is like to be dead when, logically, the fact of being dead implies that we can have no knowledge of what it is like.

> **?** We fear many things because they are unknown (e.g. ill health, poverty, loss of a loved one). We know with certainty that we will die. Is it therefore less rational to fear death than fear the loss of something we treasure when we are alive?

Fear of death is irrational. For example, we do not fear not having existed before we were born so we have no reason to fear not existing after our lives have ended. Against this, of course, the asymmetry of time means that although we can anticipate the loss of our own life in the future, we cannot regret in any meaningful way non-existence before we were born. At the same time, we can only experience being alive; we cannot experience not-existing (i.e. 'being' dead). Because 'I' can only experience 'being' alive, 'I' cannot claim any link to whoever or whatever it is that is dead after 'I' have finished being alive. 'Who' (if anyone) or 'what' (if anything) it is that is dead when 'I' die must remain unanswered (and unknown).

> **?** I experience things when I am alive. I do not experience things when I am dead. When my life ceases, have 'I' actually died?

It may be that if we did not fear death (as a fear of loss), we would not treasure life, and without the fear of losing existence, the benefits we experience during our existence would lose their attraction. Coming to terms with a rational understanding of the loss that death brings about, together with the knowledge that we cannot experience death, rids us of unnecessary anxiety and places our life firmly and properly in the 'land of the living'.

> **?** Jack says he is scared of dying. What could you say to him about this?

Death as a good

Death is not always seen as bad. Others may see the punishment by death of someone evil as good (though not necessarily good for an unrepentant subject of such a sentence). Death may be seen as a relief from the pain and the suffering of illness. Death may be viewed as an appropriate conclusion after a long, successful and well-lived life. Death can be seen as heroic in that it is caused because of some particularly courageous action (though it is questionable whether all heroes themselves actually feel heroic). Death can be personally heroic inasmuch as we may face our own deaths with courage and fortitude. More radically, there may simply be times when suicide (as Arthur Schopenhauer (1788–1860) thought) is preferable — death taking favoured precedence over life.

> **?** It seems tragic that a child aged 10 dies and not tragic that a person aged 90 dies. Is there any way that the loss of one life is qualitatively different from another?

The nature of immortality

When we talk of immortality, we are talking about the continued existence of the person, about the way that the personal identity of the individual continues beyond this one life. If there is a continued existence of something of the individual (e.g. a person's thoughts on something), this does not constitute immortality of the individual ('I' constitute more than just my thoughts). Neither can immortality be part of continued bodily existence. Some bodies are destroyed beyond the possibility of reassembly and some bodies could not sustain a continued existence anyway (e.g. the very young, the very old, the very sick). Indeed, this applies to all bodies that die because at death bodies have died of something which precluded their continued survival in the last moments of their life.

Plato (c.428–347 BC) took an idealistic view. He believed the soul was not material, that it occupied no place in space, and therefore could not be destroyed. Kant believed that there could be no purpose in the person acting morally unless the person was progressing towards a higher moral good (for which he or she would need an unending existence to attain). Some Christians would take a view that we are caused to act morally because of the prospect of either heaven or hell. Modern Christianity teaches that resurrection is the message of Christ rather than a concept of inherent immortality (this was the message of the New Testament and the Christian Fathers). Hindus believe our soul is reincarnated according to how we perform in each recurring life, Buddhists that we continue in some form of continuous experience. Many Eastern beliefs hold that ultimate liberation from the cycle of life takes a variety of forms (according to belief), ranging from a whole, unending consciousness to nothingness. In Western Christian theology, God is immortal either in that he is everlasting (exists at one and all times) or is eternal or timeless (exists somehow outside time). Following from this, Christianity considers souls immortal in the sense that they last until God (if he should choose) decides otherwise.

Survival after death
Disembodied existence

All living things die, I am a living thing, therefore I will die. This is true for bodies, but if 'I', as a living human thing with a personal identity, am somehow different from 'my' body, then this may mean that 'I' might not die. Plato and Aristotle both held this view; indeed Plato believed that our 'intellect' (our 'self') existed even before we were born.

> **?** In the future, it may be possible to swap bodies just as today we can swap bodily organs. If I swapped bodies with someone, would 'I' have died?

Reasons for believing that bodily death does not mean the death of 'me' are many and have strong philosophical, religious and psychological foundations. Some people believe it is perfectly reasonable that 'I' should survive the death of my body. There are many accounts of near-death experiences where people believe they have experienced something of death before returning fully to life. Some people believe that my own non-existence is inconceivable to me and that this level of inconceivability guarantees that it cannot be so. However, we have no problem conceiving of our non-existence before we were born (nor, indeed, does the likelihood of any pre-birth non-existence make us anxious), and it is a weak argument to use future inconceivability in a way that we do not use past inconceivability. Some people believe that even though personal death is usually so emotionally and intellectually difficult to come to terms with, this should not give us reason to believe in continued existence (which is amenable to think about) over annihilation (which is not so amenable).

> **?** John was a happy young man but a very miserable old man. He died ill and depressed. Which is the 'John' that might survive his bodily death? If John survives his bodily death, it may well mean eternal existence. Would this affect the view we might have about which John survives?

In the modern scientific world (where we are increasingly seen as a purely physical thing) we are encouraged to believe that death means personal non-existence — annihilation. Physicists say that all human traits (i.e. emotions, beliefs, fears) can be reduced to something physical, and when the body dies everything associated with it must necessarily die. Even if my personal identity operates as something seemingly separate while I am alive, this is no reason (according to the physicalist) to believe that it will continue to do so after I am dead. All living things die and we do not entitle bacteria, for example, with a continued post-death existence in the same way we imagine possible for ourselves.

> **?** Describe what it might be like to continue to exist after you die. Bear in mind you have no sensing apparatus and no brain to store memories (of any kind).

Reincarnation
Moving to a new body
In order to be reincarnated something that seems like 'me' needs to continue after my present body dies. In other words, although my body is mortal something that I call 'me' is not.

Reincarnation can be seen as the 'life force' or 'divine spark' reincarnated in a human body. While this life force or divine spark 'inhabits' a human body, the human person lives. When the human form dies, the life force or divine spark moves on (to another body). In this case, the spiritual entity, the life force, is not the 'I' because this only exists when the spiritual force and human form are combined. The life force or vital spark can exist separate from the human form. This is not, therefore, a personal reincarnation of the individual.

Alternatively (and more commonly), reincarnation is seen in a more personal way as 'me' moving from one mortal body to another. It is difficult to imagine how this can happen, though. Either 'I' can exist without a body for the time it takes to transfer to the other (in which case why do I inhabit bodies anyway?) or I need to go to another body the instant my old one dies. In either case, I also need to decide at what stage in the life with my new body do I begin to inhabit it? Is it when it is conceived? When it is born? When it is a few days old? And is it possible to apply any of these considerations if I am to live in a very basic form of life (e.g. a bacteria)?

In addition, personal reincarnation implies that there are a fixed number of selves who must continue to inhabit a fixed number of bodies (if not, there would be bodies without selves). This does not square with the idea that life has evolved from origins which were quantitatively less or that the number of humans, for example, continues to increase (although humans could be a higher tier of existence for previously lower and more prevalent life forms, all of which add up to the same total number).

That I cannot remember anything of any previous lives means either that I have not had any previous lives or that memory (in the form of a continuous memory) does not (for any reason) form part of my continuing immortal self. If memory is not part of my immortal self, it is hard to see how continued individual existence has any worth or meaning.

> **?** How can reincarnation into a lower life form (as some religions believe possible) be a punishment or retrograde step if I remember nothing of my previous life?

Supply of new bodies
If we survive in a new body then we also have to answer the problem of the endless supply of new bodies to which we can migrate; after all, immortality implies (indeed means) endlessness.

> **?** If you survived in your body, which of the phases of your body over a lifetime would you chose to survive in and why?

Endlessness
As well as an endless supply of new bodies (be they human, bacterial or whatever), the universe itself must also be endless. If the universe is finite, then we cannot claim immortality. The question of such an endless existence makes us wonder about the point of such an existence. Would it truly be to our benefit to exist endlessly (as it is generally thought in Buddhism)? This would mean that there must be a supply of better bodies available for everyone in the end. And this seems unlikely as it would mean the annihilation of all other life forms, on some of which, the better life forms (certainly humans) depend. The question of whether existing like this would lead to endless tedium is also a concern. It is hard to imagine how continued life could hold much meaning when, as it progressed, we would come to know all that it had to offer.

> **?** If immortality is endless, then what is the point of it?

Further questions

It is generally acknowledged that young people have little true sense of their own mortality (the necessary youth of the combatant soldier is not merely a physical requirement). They know they are going to die but only in some rather remote sense. They often do not seem to link this with the deeply felt sense of awareness we have in later life when we realise that we actually *are* going to die. However, religious belief and the plight of relatives and friends (and perhaps popular heroes) can affect how everyone reacts to this subject and this must be taken into account.

1. 'I' am a living organism, but is the 'I' to whom 'I' refer the same thing as the organism or something different?

2. After an accident, someone's bodily functions have all ceased but there is a mysterious trace of mental activity. You are asked to decide if this person is dead and to give reasons for your decision.

3. One day a dog speaks to you and tells you he is the soul of Louis XV reincarnate in a dog. What questions would you put to him in order to test his claims? Could you prove that his claim was not true?

4. A person who looks like Louis XV suddenly appears in the room and claims to be Louis XV reincarnate. Another, then another, closely follows him until there are 10 of them. They each back up their claim with detailed knowledge of their lives in eighteenth-century France and can produce documentary evidence in support. What do you think they are: ghosts, imposters, identical reincarnations, multiple images of the same person or what?

5. John's brain is preserved in a jar. All the information that his brain contained (i.e. memory, self-awareness, feelings of personal identity, awareness of the world) is stored on computer memory chips, one set for his first 10 years of life, one set for the second 10 years of his life and so on. One thousand years later his brain is taken from the jar and implanted back into his body (which has been kept working by machines) and the information on the memory chips progressively downloaded back into the brain. Are there any questions you can raise about John's personal identity? What are the implications if the information on one of the sets of memory chips is put out of sequence with the rest? What if one of the memory chips is mixed up with someone else's?

6. Mary has a heart attack and, although her heart stops, she is resuscitated successfully. Mary says that while she was being resuscitated she felt herself moving up towards the ceiling of the Accident and Emergency room, watching what was happening to her body and not feeling worried by her plight. She felt herself pass through the ceiling until she was high above the earth. She saw a bright white light and drifted towards it. She saw someone waiting for her, holding out his hands in welcome. She felt very calm and peaceful. When she felt herself being dragged back to her body she did not want to return. Mary says she believes she experienced being dead. The doctors confirm that her heart was not beating for one minute and that during this time her body was not fully functioning. If Mary died, she has come back to life. If she did not die then it was just a dream or a hallucination. What do you think?

7. Most things that we value have purpose. Purpose implies some end to a process. If immortality is endless, does this mean that it is both purposeless and valueless?

8. A woman tackles a murderer and although she is brutally killed, she saves the lives of her three children who, as she fights the attacker, have time to escape. Was her death a good death?

9. If God's purpose is beyond our understanding, how can it have meaning in our lives?

10. When I die, my brain is scanned and all the information it contains (i.e. memories, hopes, concerns, sense of self) is loaded onto a computer chip. The computer chip is installed in a massive computer, called 'Rreligionn', which creates a virtual world, called 'Hheavenn', which the contents of my computer chip now inhabit. I think my existence in Hheavenn is good. What is going on here? Am I alive? Am I dead? Am I deceiving myself? Am I being deceived?

Further reading

Thomas Nagel, *Mortal Questions* (Cambridge: Cambridge University Press, 1979), Chapter 1.

Thomas Nagel, *What Does It All Mean?* (Oxford: Oxford University Press, 2004).

Robert Nozick, *The Examined Life* (New York: Simon and Schuster, 1989).
Roger Scruton, *Modern Philosophy: An Introduction and Survey* (London: Pimlico, 2004), Chapter 21.

23

Evolution

According to Philip Henry Gosse (1810–1888), God created the world about six thousand years ago. What reasons might you have for believing that this is not true?

Introduction

If we believe that we have a history either remembered or recorded, and we believe that every event has a preceding cause, then we must conclude that the universe and its living inhabitants have antecedence — a previous history of causes. If we accept this then we are faced with two choices: either a supernatural being (God) created us, or we were generated from lesser beings whose origins are no longer evident. Such origins may be a life-energy that is coexistent with matter and energy, it may have arrived from another planet (e.g. on a meteorite) or it arose from inanimate chemicals in accordance with known physical laws. The first theory is called 'creation', the second 'evolution'.

> **?** If God created us, then why did he not give us certain knowledge of this? If God did not create us, then why do some people suspect that he did?

Origin of life

Aristotle (384–322 BC) believed that life arose from spontaneous generation, a theory still defended in the seventeenth century by Alexander Ross (*c*.1590–1654). Fransesco Redi (1626–1697) successfully debunked this theory when in 1668 he showed that maggots did not arise if flies were prevented from laying eggs. After that two theories arose: 'biogenesis' is the theory that living things originate only from pre-existing living things, 'abiogenesis' that life may also arise from inorganic matter. In 1862, Louis

Pasteur (1822–1895) showed conclusively that life only arises from life — *omne vivum ex vivo*, 'all life is from life'.

> **?** If inorganic matter cannot be motivated (because it is not sentient), what motivated it to become a living form?

Creation

There are two separate creation myths described in the Bible's Book of Genesis. In Genesis 1, humankind is created to oversee God's creation of six days. In Genesis 2, God first creates man, places him in a garden east of Eden, and forms woman from him. In the Western Christian world creationist views range from a literal belief in the six-day creation story described in Genesis 1, to a view that, while still maintaining God as the supernatural causal agent, holds the story in Genesis 1 to be a metaphor of geological periods. Some creationists, as convicted Christians, also hold orthodox evolutionary views but believe that God, as creator of everything, is responsible for the changes of natural selection. This opinion includes the idea that although there may be heredity common to all animal species the human race was separated by God's will, whose particular interest imbued human beings with a soul and special relationship with God.

> **?** What reasons could there be to explain why the creation story in Genesis 1 follows an evolutionary pattern? What reasons do you think God may have had for creating human beings anyway?

Though Christians form a large body of anti-evolutionists, holders of such views are by no means restricted to Christians. There are strong creationist bodies of thought, some of which aim to demonstrate that evolution theory is not in keeping with scientific fact, while others seek to harmonise the Bible and science.

> **?** If we accept the geological process as indicative of evolution, why do you think God left the creation of human beings until the very latest stages of creation?

Evolution

Humans have known for thousands of years how to alter animal species by selective breeding. The method, however, was hit or miss. Even so, all domesticated animals have been bred by this means. Since the pioneering work on genetics by Gregor Johann Mendel (1822–1884), the process has become increasingly certain, and modern methods combine selective breeding with artificial insemination to produce the most desirable breeds. The current methods of selective breeding involve genetically modifying plants and animals, and this has led to cloning whole plants and whole animals.

Evolution theory

It is an extension of our understanding of the breeding process to interpret how all species (there are presently around three million known species on earth) came into existence that we call 'evolution theory'. Although modern evolutionary theory is attributed to the work of Charles Darwin (1809–1882), there were others before him who had similar ideas. Alfred Russell Wallace's (1823–1913) work on natural selection was published in 1855, Darwin's *On the Origin of Species* in 1859. The theory relies on the principle of biogenesis, a hypothesis proved by Pasteur, which holds that living things can come only from other living things (which is similar, though opposite, to the principle of non-emergence which holds that no thing can arise from nothing). Since Aristotle proposed the idea of spontaneous generation of living things, it was not until Redi said that no living things arise if living things are excluded, that Aristotle's view was doubted (to deny Aristotle up until the Renaissance, and indeed after, was to deny the very processes of reason).

> **?** If the universe was created from nothing (as some Big Bang cosmologists believe), why is the principle of spontaneous generation so unreasonable? After all, if the universe were created ex nihilo then surely spontaneous generation would be its fundamental principle.

Continental drift

The principle of continental drift, first proposed by Alfred Lothar Wegener (1880–1930) in 1912, both supports and is supported by the theory of evolution. First, it shows that separated groups of animals can evolve in ways peculiar to their being in that location (e.g. the high proportion of marsupials in Australia) and second, that this sort of distribution is the case supports the claim that from a common heredity and physical landmass (Pangaea) all varying species evolved.

> **?** How much a theory can depend on other theories bears on how well the theory works out. How strong does a theory have to be (i.e. how many times does it need to be repeated or how difficult is it to falsify) in order to support another theory? Under what circumstances is it reasonable that a theory can be given extra support by another theory (bearing in mind that a theory is not a fact)?

Extinction
The Ancient Greek philosopher Anaximander (c.610–540 BC) proposed that the first life forms lived in water and that from these creatures arose human beings. Gideon Mantell (1790–1852) was probably the first to find proof that prehistoric reptiles existed (he named his find 'iguanodon'). Baron Georges Cuvier (1769–1832) was the first to demonstrate that extinctions had occurred ('catastrophism') and was the first to identify a flying reptile (a 'pterosaur'). In 1842, Richard Owen (1804–1892) coined the word 'dinosaur'.

The evolutionary trail has passed through at least five major catastrophic bottlenecks and it is estimated that in our present time 99.9% of all previously living life forms are now extinct.

> **?** If most living life forms are a small proportion of all life forms that have ever lived, is it reasonable to suppose that the best life forms have already died out?

Evolutionary change over time
In 1809 Jean-Baptiste de Monet, Chevalier de Lamarck (1744–1829) proposed a detailed theory of evolutionary change over time in animal species. This was based on change in relation to use or disuse (e.g. of a particular body part). Over a long period of time he foresaw an environmentally driven change in the species. For example, he believed that a giraffe might

stretch its neck to reach the leaves from high tree branches and this modification could be passed on to its progeny. Charles Lyell (1797–1875), a great populariser of geology, found inconsistencies in Lamarck's theory of constant change and was an opponent of Cuvier's theory of catastrophism. His uniformitarianism proposed that forces still in existence (earthquakes, volcanoes) could explain changes in the earth's history and that changing fossil records indicated changes in the rock strata laid down over time.

Lyell's ideas influenced Darwin and ultimately lent support to Darwin's theory. Wallace arrived at much the same conclusion about evolution as Darwin, indeed Darwin was prepared to concede first publication of the ideas but, although they read their papers at the same meeting, Darwin went on to publish *On the Origin of Species* and Wallace took a back seat. Wallace embraced spiritualism and supported the idea that natural selection was what drove evolution forward (Stephen Jay Gould (1941–2002) calls this 'hyperselection'), whereas Darwin included competition and choice as part of sexual selection (e.g. competing males chosen by females in animal species, males making choices in the human species). Wallace subordinated humans to merely a part of 'living things', whereas Darwin accepted a fundamental distinction between humans and other animals (e.g. humans have language whereas other species merely vocalise sounds).

Darwin described an evolutionary mechanism where species that adapted successfully eventually came to dominate those that did not. Darwin's theory suffered from two central difficulties. First, he could not explain how the variation (upon which natural selection acts) could be generated; second, he had no experimental evidence. In the late 1890s, August Weismann (1834–1914) claimed it was the cells of organisms that carried the information which formed the nature of the organism and not its body in its environment. Mendel's theory of how genes are inherited answered the first of Darwin's difficulties (first published in 1865 and 1866, rediscovered in 1900) and Darwin's own work on the selective breeding of pigeons answered (in his view) the second. In this (his only experimental work) he argued that nature could take the place of man in a similar selective process to the one he demonstrated.

The Hardy-Weinberg law (named after the independent work of Godfrey Harold Hardy (1877–1947) and Wilhelm Weinberg (1862–1937) in 1908, though also formulated earlier by William Ernest Castle

(1867–1962)), is an algebraic equation which describes that in large sexually reproducing populations with equal opportunity for survival and reproduction, and in the absence of selection, genes will, by chance (where mutation is at a minimum and mating is random), remain unchanged. However, in small populations, random mating is unlike that in large populations and change is caused not exclusively by natural selection but by 'genetic drift' (the Sewall Wright effect named after its originator Sewall Wright (1889–1988)). Small populations (either by geographical isolation, reproductive isolation, catastrophe or bottle-necking) also suffer from small gene pools. Since the early work, many have consolidated and expanded the view to create what has become an overarching evolutionary context for much of contemporary scientific thinking.

> Evolution theory itself has evolved. Is evolutionary thinking an aspect of human rationalising that may be imposing itself on the world more than merely interpreting what the world is like? Are there any other examples of this as a form of human thinking?

Darwin's theory of natural selection

Darwin's theory works like this. Observation 1: organisms have a tendency to multiply in geometric progression (first stated by Thomas Malthus (1766–1834) in his *Essays on the Principles of Population*). Observation 2: numbers of species tend to remain constant over long periods. Deduction 1: organisms are in continual competition for the chance to reproduce and so there is a constant struggle for existence. Observation 3: all living things vary. Deduction 2: varying individuals with favourable characteristics are more likely to succeed in the competition for survival than others, thus there is a process of natural selection.

> What attacks can be made on either the formulation or the content of Darwin's argument?

Objections

The pace of change — punctualism and gradualism

Progressive mutation that is preserved and transmitted by the mechanism of particulate inheritance eventually leading to new species is the governing framework of evolution theory. However, evolution seems not to have the regular slow-paced effect supposed by the theory. There have been long pauses of evolutionary inactivity as well as sudden outbursts of activity. The former could be explained by environmental factors, but the latter would seem to require much larger scale changes than the theory allows.

In the early 1940s, Ernst Mayr (1904–2005) suggested that in small localised populations evolution could occur rapidly, indeed too rapidly to leave a fossil record of the change. This view was strongly supported in the 1970s by Niles Eldredge (1925–) and Gould, and the debate continues, sometimes incorrectly typified as representing the polarised camps of evolutionists and anti-evolutionists. The notion of an episodic (as opposed to a gradual) change is called 'punctuated equilibrium' and is in contrast to the orthodox Darwinian theory of gradualism in evolving change. The argument is, however, about the mechanism of evolution, not whether or not evolution did or is taking place. The punctualist view is often taken by evolutionary-creationists, who believe that the sudden appearance of new species in the fossil record should be taken as evidence of the work of God.

> **?** Evolution theory relies heavily on the fossil record. If this shows periods when no evolution took place and does not reveal changes that happened too quickly to become embedded in the record, is the theory still intact?

Direction of change
Random changes that coincide with greater environmental success do not explain the apparent trend or direction of change that occurs. Part of Lamarck's theory was that organisms have an innate urge to increase in complexity. Darwin rejected this, believing instead that change is brought about by success. Such trends are made more puzzling by the apparent fact that related groups of organisms evolve in the same direction (e.g. the evolution towards hooves as opposed to fingers or toes in more than one sub-species) and this is not determined by natural selection. This process, called orthogenesis, does not follow conventional natural law and is therefore not available for empirical testing. Creationists, who, particularly

when the fossil record is largely incomplete, see change as the work of God, favour orthogenesis. Evolutionists point to a more complete fossil record which shows many adaptive branches that ultimately became extinct but are sufficient to provide heritage to successive adaption in others.

> **?** There are many ways that the world can be sensed (e.g. proximity, radar, heat, ultraviolet or infrared radiation). Why should so many different species independently evolve an eye which is sensitive to light waves?

Preceding states in the process
Slow progressive change requires a large number of preceding intermediate stages. Evolution theory requires that all of these superseded stages must have been inferior and yet each subscribes to a superior successor. The difficulty of trend, and how the organism can recognise such a trend, is difficult to understand. For example, how could a half-developed eye (which, say, only distinguished light from dark) be the precursor to an advanced human eye today? Although any increase in acuity would presumably be a survival advantage, what, we must ask, leads the modification in the construction itself (i.e. towards a fully functioning eye) where most intermediate phases would have no meaningful effect on success?

> **?** The evolution of, say, the human toe, requires millions of intermediate sub or pseudo-toes. Is it reasonable to suppose that each of these phases benefited the individual organism so much that it was more successful? If not, then why did the trend continue? If the evolutionary trend continues (which it must for evolution based on success to occur), then what might be the ultimate product of the human toe?

Enough time?
Because evolution theory requires slow progressive change, it is arguable as to whether there has been sufficient time for the existing complex organisms to come about. Although there are examples of very quick adaptive

change in animals (e.g. Warfarin, an anticoagulant pesticide against rats, was introduced in the UK in 1950 as a poison and by 1958 a resistant strain of rats had evolved in Scotland), because evolution is based on chance success of random mutation, the amount of time needed to produce, say, an effective human eye from first principles would seem too immense (even in geological time).

> **?** For every successful step in evolutionary change, there must be millions of unsuccessful steps that take the process in the wrong direction. Each unsuccessful step will evolve further unsuccessful steps until ultimately the newly evolved species will die out. What are the chances of success in such an environment? How big must populations be to accommodate this?

Embryological recapitulation

There is a great amount of external and internal similarity between all vertebrate species in their embryo stage. This led Karl Ernst von Baer (1792–1876) to propose a Law of Recapitulation, which implies that during its embryological stage an animal somehow ascends its own evolutionary tree. These days it is accepted that while there is undoubtedly some degree of recapitulation evident in animals, it is too simplistic to think that we go through all previously evolved phases (i.e. fish, amphibian, reptile and so on) before we are born.

> **?** If we inherit the genetic code of our ancestors, does this mean we also inherit a memory of them?

Purpose

The explanations we use to characterise the existence of organic things is quite different from how we characterise inorganic things. Although we may wonder whether the existence of the universe has a purpose, we do not usually attribute the idea of purpose to particular inorganic existents (e.g. we would not ask what purpose a planet has for going around a star). However, we commonly describe living creatures as if they have, or their characteristics derive from, a sense of purpose (e.g. the purpose of the arctic fox being white is to blend into its background). Indeed, we remain puzzled about something in the organic world until we resolve its purpose or previous purpose (e.g. the purpose of the human appendix). However, there is an evolutionary interpretation for most of these apparent purposes (e.g. the arctic fox is white because more of them have survived because they blend into their background). Even so, purpose remains a characteristic requiring knowledge of the future, and it is hard to see how, for example, the arctic fox discerns that its best purpose is to blend into its environment.

Purpose can be seen as that which we intend. For example, we turn left not right because where we want to go is left. This human trait is extended to animals on a reducing scale: that is, we see this sort of purpose in higher species but not perhaps in bacteria. Purpose can also be seen as being contained in an inorganic thing that we create in order to do something. For example, the purpose of the computer is to perform calculations, store and process information, and retrieve data, and that is why human beings created it. Things may have a divine purpose. For example, the human heart does not have a conscious purpose nor is it a thing created by humans to fulfil a certain human purpose. However, God may have created it in order to fulfil the purpose of pumping blood. Evolutionary theory says that the purpose of a thing is bound up in the fact (the outcome) that a certain thing survives. In other words, the thing does not have any purpose at all but simply appears to have one because it has survived where others have not. But this does not satisfactorily explain why anything lives in the first place, why anything that lives seems to have a need to diversify and why anything that lives seems to want to survive.

> ❓ Viruses are part of evolutionary process (indeed they evolve very rapidly according to their circumstances), although it is unclear if they are living things (in that they do not fulfil all the main functional activities of a living things, i.e. metabolism, growth, reproduction and responsive adaptation). What could be the purpose of a virus when it infects a host that it kills and the consequent death brings about its own destruction?

Creation versus evolution

Evolutionists tend to see creation theory as intellectually regressive. Creationists tend to see evolutionary theory as resting on almost inconceivable odds. The creationist would say that the odds of life arising from inorganic material are so small as to be inconceivable. Charles-Eugène Guye (1866–1942) calculated the mathematical odds against the random formation of a single protein molecule at 2.02×10^{321}. Using Guye's figures Pierre Lecomte du Nouy (1883–1947) concluded that it would take 10,243 billion years to produce one protein molecule by chance from something the size of the earth. Although such odds seem (unimaginably) small, an evolutionist would point out that the possibility of God creating it out of his mind would also seem inconceivably small (if not smaller because, presumably, the creative act was an original thought on the part of God with no preceding model from which to work, inorganic or otherwise). Evolutionary theory, no matter how improbable, can be scientifically tested (if not proved), whereas creation theory cannot. Indeed, if creation theory is true, then the fossil record is either a falsehood or completely unnecessary (if God wanted to create life why did he want to create the appearance of previously evolved life?). The evolutionist, though, finds it difficult to account for certain human traits, for example, a sense of beauty or moral purpose, neither of which seem to have any evolutionary meaning, and, indeed, belief in God would seem to have no evolutionary purpose at all. On the other hand, evolution theory does not need God and can reject creation theory because it is not scientifically testable. Whereas a scientist can plot the fossil record and test its age by various means, the creationist has nothing comparably factual to offer. What the creationist might refer to as the unfolding 'drama of life' the scientist would call the 'struggle for survival'. There is a commonality in both these ways of thinking. Indeed, it is possible to hold both views, as evolution theory and creationism do not mutually exclude each other.

> **?** Which appeals more to common sense: evolution theory or creation theory? Is one more comforting than another?

Evolutionary success versus social conscience

Evolution theory tells us that organisms which best suit the environment (and its risk and reproductive factors) are those destined for success. We commonly understand human beings to be at the top of the evolutionary tree. One of the features of human beings is their ability to think rationally and to be aware of the condition of others. From this has developed a moral view that encourages us to have regard for those less fortunate than ourselves. Because of other influences (including medicine which holds a fundamental belief in the saving of human life) this has led contemporary Western society to hold the sanctity of life itself above any judgement about the value of that particular life. This means that an important trait of contemporary civilised life is to nurture individuals who do not share the same inherited successful gene pool as others, and this necessarily weakens the race and should (on evolutionary theory) ultimately lead to its downfall.

> ❓ Should the human race allow evolutionary processes to decide on the fate of members of its species, or should it intervene even though this means that an increased number of weakened gene permutations will follow?

The effects of evolution on religion

After the publication of Darwin's work in 1859, there was much ridicule of evolutionary theory from religious thinkers (e.g. mocking the characterisation of humans as bestial apes). During the twentieth and into the twenty-first century, with science always on the ascendant, the acceptance of evolutionary theory has spread beyond its use as a tool for interpreting the heredity of living things into a general method of interpreting anything which alters organically in the broadest sense (e.g. a society might be said to evolve in the same way that a new motor car design may be seen as a further evolution). Such deeply ingrained evolutionary thinking, although accommodated by some Western Christianity (which has bent to accommodate evolution), has become polarised by others in defence of creationist thinking. This has led to a deep rift between science and non-science.

? How can the idea of a personal spiritual afterlife be reconciled with an evolution from lower forms (indeed the lowest forms) of life?

Further questions

The initial question (Gosse's proposal that the earth was created by God about six thousand years ago) is difficult (if not impossible) to answer, and can be returned to without fear of not finding a solution. If it is proposed that God has laid a trail of evolutionary, geological and archaeological artefacts simply to comfort us with a sense of history and belonging, it is hard to argue that this is impossible. It is a good proposition against which to test your analytical skills.

Although evolutionary theory is (to some extent or another) broadly accepted, and as a general principle has found application as an interpretive theory in many other scientific fields, it has also brought about a heightened adherence to a theological view of divine creation as a meaningful alternative. This has led to some intolerance where loyalty to belief can take precedence over sense. Because evolutionary thinking and creationist thinking remain theories, all the questions here offer a chance for criticism.

1. In his *Omphalos*, Gosse claimed that the earth, although appearing old, was actually young, and that the apparently ancient geology of the earth, together with its fossil record, were put there by God in order to provide us with a sense of history. Can you say that this is untrue?

2. Is it possible to explain the notion that the evolutionary purpose of all living creatures was originally contained in the simplest forms from which life evolved? If it was not, then from where could this purpose derive?

3. If God created the earth and all its creatures (including humans) in six days, then why did he complicate the situation by laying a (false) geological and evolutionary trail?

4. If a theory calls for evidential support, is it reasonable to accept such partial, non-resembling evidence as the fossil record? After all, such a record tells us little or nothing of an organism's soft tissue or behaviour.

5. That the evolutionary trend follows successful adaptation to the demands of the environment is a justification for evolutionary process. What reasons do we have for believing that animal and plant species want to succeed when faced with an adverse environment?

6. Logically, on evolution theory, in the absence of environmental change and with sufficient time, a species must evolve to perfection. Is there any evidence that this is or has been the case? What would be a fully evolved, perfect state for human beings?

7. How do we judge that evolutionary change is a change for the better as opposed to a change for the worse?

8. Our assessment of the past suggests that large species populations that are no longer evolving soon die out. Human beings are a large species that (apparently) is no longer evolving. Should we take steps to reduce the population in the hope of saving the species?

9. Other than human beings, the New Caledonia crow is the best tool-maker in the living world (not a monkey or an ape). Should this mean that it would be reasonable to consider the New Caledonia crow as our nearest evolutionary relative and treat it accordingly?

10. Is it possible that human civilisation will halt evolution?

11. That something survives does not mean it has a purpose. Unless something has a purpose, there is no reason why it should survive. Are these two propositions reconcilable?

12. For humans, the act of creation is usually something to be proud of (e.g. we invariably claim our own creations if they are merit worthy). Why does God not make an obvious claim on his creation? Does this mean he is not proud of it?

Further reading

Charles Darwin, *On the Origin of Species by Means of Natural Selection or The Preservation of Favoured Races in the Struggle for Life* (Mineola, NY: Dover, 2006).

Genesis 1–2.

Stephen Jay Gould, *Wonderful Life: The Burgess Shale and the Nature of History* (London: Vintage, 2000).

Julian Huxley, *Evolution: The Modern Synthesis: The Definitive Edition* (Cambridge, MA: MIT Press, 2010).

Steve Jones, *Almost Like a Whale: The Origin of the Species Updated* (London: Doubleday, 1999).

24

Cosmology

Where did the universe come from (if indeed it has to come from somewhere)?

Introduction

Cosmology is a branch of speculative metaphysics concerned with theories about the large-scale space-time nature of the universe. It brings together thinkers from many disciplines including philosophers, physicists, mathematicians, astronomers and theologians.

There is some contemporary philosophical and scientific agreement on the conclusion that the universe probably began to exist (perhaps even in the 'Big Bang' about 15 billion years ago), but less agreement as to whether or not the creation of the universe was caused. This modern understanding of cosmology is only the most recent of a long heritage of beliefs about how the universe came to be and what it may constitute. If it was caused, we have to deal with the problem of what caused it and therefore the puzzling idea that the universe had some content before it began. If it was not caused, we are faced with a universe that arose from nothing for no reason and this is not in keeping with universal nature in general. An infinite number of Big Bangs get around the difficulties of cause, but an infinity of un-caused causes (even if they are Big Bangs) presents many (perhaps too many) psychological difficulties.

Cosmological theories

There are three identifiable phases of cosmological theory preceding the modern view.

First theory phase

Although the Babylonians and Egyptians knew of the rhythmical movements of the heavenly bodies, it was the Pythagoreans (sixth century BC) who put forward the idea of a spherical earth contained within a system of natural laws. The ancient Greek atomists Leucippus (fifth century BC) and Democritus (c.460–c.370 BC) proposed countless worlds, all with living things, that had come about by the chance formation of atoms. Aristotle (384–322 BC) placed the spherical earth central to a universe made up of translucent spheres to which were attached the sun, planets and stars. Ptolemy (c.90–c.168) modified this with a still geocentric system about which the planets and the sun revolved in circles (and within them some in epicycles). St Thomas Aquinas (1224/5–1274) adapted the Aristotelian model that was then adopted by Christianity.

Second theory phase
Aristotle's ideas were central to the European renaissance of classical thought. Nicolaus Copernicus (1473–1543), using early astronomy, developed Aristotle's ideas and in a revolutionary 'heliocentric' system placed the sun at the centre of the universe. From this, Isaac Newton (1642–1727) postulated an integrated mechanistic universe in which space and time were separate and in keeping with Euclidean geometry (Euclid flourished c.300 BC). Newtonian mechanics remained the dominant theory of universal order until the early 1900s. During this time, Thomas Wright (1711–1786) theorised that the universe was filled with galaxies.

Third theory phase
At the beginning of the twentieth century, our view of a universe governed by Newtonian mechanics changed with Albert Einstein's (1879–1955) theories of special and general relativity. Astronomy advanced rapidly with both larger optical then radio telescopes. Vesto Melvin Slipher (1875–1969) discovered that objects travelling away from the observer at high speed appear at the redder, longer wavelength end of the spectrum. The discovery of more galaxies led Edwin Powell Hubble (1889–1953) to calculate their distance away from us. Using these measurements within the mathematical theories of general relativity, Willem de Sitter (1872–1934), Aleksandr Aleksandrovich Friedmann (1888–1925) and George Lemaitre (1894–1966) came to the contemporary view that the universe is expanding. Based upon the field equations of Einsteinian general relativity,

it is possible to extrapolate a variety of different space-time (non-observer dependent) universes. Such ideas only work on the huge scale of galaxies and the greater universe and any conflict between Newtonian (Euclidean) space and time and Einsteinian (non-Euclidean) space-time only has true meaning on this macro-scale.

Modern cosmology
Modern cosmology envisages a universe of stationary galaxies set in an expanding space that is curved (the way in which it is curved prescribes whether it is finite or infinite). Relative to all other galaxies, all galaxies are moving away from each other equally and at the same speed that is not constrained by the velocity of light. This expansion indicates an explosive beginning (a 'big bang') from a dense state 10–15 billion years ago. This theory is further supported by the discovery by Arno Allan Penzias (1933–) and Robert Woodrow Wilson (1936–) in 1965 of a cosmic background radiation at a temperature of 2.725 K with a peak microwave frequency of 160.2 GHz that is deemed left over from the Big Bang itself. There is presently no solution to the question whether the universe if finite or infinite or whether the universe will continue to expand or eventually fall back in on itself, or indeed, that it will remain in some middle non-expanding-non-contracting mode.

> **?** If there are an infinite number of universes, then there are an infinite number of each of us leading identical lives. If this is the case, could I reasonably claim to be me or would I be someone else?

Any of these theories lead naturally to the question of creation and design.

A creator
Those who oppose the idea of a creator favour the idea that the universe is in a steady state (neither expanding nor contracting). However, on this view it is not possible to explain the background microwave radiation. Added to this, Stephen Hawking (1942–) and Roger Penrose (1931–) predict mathematically that we should expect a Big Bang (a singularity) to exist in any relativistic model of the universe and such a singularity implies creation. On the other hand, and pushing out a creator, Hawking

and James Burkett Hartle (1939–) have proposed a quantum mechanical model of an expanding universe which does not require a singularity.

> **?** Is there anything sufficiently convincing about mathematics which might eliminate the probability of a creator?

A design
Intelligent design
The argument for intelligent design (the teleological argument) says that things are so perfectly put together (the universe seems so precisely designed) that there must be a designer. In ancient times, the Roman philosopher Marcus Tullius Cicero (106–43 BC) strongly supported this view, comparing the workings of the heavens with human artefacts such as sundials and water clocks. In the seventeenth century, there was a revival of atomism (the view of the world constituted by an infinite number of indivisible corpuscles proposed by the ancient Greeks Leucippus and Democritus) as 'corpuscular philosophy'. Newton proposed a deity highly skilled in mathematics and the scientific arts. Corpuscular philosophy together with Newton's ideas, combined with the invention of the microscope and scientists' general wonderment with the minutiae of creation (e.g. Robert Boyle (1627–1691) was amazed by the exquisite, precision design of the house-mite) to produce a committed belief that a designer's hand was at work. A contemporary view might suggest (against this) that with so many universes to choose from it is not surprising that ours just happens to be the way it is (i.e. apparently but not necessarily designed).

> **?** Who, or what, could the cosmic designer be? What could be the motivation for such a designer to design?

Evolutionary change is itself a design
Charles Darwin (1809–1882) believed that evolution was a process of designed laws but with the rest left to chance. This view can be applied to cosmology. Although evolution is random, there are so many constraints on the nature of things (e.g. olfactory processes, sensing mechanisms, social structures, genetic continuity) that even if evolution was re-run we would end up (it is claimed) with more or less the same make up of

species we have now. On this argument, randomness, although based on some specific random events, deals with those initial random events in fairly standard (and non-random) ways. Features of living things in this way are termed 'emergent' (i.e. emerging from previous given situations) and 'convergent' (inasmuch as many features of living things are similar or parallel).

> **?** If evolution were re-run and brought about more or less the same result, would that still be evolution?

Creation ex nihilo

It is uncertain whether the universe is finite or infinite (i.e. if it came from nothing or has always been there). If the universe emerged from nothing (i.e. was created *ex nihilo*), then we would expect to find evidence of 'emergence from nothing' in much of the universe (i.e. it would be normal and part of the universal structure for things simply to appear from nowhere), but we do not. In addition, the idea of something that contains the potential for everything which is the universe is both counter-intuitive and difficult to comprehend (though neither would make it untrue). On the other hand, it is also difficult to believe that the universe has always been (and will always be). Nothing in our experience exists eternally — everything ends — and it is hard to believe that the universe itself (and not its contents) somehow exists under a different set of rules to the things that it contains.

> **?** If the universe ended, what would happen next?

Further questions

Physicists, astronomers and mathematicians think that the ultimate cause and meaning of the universe is to be detected in its fundamental ingredients and patterns, and this has become dominant in cosmological thinking. Because we live in a scientific age, it is difficult to resist scientific pronouncements on this subject. Because cosmology is an area of the most speculative metaphysics, an open-minded philosophical scepticism should be developed to challenge any religious and scientific views.

1. As far as we know, there is no obvious evidence in the universe of anything having come from nothing. The Big Bang is the creation of the universe and its contents. If it was the creation of the universe (i.e. space, time and all substantial content), then where did the Big Bang itself come from?

2. If there is a creator, then the creator exists. If the creator created the universe, then the creator existed before the universe. If the creator existed before the universe, then where did the creator come from? By invoking a creator, have we simply answered the question of creation (of the universe) with the same puzzle (this time of the creation of the creator)?

3. Is it possible for time to begin? If you think it is, then how (or where) was the event of change from 'no time' to 'time' accommodated? (It could not be accommodated in 'time' as there was not any 'time' at this 'time'.)

4. If space-time is positively curved (Einstein's preference), then time is finite. If space-time is negatively curved, then time is infinite. Is there any way in which either of these could be true? Explain how (there is no need to know about positively or negatively curved space in order to analyse the likelihood of finite or infinite existence).

5. If everything is random, we might accept that an aeroplane (e.g. a Boeing 777) could be created by a tornado passing through a (very large and diverse) scrap yard. At the same time, even though many microbiological features have designs that are unexplainable by purely evolutionary theory, such a proposition seems preposterous. However, to say the 777 argument is preposterous is merely a way of saying it is beyond our understanding (in just the same way we might say that some features of living things are amazing). What are your thoughts on this?

6. It may be the case that the Universal Law of Gravitation has held for 15 billion years. However, should it change from this moment on (so that gravity did not operate as it does), and continued in that way for the next 15,000 million billion years, then from that future point the current situation would seem only a distant (and trivial) anomaly. Does this seem reasonable and does it affect the way we should look at other (so far) highly repeatable events?

7. Why would a creator want to create?

8. Why would a designer want to design?

9. Why would a universe, which was neither designed nor created, come into being?

10. If there were a God with enough power to create, would he not create something that was perfect in every way? Do you think we live in a perfect world?

11. An accident occurs when an event arises without apparent cause — it is something unexpected and unforeseen although after it has occurred its causes may be identified and an explanation provided. No accident can occur unless there is a pre-existing set of circumstances made up of things and events. For example, if two cars collide there is an accident, but without the two cars, the road, the drivers and so on, coming together at a particular moment in time the accident could not have occurred. Is it intelligible that the universe could have arisen by accident out of nothing? If you think it is, explain what elements of nothing might constitute the preceding causal chain. If you think not, explain what you think could have caused it.

Further reading

William Lane Craig and Quentin Smith, *Theism, Atheism and Big Bang Cosmology* (Oxford: Clarendon Press, 1995).

John Leslie, *Universes* (London: Routledge, 1989).

M. K. Munitz, *Theories of the Universe from Babylonian Myth to Modern Science* (New York: Free Press, 1957).

25

The Meaning of Life

'He had a long and meaningful life.' Assuming that he lived to an old age, what could the rest of this statement mean?

Introduction
The meaning of our life is generally a measure of its value. All things measured are measured in respect of something else (even if that something else is the measure used). Most ideas of life's meaning measure our life against such things as its inherent value, its value in respect of others, its value in respect of the greater good or perhaps in respect of God. The meaning of life might also be measured by success. It is held by some that the true meaning of life is not known until we are dead. Others think that life is absurd and has no meaning beyond the experience of living it.

Impermanence of achievement
In 150 years' time we will all be dead. This fact seems enough in itself to make us think that nothing we achieve in our lives that satisfies us is worthwhile because none of these achievements will be permanent. If there is any meaning to our personal experience of life, we must find it in the context of our transitory life itself. Many of our functions have meaning (e.g. eating when we are hungry, resting when we are tired), but, on the face of it, our whole life, as a thing in itself, does not. Our life may have meaning beyond our own life (e.g. we may do something that benefits others), but any sense of personal satisfaction we gained from this would not extend beyond our impermanent existence.

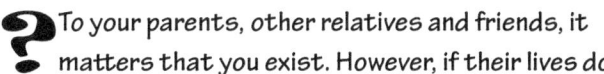
To your parents, other relatives and friends, it matters that you exist. However, if their lives do

not mean anything (other than to you and their other relatives and friends) then outside of your (and the others) significance to them (and vice versa) there is still no meaning to your life. Is this a reasonable view?

Ultimate destiny

Even if we extend the meaning of our lives beyond our own life (and its relationship to parents, other relatives and friends) and take part in large scale enterprises (e.g. economic, political or religious movements), we must still face the seeming fact that, if we look at the context of the whole (i.e. the earth will ultimately cool down and be destroyed), even that must be meaningless.

> *In what ways might taking an active part in a political movement fulfil us? Could this give our lives true meaning?*

God's purpose

Plato (c.428–347 BC) believed that the meaning of our life was a recurring system of re-birth ultimately leading to perfection. Friedrich Wilhelm Nietzsche (1844–1900), on the other hand, did not accept any objective reality in our lives (nor, indeed, the reality of God). If an individual believes that his life has meaning because he is fulfilling the purpose of God, we are still entitled to ask what the point of God's purpose is. Answering that it is 'God's purpose' does not bring the questioning process to an end (i.e. God's purpose is not immune from such a question or further questioning). If God really can give purpose to our lives, then it seems reasonable to suppose that God must have his own purpose beyond giving purpose to our lives.

> *If God provides ultimate justification for our existence and we cannot understand God's purpose, can such a justification provide us with a personal sense of purpose?*

Taking life's meaning too seriously

It may be, as Nietzsche thought, that our lives have no meaning beyond ourselves (i.e. our relationship with ourselves and others) and we are mistaken in looking for one. Henry Sidgwick (1838–1900) believed that the only things of value were conscious states (after all, conscious states formulate values). In looking for a sense of purpose in our lives we may be regarding ourselves as too self-important — we are taking life (and our possible purpose beyond what we can see) too seriously. Thomas Nagel (1937–) believes that if we cannot accept that we take life too seriously we have to put up with our lives being ridiculous, meaningless and absurd.

> *'You take life too seriously,' said Charles' grandfather. 'You'll worry yourself to death if you're not too careful. Here, leave your homework, take this and buy an ice cream. Enjoy yourself!' What do you think of Charles' grandfather's advice? Is it taking a sufficiently serious view of life?*

Love of life

Aristotle (384–322 BC) said that life is never about ends but always about means, and that the process of 'recontouring' the ultimate meaning of our life (as an end) is pointless (what modern philosophers call 'cospecification'). A person, according to Robert Nozick (1938–2002), may feel that his or her own philosophy of life (e.g. Buddhism, existentialism, Marxism) may be more than any theory of meaning could ever encompass: that is, that our own view of our own particular life and its spontaneous living is the most important thing. Nozick recommends focusing upon the major benefits of life (i.e. being alive, being human, being reasonably competent). He believes that even if ultimately we enter some spiritual realm (which may contain many things beyond what we presently know) we would, because of our need to explore and investigate, still end up in the (pointless) spiralling search for meaning.

The best place to live out our philosophy of life is the here and now. Love of life and love of the world is our fullest response to being alive (itself the most important benefit of life). Acceptance of our place in nature, and the debt we owe to the nature that sustains us, is the fullest recognition of meaning. Recognising that we are small parts in a vast whole and identifying with being part of it, together with an acceptance of the unavoidability of our spiralling search for our own reality can be satisfaction enough for our living.

> **?** 'Life is what you make it.' What does this mean? Can it possibly be true?

Further questions

1. What is the meaning of your life: to yourself, to others, to your pet, to the rest of the universe?

2. Will me thinking that my life has meaning cause it to have meaning?

3. Mary won £10,000,000 on the lottery. Will this help her life have meaning?

4. 'I believe in God.' If this is a truly held belief and there is a God, does this belief give my life meaning? If this is a truly held belief and there is no God, does this belief give my life meaning?

5. Has your life become more meaningful now that you have finished this book?

6. Do you feel any wiser now that you have finished this book?

7. Do you think philosophy is worthwhile? If so, why? If not, why not? If you answered this question in Chapter 1, has your response changed?

Further reading

Thomas Nagel, *What Does It All Mean?* (Oxford: Oxford University Press, 2004).

Robert Nozick, *The Examined Life* (New York: Simon and Schuster, 1989).

Annotated Bibliography, Extended Reading and Internet Resources

Annotated bibliography

George Berkeley, *Principles of Human Knowledge and Three Dialogues*, Oxford World Classics (Oxford: Oxford University Press, 2009). Berkeley was one of philosophy's most daring thinkers. This is his argument against Locke on the nature of perception that seeks to prove that the world 'outside' our senses is also made up of 'ideas'. The unfavourable response to this argument caused him to write the *Three Dialogues between Hylas and Philonous*. Get used to the eighteenth century style and this will bring great rewards.

Paul M. Churchland, *Matter and Consciousness* (Cambridge, MA: MIT Press, 1988). Well organised, this covers most of the fundamental areas of the philosophy of mind. Includes an interesting chapter on artificial intelligence.

A. J. Coates, *The Ethics of War* (Manchester: Manchester University Press, 1997). Authoritative and accessible, Coates' work analyses all the important areas of this subject and provides good advice on further reading.

William Lane Craig and Quentin Smith, *Theism, Atheism and Big Bang Cosmology* (Oxford: Clarendon Press, 1995). An out-of-the-ordinary piece of philosophy where the two authors alternately take a different view: Craig that the Big Bang was created by God; Smith that it was uncaused.

Charles Darwin, *On the Origin of Species by Means of Natural Selection or The Preservation of Favoured Races in the Struggle for Life* (Mineola, NY: Dover, 2006). The published origin of modern evolution theory is elegantly written and classic.

René Descartes, *Meditations on First Philosophy, with Selections from the Objections and Replies*, trans. Michael Moriarty, Oxford World Classics (Oxford: Oxford University Press, 2008). A particularly accessible work written in non-technical, common-sense language.

R. A. Duff, *Trials and Punishment* (Cambridge: Cambridge University Press, 1986). Arguing for the Kantian view that we should treat people as ends not means, Duff criticises theories of both retributivism and deterrence. Excellent and diverse bibliography.

Richard Feldman, 'Evidence', in Jonathan Dancy and Ernest Sosa (eds), *A Companion to Epistemology* (Oxford: Basil Blackwell, 1993), pp. 119–22. An interesting short article on the evidence of our senses.

David Fisher, *Morality and War: Can War be Just in the Twenty-First Century?* (Oxford: Oxford University Press, 2011). Written with much insight, this is a particularly clear and up-to-date account of the morality of war. Extensive and broad-ranging bibliography.

Raymond Flood and Michael Lockwood (eds), *The Nature of Time* (Oxford: Basil Blackwell, 1988). A collection of authoritative articles on time, this is a sound introduction to important aspects of this puzzling subject.

Genesis 1–2. The creation myths of Genesis 1 and 2 provide the essential background to the Western counter view of evolution theory.

Stephen Jay Gould, *Wonderful Life: The Burgess Shale and the Nature of History* (London: Vintage, 2000). A marvellous illustration of the careful work of the palaeobiologist, as well as an interesting argument for outcomes as contingent (in the same way the lives of others are affected by the existence of George Bailey in the film from which Gould draws his title, *It's a Wonderful Life*).

Ronald Grimsley, *The Philosophy of Rousseau* (London: Oxford University Press, 1973). A sound introduction to Rousseau's philosophy.

Susan Haack, 'Pragmatism', in Jonathan Dancy and Ernest Sosa (eds), *A Companion to Epistemology* (Oxford: Basil Blackwell, 1993), pp. 351–7. A succinct review of the pragmatism of Peirce, James and Dewey.

Edith Hamilton and Huntington Cairns (eds), *The Collected Dialogues of Plato including the Letters* (Princeton: Princeton University Press, 1961). The *Republic* demonstrates Socrates' outstanding skill in argument and develops not only the plan for the perfect state and how it should be run but also the best possible standards for human life. Although a complete book in itself it is best accessed in parts. Plato's views on knowledge can be found in Chapter 7 (which includes the 'Allegory of the cave') as well as in *Meno* and *Theaetetus*.

Paul Helm (ed.), *Faith and Reason* (Oxford: Oxford University Press, 1999). An excellent and broad-ranging collection of abstracts covering aspects of God and faith.

Ted Honderich, *Punishment: The Supposed Justifications* (Cambridge: Cambridge University Press, 1989). Thorough philosophy covering all the important areas of the subject, this book brings out the writer's views in a deliberate and straightforward manner.

Ted Honderich (ed.), *The Oxford Companion to Philosophy* (Oxford: Oxford University Press, 2005). An excellent compilation of information with authoritative and easily accessible articles. If in doubt about anything philosophical, reach for this.

John Hospers, *An Introduction to Philosophical Analysis* (London: Routledge, 1997). The latest edition of Hospers' easily read and classic introduction to philosophical analysis.

David Hume, *A Treatise of Human Nature*, 2nd edition, (ed.) P.H. Nidditch (Oxford: Oxford University Press, 1978). This standard edition of Hume's great work covers a wide range of topics. Although Hume's language is old-fashioned, his concepts are penetrating and crisply expressed. Recommended to be taken a part at a time.

Julian Huxley, *Evolution: The Modern Synthesis: The Definitive Edition* (Cambridge, MA: MIT Press, 2010). An easy-to-read popular exposition of evolution theory and some of its more confusing details. First published in 1942 with new editions in 1963 and 1974, this book remains highly relevant today.

Steve Jones, *The Language of Genes: Solving the Mysteries of Our Genetic Past, Present and Future* (London: Anchor, 1994). High-quality popular science that discusses all areas of interest in this subject.

Steve Jones, *Almost Like a Whale: The Origin of the Species Updated* (London: Doubleday, 1999). Jones rewrites Darwin's argument with the benefit of science not available to

Darwin. Easily read and scholarly.

Hugh LaFollette (ed.), *Ethics in Practice: An Anthology* (Oxford: Blackwell, 2002). An indispensible collection of articles by major philosophical thinkers on contemporary ethical issues.

John Leslie, *Universes* (London: Routledge, 1989). A carefully worked philosophical argument in support of the anthropic principle that as conscious beings we live in a finely tuned world.

John Stuart Mill, *On Liberty and Other Essays*, (ed.) John Gray, Oxford World Classics (Oxford: Oxford University Press, 1991). Much of our modern Western thinking on what it is to be human and a member of society owes something to Mill. Any reading will be rewarded.

M. K. Munitz, *Theories of the Universe from Babylonian Myth to Modern Science* (New York: Free Press, 1957). A collection of cosmological thinking over history, this book provides a first-class background to the subject.

Thomas Nagel, *Mortal Questions* (Cambridge: Cambridge University Press, 1979). Nagel's famous book deals with important questions concerning personal meaning, nature and value in both practical and abstract forms. His human approach to philosophy is easy to identify with and his clear and concise authority is a striking example of doing philosophy from one of the world's most enlightened living philosophers.

Thomas Nagel, *The View from Nowhere* (Oxford: Oxford University Press, 1986). A clear, thought-provoking and highly insightful analysis of what it is to exist as a human being. Essential reading on the human condition.

Thomas Nagel, *What Does It All Mean?* (Oxford: Oxford University Press, 2004). A brief and elegantly written introduction to all the major topics of philosophy.

Robert Nozick, *Anarchy, State, and Utopia* (Oxford: Blackwell, 1974). A seminal philosophical work that first appeared as an argument against Rawls, it describes Nozick's conservative views of the state and is a central (and crucial) piece of twentieth-century philosophy. Nozick analyses the place of the individual in the state and in so doing covers most of the aspects of human concern in the larger social environment. This dense book is highly readable. Its contents form the pattern of a whole argument that can be separately accessed via its full table of contents.

Robert Nozick, *The Examined Life* (New York: Simon and Schuster, 1989). Written in a personal and accessible style, this challenging book discusses (and makes clearer) many of the doubts and concerns we have as individuals in a confusing world.

Anthony O'Hear, *An Introduction to the Philosophy of Science* (Oxford: Clarendon Press, 1989). A balanced analysis of the main topics of the subject. His *Beyond Evolution* (Oxford: Oxford University Press, 1997) may also be of interest but it is not easy to read and, because it is a complete argument, should be treated with care if looked at only partially.

Hilary Putnam, *Reason, Truth and History* (Cambridge: Cambridge University Press, 1981). One of today's outstanding philosophers expounds many of his influential views in this dense but readable book.

John Rawls, *A Theory of Justice* (Oxford: Oxford University Press, 1971, revised 1999). Probably the most important contribution to political philosophy in the twentieth century, Rawls describes two principles of justice by which a state can regulate liberties, social and economic goods. It is a difficult book but has a detailed contents list that makes it more accessible.

Tom Regan and Peter Singer (eds), *Animal Rights and Human Obligation* (Englewood

Cliffs, NJ: Prentice-Hall, 1989). An updated collection of the original (1976) version edited by the two foremost philosophical authorities on the subject.

Tom Regan, *The Case for Animal Rights: Updated with a New Preface* (Berkeley, CA: University of California Press, 2004). Regan's original (1974) case for animal rights updated.

Gerald Rochelle, *Behind Time* (Aldershot: Ashgate, 1998). My own account of the unreality of time and McTaggart's system of an atemporal world including analysis of the nature of past, present, future, and before and after.

Bertrand Russell, *The Problems of Philosophy* (Oxford: Oxford University Press, 1986). First published in 1912, this is still one of the best introductions to philosophy available.

Roger Scruton, *Modern Philosophy: An Introduction and Survey* (London: Pimlico, 2004). A fine and easily read book providing a philosophical account of most subjects of human interest.

Peter Singer (ed.), *Applied Ethics* (Oxford: Oxford University Press, 1986). An outstanding collection of essays on applied ethics.

Peter Singer, *Practical Ethics* (Cambridge: Cambridge University Press, 1993). A clear and comprehensive coverage of all the difficult and controversial ethical issues facing us today from one of the world's philosophical authorities on the subject.

Peter Singer (ed.), *Ethics* (Oxford: Oxford University Press, 1994). A stimulating anthology of the thoughts of philosophers on a wide range of ethical topics.

Judith Jarvis Thomson, 'A Defence of Abortion', in Peter Singer (ed.), *Applied Ethics* (Oxford: Oxford University Press, 1986), pp. 37–56. The seminal and widely referred to defence of abortion.

Douglas N. Walton, *Informal Logic: A Handbook for Critical Argumentation* (Cambridge: Cambridge University Press, 1989). A technical book that, if used with care, is excellent. There are many very good examples.

Nigel Warburton, *Thinking from A to Z* (London: Routledge, 2007). Using interesting examples, Warburton provides a concise alphabetically arranged run-through of argument types and their problems.

G. J. Whitrow, *The Natural Philosophy of Time* (Oxford: Clarendon Press, 1980). A comprehensive account of the concept of time and its role in the different sciences.

G. J. Whitrow, *Time in History: Views of Time from Prehistory to the Present Day* (Oxford: Oxford University Press, 1988). A concise appraisal of the changing nature of our concept of time in history, this elegantly written book highlights the artificiality of many of our views on time.

Jonathan Wolff, *An Introduction to Political Philosophy* (Oxford: Oxford University Press, 2006). A clear exposition of the essential ingredients of political philosophy that sets out under sensible and accessible headings the ideas of major thinkers. Includes some good further reading advice.

Extended reading

Doing philosophy necessarily leads to looking at the original works of major philosophers. These can be found as abstracts in collections of classical or topic-based texts or by referring to the entire work. It should be emphasised that philosophical works, though often expounding complete arguments, are sometimes best accessed in small doses. Particularly dense works, such as those by Aristotle or Kant, say so much in a short space that the best

Annotated Bibliography, Extended Reading and Internet Resources

benefit can be had from looking carefully at only one particular section, then thinking about it or discussing it before moving on. The recommendations here are an initial selection of possibilities.

Aristotle, *Physics* and *Metaphysics* contain much of Aristotle's thoughts on the nature of the world and reality. The works of Aristotle are most likely copies of his lecture notes or academic papers (whereas the works in existence of Plato were intended for a broader more general audience) and, as such, give an impression of dryness. He is, however, very readable. Aristotle's thoughts are supremely incisive and compact and his work lends itself well to close reading of small passages. Anyone wishing to look more closely at Greek philosophy will get a feeling for some names and concepts by looking at J. V. Luce, *An Introduction to Greek Philosophy* (London: Thames and Hudson, 1992), an excellent introduction to all the major topics of Greek philosophy and for someone new to Greek philosophy, probably the best place to start. Jonathan Barnes, *Early Greek Philosophy* (London: Penguin, 2001) is very accessible and easy to read. Anyone wanting to be introduced to this fascinating (and fundamental) grounding to philosophy would be well advised to delve into these. The finest compilation of Aristotle's work is R. McKeon (ed.), *The Basic Works of Aristotle* (New York: Random House, 1941).

René Descartes, *Descartes: Selected Philosophical Writings*, trans. J. Cottingham, R. Stoothoff and D. Murdoch (Cambridge: Cambridge University Press, 1988). Descartes is very easy to read and this anthology of his work is essential reading.

Iain Hampsher-Monk, *A History of Modern Political Thought: Major Political Thinkers from Hobbes to Marx* (Oxford: Blackwell, 1992). One of the best introductions to the history of political theory that includes accounts of most of the philosophers mentioned here.

Immanuel Kant, *Groundwork of the Metaphysic of Morals*, in H. J. Paton, *The Moral Law* (London: Routledge, 1991). This is more accessible than his masterpiece the *Critique of Pure Reason* and is introduced extensively and analysed carefully by Paton.

Eugene Kelly, *The Basics of Western Philosophy* (New York: Humanity Books, 2006). A succinctly written history of both the activity and problems of philosophy that introduces all the major philosophers. A solid resource with a good index, bibliography and useful timeline.

E. D. Klemke (ed.), *The Meaning of Life* (New York: Oxford University Press, 2008). An outstanding collection of pieces by some of the most accomplished philosophical thinkers in recent history. The chapters are grouped under theist and non-theist arguments and arguments that question the idea of enquiring about life's meaning.

John Locke, *An Essay Concerning Human Understanding*, (ed.), P. Nidditch (Oxford: Oxford University Press, 1975). Locke's hugely influential work, like Hume's, is best taken in small doses.

Plato, *The Last Days of Socrates*, trans. Hugh Tredennick and Harold Tarrant (London: Penguin, 2003). Brings together Plato's works connected with the imprisonment and death of Socrates. The biographical work on Socrates is deeply moving and provides one of the best examples in history of a happy and good death. The individual books concerned are *Euthyphro, Apology, Crito* and *Phaedo*. Any of Plato's work is easy to read (it is stylish literature with a flowing and engaging style), however, the concepts are difficult and need to be studied with care. The best full collection of Plato's work is found in Edith Hamilton and Huntington Cairns (eds), *The Collected Dialogues of Plato including the Letters* (Princeton: Princeton University Press, 1961).

Nigel Warburton, *Basic Readings* (London: Routledge, 2004). A collection of well-chosen extracts by important philosophers on 'What is Philosophy?', 'God', 'Right and Wrong', 'Politics', 'The External World', 'Science', 'Mind', and 'Art'.

Nigel Warburton, *The Classics* (London: Routledge, 2006). Outlines the arguments together with criticisms of important philosophers including: Plato, Descartes, Locke, Hume, Kant, J. S. Mill and Wittgenstein.

Ludwig Wittgenstein, *Philosophical Investigations*, trans. G. E. M. Anscombe (Oxford: Basil Blackwell, 2001). This is an unusual book (it is broken down into brief, numbered propositions), but it is worth looking at very closely. Wittgenstein was one of the most influential philosophers of the twentieth century.

The Oxford Past Masters Series gives excellent, authoritative and brief introductions to most notable philosophers including Aquinas, Aristotle, Berkeley, Bentham, Descartes, Hegel, Hume, Kant, Leibniz, Locke, Mill, Nietzsche, Plato, Rousseau, Schopenhauer, Spinoza and Wittgenstein.

Internet resources

At the beginning of the twenty-first century, there is a vast (and growing) array of information resources available via the Internet. Those shown here are acknowledged as contributing to data contained in the topics of this book. They can all be used effectively to deepen and extend the range of the ideas presented here.

British Library (www.bl.uk). An easy-to-use research tool backed up by a massive catalogue and resources. Particularly impressive (and useful) is the 'Help for Researchers' section.

Commonwealth War Graves Commission (www.cwgc.org). Holds detailed records of service casualties in both World War I and II.

Encyclopaedia Britannica (www.britannica.com). A huge, highly authoritative and easily accessible resource.

Equality and Human Rights Commission (www.equalityhumanrights.com). A complete resource for all aspects of human rights in the UK.

Gerald Rochelle's Practical Philosophy (www.practicalphilosophy.org.uk). This comprehensive website looks at various ways of doing philosophy, especially Reflective Practice as a means of achieving philosophical understanding. There are some useful links and a picture gallery of philosophers.

Google Scholar (http://scholar.google.co.uk). Affords quick access to the range of available scholarly and academic work in all fields.

Government Equalities Office (www.equalities.gov.uk). Provides background and application of equality legislation in the UK.

Internet Encyclopedia of Philosophy (IEP) (www.iep.utm.edu). A huge resource of peer reviewed and thoroughly referenced philosophical topics edited by James Fieser (who was also the founder) and Bradley Dowden.

Library of Congress (www.loc.gov). A vast information portal including an effective 'Ask a librarian' function. Contains much on North American history and culture together with an extensive and culturally comprehensive digital collection.

David McCandless, *Information is Beautiful* (London: Collins, 2009 and www.informationisbeautiful.net). A highly original source of information displaying facts, figures and ideas in thought-provoking graphics. Not to be missed.

Pathways School of Philosophy: Ask a Philosopher (www.philosophypathways.com/questions). Geoffrey Klempner's excellent site allows you to submit questions for a philosopher to answer. Also contains a bank and searchable knowledge base of previous questions and answers. A great place to test out your philosophical thoughts.

US Congressional Research Service (www.loc.gov/library/libarch-digital.html). An immense data collection that also provides a good starting point for details of war casualties.

United Nations (www.un.org/en/). This site contains all information on the work of the UN since its inception.

Wikipedia (en.wikipedia.org). A vast and continually growing encyclopaedia of information. Contributions vary in quality, though constant editing to articles takes place. The best contributions are provided with extensive references and links.

Index

abiogenesis 220
abortion 161
   Aristotle 203
   backstreet objection 171
   as birth control 163
   consent for 161
   killing 162–3, 164, 170
   language used 163
absolutism 58, 60, 144, 164
abstract thinking 29, 48
adaptive modification 197, 227–8
adoption 162, 163
Afghanistan 145, 147, 150
agnostics 74
AIDS 71, 170, 202
alleles 196
alphalactalbumin 201
altruism 50
Amazon Basin 131
American Civil War 106
American Revolution 105
Amnesty International 106
analogy 45
Anaximander 223
animal liberation movement 183
animal rights 183–4, 186, 192–3
animals
   consciousness 185, 186
   experimenting on 193
   free-will 192
   genetic modification 200–1
   killing 193
   life 209
   pain 187
   pairings for life 187
   as pets 193–4
   self-consciousness 189–90
   self-defence 190–1
   social groups 187
Anselm, St 76
anthropomorphism 186, 195
anti-abortionist argument 164–5
   see also pro-life views
anti-evolutionists 221
anti-government feeling 106, 126–7
anti-Vietnam War protests 106
Aquinas, St Thomas
   cosmological argument 77, 235
   design argument 78
   evil 82
   on homosexuality 70
   humans/animals 209
   just war 137
   kindness to animals 183
   lex talionis 158
   ontological argument 76
   religious/political authority 126
Arab Spring 147
Aristotle vii
   abortion 203
   cosmological argument 77, 235
   eugenics 206
   final cause 185
   future determined 123
   gender differences 69
   good 50
   humans/animals 209
   life 220, 222
   life, ends/means 243
   logic 12, 14
   a posteriori knowledge 30
   science 86
   state/individual 125–6
   survival after death 214

Index

virtue 56
assisted suicide 175, 177–8, 180
assumption 93, 94
astronomy 235
atheists 74
atomism 237
Attard, Mary and Jodie 179–81
Augustine, St 41, 81, 99, 126, 137, 183
Austin, J.L. 153
authority 119–20, 133, 134
Ayer, A.J. 29, 58

Bacon, Francis 86
bacteria 215, 229
Baer, Karl Ernst von 228
banishment 156
Barrett, Justin L. 80
Beauvoir, Simone de 70
behaviourism 43–4
Belgium 178
belief 11, 28, 82, 84
Bentham, Jeremy
   equal distribution 66
   kindness to animals 183
   protection of society 155
   utilitarianism 54, 105, 153
Bergson, Henri 208
Berkeley, George 35
Beyond Good and Evil (Nietzsche) 50
Big Bang theory 79, 101, 222, 234, 236, 239
Bijani, Ladan and Laleh 178–9
bin Laden, Osama 149
biogenesis 220
black holes 101
blood-clotting agent 200
Boyle, Robert 237
brain 40–1, 166, 210
brain-dead people 46, 166
Brave New World (Huxley) 205
Bt Potato 202
Buddhism 75, 213
Bunker, Eng and Chang 179
Butler, Joseph 209–10

Calvinism 116
Cambridge change 96, 100
camouflage 190

Campaign for Nuclear Disarmament 141
Camus, Albert 158
Cancun Agreement 132
capital punishment 158–9
capitalism 127, 129–30
carbon dioxide emission 131, 134
Cartagena Protocol on Biosafety 131
Castle, William Ernest 224–5
catastrophism 223, 224
categorical imperative 53–4
causal chains 28, 115, 116
cause 93, 94, 100, 115, 116
cell division 168
child-bearing 71
chimpanzees 189, 190
China, People's Republic of 127
Chinese room experiment 44
Christianity
   ethics 51–2
   euthanasia 176
   evolution theory 231
   God 74, 75
   homosexuality 70
   resurrection 213
chromosomes 196, 199
Cicero, Marcus Tullius 237
citizenship 119–20, 126
civil disobedience 140, 144, 156–7
class conflict 127
Cleckley, Hervey M.: *The Three Faces of Eve* 46
cloning 168, 199–200
coincidence 93, 94
Cold War 127, 130, 146–7
collectivism 121
common-sense philosophy 29
communism 129
communitarianism 128
compatibilists 117
Concept of Mind (Ryle) 43
conception 163
conclusions 3, 13
conjoined twins 173, 178–80
conscience argument 80
consciousness 185, 186, 188, 209
consequence 53, 54–6
consequentialism
   deterrence 154

253

euthanasia 176
  protection of society 155
  reform 155–6
  retribution 154
  vegetarianism 192
  violence 144
Conservation of Energy, Law of 91
Conservation of Matter, Law of 90–1
Constant de Rébecque, Henri Benjamin 118–19
continental drift 222–3
continuity, bodily 46
continuous processes 167, 210
Conventions: *see* United Nations
Copernicus, Nicolaus 235
corpuscular philosophy 237
cosmological argument 77, 235
cosmology 234–6
cospecification 243
creation ex nihilo 238
creation theory 220, 221, 226–7, 230, 236–7
creator 220, 221, 230, 239, 240
Crick, F.H.C. 196
crimes 152
criminals 155–6
Cuba 129
Cuvier, Georges 223, 224
cystic fibrosis 204, 205

Darrow, Clarence 158
Darwin, Charles 88, 203, 222, 224, 225, 237–8
death 210–12, 214–15, 218
Declaration of the Rights of Man and of the Citizen 105
deductive argument 13, 14, 15–16, 17–18
democracy 67–9, 118, 128, 157
Democritus 235, 237
Descartes, René
  animals 183
  certainty 31
  cosmological argument 77
  dreams/reality 36
  Meditation 76
  mind/body 41
  as rationalist 30
  scepticism 28

design argument 78–9
desires, hierarchy of 193
determinism 115, 116–17, 118, 122, 123, 153
deterremce 154–5
Dewey, John 31
diminished responsibility concept 123
disabilities, people with 203
discrimination 66
  reverse 67, 72–3
distributive equality 65–6
DNA 196, 198, 205
DNA Database 205
Dolly the sheep 199
Dostoevsky, Fyodor 52, 158
double effect principle 170
dreaming 36
dualism 41–2
duty-based theories 51–4, 176–7
Dworkin, R. 128

Earth Summit 131
egoism 50
Einstein, Albert 21, 101, 235
Eldredge, Niles 226
embryological recapitulation 228
emotivism 58
empiricism 29–30
employment 66–7
encephalitis virus 200
endlessness 216
Engels, Friedrich 127
An Enquiry Concerning Human Understanding (Hume) 79
environmental movement 130
Enviropig 201
Epicurus 81, 211
epiphenomenalism 41
epistemic necessity 10
epistemology 7, 27–9
equal opportunity 63, 66–7
equality 62–3, 65–6, 67–70, 72, 73, 124–5
ether 91
ethical progress view 192–3
ethics 50
  applied 57
  Christian 51–2
  environmental 130

Kantian 53–4
killing 169
politics 125
warfare 138–9
Euclid 235
eugenics 178, 203, 205–6
euphemisms for warfare 143–4
European Convention on Human Rights 112–13, 141
euthanasia 175, 176, 177, 178
event horizons 101
evidence 2, 10, 17
evil 81–2
evolution 227, 228–9, 230
evolution theory 196, 220, 222–5, 226–7, 231, 237–8
excluded middle, law of 14
existence, disembodied 214
existentialism 57
experimenting on animals 193
extinction 223
eye, evolution of 227

faith 82, 84
fallacy 90
fatalism 118
fate 93, 94, 117
FBI CODIS 205
feminism 69, 169
fertilisation 168
final cause (Aristotle) 185
first-order theories 51
fission 168
Flavr Savr tomato 202
foetus 164–5, 166
Foglia, Giuseppina and Santina 179
fossil record 226, 227
Foucault, Michel 70
freedom 115, 117, 118–19, 120, 122, 152
freedom of action 120–1
freedom of speech 120, 121–2
free-will 81–2, 115–16, 185, 192
Frege, Gottlob 12, 76
French Revolution 104, 105
frequency probability 22, 23
Freud, Sigmund 38, 70
Friedman, Milton 129
Friedmann, Aleksandr Aleksandrovich 235

functionalism 44
future 98, 101, 118, 123

Gadarene swine 183
Gaddafi, Muammar 114, 139
Galton, Francis 203
Gandhi, Mohandas Karamchand 105, 106, 140, 157
Gaunilo 76
gender bias 66–7
gender discrimination 111
gender selection 204
gene cloning 199–200
gene pool 197–8
gene therapy 203–4
General Theory of Relativity 91, 93, 101, 235
generalisation, high-/low-level 91
genes 196, 197
Genesis 183, 221
genetic code 228–9
genetic drift 225
genetic engineering 178, 198–9
genetic forensics 205
genetic modification 199, 200–1, 206, 222
genetic population 197–8
genetic screening 205
Geneva Conventions for the Protection of Prisoners of War 139, 145–6
Geneva Conventions on the Treatment of the Victims of War 110
geology 224
geometry 235
ghost in the machine (Ryle) 43
global wealth 127
globalisation 125, 147
GM food: *see* genetic modification
God
  attributes of 74–5
  Christian ethics 51–2
  as creator 220, 221, 230, 239, 240
  evil 81–2
  existence of 52, 74, 75–81
  humans' conception of 76
  immortality 213
  purpose 242
  supernatural 74
  will of 52, 115

good 50
Goodall, Jane Morris 189
Goodman, Nelson 87
Gosse, Philip Henry 220, 232
Gould, Stephen Jay 224, 226
gradualism 226
gravity 14, 21, 30, 85, 88, 91, 239
Greeks, Ancient
   democracy 68
   freedom 118
   genetics 205
   gods/godesses 74, 77
   homosexuality 70
   slavery 58
green climate fund 132
greenhouse gases 131
Guantanamo Bay 146
Gulf War 150
Guye, Charles-Eugène 230

hallucination 37, 75
happiness 50, 54, 55, 63, 66
Hardy, Godfrey Harold 224–5
Hardy-Weinberg law 224–5
harm principle 127
Hart, H.L.A. 128, 154
Hartle, James Burkett 237
Hawking, Stephen 101, 236–7
hedonism 54
Hegel, G.W.F. 69, 121
heredity, genetic 196, 221
heterosexuality 71
Hinduism 74, 213
Hipppocratic oath 176, 178, 179
Hiroshima 146
historical materialism 127
Hitler, Adolf 178
Hobbes, Thomas 64, 120, 126
Hofmeister, W.F.B. 196
homosexuality 70, 71
Honderich, Ted 117
Hubble, Edwin Powell 235
human cloning 199
human difference 3, 62–3
human genome 198
human nature 57
Human Rights Act 112–13
humans

evolution theory 231
foetus 165, 166
genetically modified 201
sorites paradox 167
Hume, David
   determinism 116
   empiricism 30
   An Enquiry Concerning Human
      Understanding 79
   God 78
   induction 87
   perceptions 40
   scepticism 28–9, 30
Hussein, Saddam 139, 148–9
Huxley, Aldous: *Brave New World* 205
hypothesis 93, 94

idea 93, 94
idealism 9, 35, 37–8
identity 14, 72, 73, 209–10, 214, 216, 217–18
ill health/poverty 202
immortality 213, 216
impermanence 241–2
incompatibilists 117
individual
   community 128
   state 124, 125, 126, 142
inductive argument 10, 13, 14–15, 55, 86–7
information 1, 129
intelligent design argument 237
interconnectedness 125
International Covenant on Civil and
   Political Rights 108–9
International Covenant on Economic,
   Social and Cultural Rights 109–10
in-vitro fertilisation (IVF) 201
Iraq War 139, 143, 145, 147, 150–1
Islam 74
Israel 145

Jainism 75
James, William 31, 117
Johannsen, W.L. 196
John, King of England 104
Judaism 74
Jung, Carl 93

Index

jus talionis 153–4
just war argument 52, 137–8, 139–40, 143, 147–8
justice 125, 158
justification 86–7, 88, 89–90, 152, 153, 156–7

Kafka, Franz: *Metamorphosis* 46
Kant, Immanuel
   duty-based view 176–7
   ethics 51, 53–4
   gender differences 69
   God 76
   humans/animals 209
   kindness to animals 183
   knowledge/experience 30
   noumenal/phenomenal world 29
   retaliation 153–4
   time 98–9
Keynes, John Maynard 129
killing
   abortion 162–3, 164, 170
   animals 55, 193
   corporate 59
   ethics 169
   God 52
   Kantian ethics 53
   for mercy 176
   unintentional 58–9
   in war 57, 138
   see also euthanasia; warfare
King, Martin Luther, Jr. 105, 157
Kinsey Reports 70
knowledge 26–7, 85, 204
   a posteriori 9–10, 30
   a priori 9–10, 29–30
Koestler, Arthur 158
Korea, North 129
Korean War 150
Krivoshlyapova, Masha and Dasha 173, 179
Kyoto Protocol 131

Lamarck, Jean-Baptiste 223–4, 226
language 188, 189
language philosophy 29
Laplace, marquis de 115
law-breaking 157

Lecomte du Nouy, Pierre 230
legal rights 104
Leibniz, Gottfried Wilhelm 30, 77, 81
Lemaître, Georges 235
Leucippus 235, 237
Lewis, David 76
lex talionis 153, 158
liberalism 119
liberty 118–19
   see also freedom
Libya 114, 139, 147, 151
life
   Bergson 208
   humans/animals 209
   love of 243–4
   meaning of 241, 242–4
   origin of 220–1
life force 208, 215
light cones 101
Locke, John
   compact with state 64–5
   cosmological argument 77
   as empiricist 30
   government 126
   identity 209
   natural rights 65, 104, 120
   politics 124
   representative realism 34
   right to life 141
logic 8–9, 12, 13–18, 21
logical positivism 29
Lyell, Charles 224

MacIntyre, Alasdair C, 127–8
McTaggart, J.McT.E. 99
Magna Carta 104
Malthus, Thomas 225
Mantell, Gideon 223
marriage, as institution 71
Marx, Karl Heinrich 69, 121, 127
Marxism 127, 129
mathematical probability 22, 23
Mathibela, Mpho and Mphonyana 179
Mayr, Ernst 226
media 129, 143
medical science 178–9
Meditations (Descartes) 76
memory 37, 45, 216, 217–18, 228–9

Mendel, Gregor 196, 222, 224
mental states 42–3
mentalism 186
mercy killing 176
meta-ethics 57
Metamorphosis (Kafka) 46
metaphysics 3, 6, 10
microwave radiation 236
Mill, John Stuart
   anti-state view 126–7
   as empiricist 30
   gender differences 70
   individual freedom 152
   liberalism 119
   phenomenalism 37
   sexual equality 69
   utilitarianism 54, 105, 120, 127, 153, 177
mind 41, 44–5, 197
mind/body dualism 41–2, 43, 46–7
Minkowski, Hermann 101
miracles argument 79–80
miscarriage 161
Moore, G.E. 29, 117
moral actions 55, 57
moral choice 185
moral dilemmas 50–1
mosquito 200
motive 93, 94
Muir, John 130
multiple personality cases 46
mutation 93, 197, 225–6

Nagasaki 146
Nagel, Thomas 41, 211, 243
Native American Indians 106
NATO 139
natural laws 91–2
natural rights 65, 104, 120
natural selection 88, 221, 224, 225
naturalism 57
nature 6–7, 91–2
Nazi Germany 203
necessity 9–10
neoliberalism 129–30
Netherlands 178
Newton, Isaac 21, 115, 235, 237
Nietzsche, Friedrich Wilhelm 56, 152, 242, 243
   Beyond Good and Evil 50
non-contradiction, law of 14
non-governmental organisations 126
Nozick, Robert 66, 127, 243
nuclear war 146–7

observation 88
On the Origin of Species (Darwin) 222, 224
ontological argument 76–7
opinion 82, 84
organ donation 201
orthogenesis 227
Orwell, George 143
Owen, Richard 223

pacifism 140–1, 143
pain 165, 175, 187, 188
Paine, Thomas 105
Pakistan 147
Palestine 145
Pangaea concept 223
Parfit, Derek 210
parthenogenesis 169
Pascal's wager 80–1
past 97–8, 101
Pasteur, Louis 220–1, 222
patents 200, 202
Paul, St 183
Pearson, Karl 203
Peasants' Revolt 105
Peirce, Charles Sanders 31
Penrose, Roger 101, 236
Penzias, Arno Allan 236
personal identity 48–9
personalist theories 23
pet animals 193–4
phenomenalism 37–8
philosophy
   defined 2–3
   as process 12–13
   reasons for studying ix
   terms 6–10
physicalism 42–3
physics 7
Pinchot, Gifford 130
Pinochet, Augusto 129–30
plant life 188

Plato
- breeding 203
- cosmological argument 77
- democracy 69
- epistemology 27–8
- eugenics 206
- evil 81
- gender differences 69
- homosexuality 70
- justice 125
- knowable things 27
- meaning of life 242
- mind 41
- natural laws 91
- punishment/banishment 156
- scepticism 30
- soul 213, 214
- time 98

pleasure-pain system 187, 188
politics 124, 125, 128–9
Poll Tax 105
Popper, Karl 87
possibility
- logical 21–2, 24
- probability 22–3

poverty/ill health 202
power 124, 133, 134
pragmatism 30–1
predetermination 118, 123
predicate calculus 12
preference utilitarianism 193
pregnancy, unwanted 162, 171
prejudice 72, 73
premise 13
present 97, 101
primary qualities 34
Prisoner's Dilemma 64
pro-abortion views 162, 166–9
probability 22–3
pro-choice 169
pro-life views 162
see also anti-abortionist argument
proof 17–18
proportionality 140
propositional calculus 12
protection of society 155
proteins, cloning 199–200
Protestantism 116, 145

Ptolemy 235
punctualism 226
punishment
- capital 158–9
- deterremce 154–5
- justification 152, 153
- protection of society 155
- reform 155–6
- retribution 153–4

Putnam, Hilary 28, 36
Pyrrho 28
Pythagoreans 234–5

al-Qaeda 145
quantum mechanics 117–18
questions 3, 4–5

racial bias 67, 203
randomness 117–18, 238
rape 163, 170
rationalism 29–30, 209
Rawls, John 127
Reagan, Ronald 129
realism 33, 34, 36–7
reality 7, 36
Recapitulation, Law of 228
Redi, Francesco 220, 222
reform 155–6
Regan, Tom 130, 184, 188, 189–90
reincarnation 213, 215–16
religion 74
- conflict 144
- determinism 116
- evolution theory 231
- experience 75–6
- terrorism 144–5
- *see also* God

representative democracy 68–9
resurrection 213
retribution 153–4
right to die 177–8
right to life 113, 164–5
rights
- civil 71, 157
- defined 184
- entitlement 194
- genetically modified animals 201
- language 189

moral 104–6
natural 65, 104, 120
responsibilities 184–5
rights-based views 191–2
rioters 155
risk assessment 179
Robespierre, Maximilien-François-Marie-Isidore de 105
Roe v *Wade* case 164
Rolston, Holmes, III 130
Rosie the cow 201
Ross, Alexander 220
Rousseau, Jean-Jacques
citizenship 104–5
freedom 118–19
gender differences 69
right to life 141
social contract 126
state of nature 65
Russell, Bertrand 12, 29, 37, 140–1, 156
Russia 106
Ryder, Richard D. 183–4
Ryle, Gilbert: *Concept of Mind* 43

same-sex marriage 71
Sandel, Michael 127–8
Sartre, Jean-Paul 57
scepticism 7, 11, 14–15, 27–9, 33
Schopenhauer, Arthur 212
science 85, 87, 88–9, 89–90
science fiction 102
scientific determinism 116
scientific method 85–6
Searle, John 44
secondary qualities 34
second-order questions 57
selective breeding 198, 204, 222, 224
self-consciousness 40–1, 189–90, 209
self-defence 141–3, 147–8, 190–1
self-harm 121
selfhood 209
self-interest, rational 119
Sewall Wright effect 225
Sextus Empiricus 28
sexual inclination 70–1
Shipman, Harold 178
Shoemaker, Sydney 210
Sidgwick, Henry 243

similarity 72, 73
Singer, Peter 130, 183–4, 192, 193
Sitter, Willem de 235
Skinner, B.F. 116
slavery 58, 106
Slipher, Vesto Melvin 235
Smith, Adam 129
social conscience 231
social constraint 124
social contract 64–5, 120, 126
society 62, 63, 156
Society of Friends 140
Socrates vii, 208, 211
solipsism 9, 35, 45
sorites paradox 167
soul 41, 213, 214
sovereignty 126
Soviet Union, collapse of 127, 147
space-time 101, 236, 239
spatial objects 95
speciesism 183–4
Spinoza, Baruch 77
Star Trek example 46
state
authority 119–20
capital punishment 158–9
citizenship 119–20
equality 124–5
force 141
freedom 118–19
individual 124, 125, 126, 142
pacifism 141
self-defence 142–3
sovereignty 126
terrorism 145
warfare 136–7, 139
state of nature 63, 104, 120
statistics 22, 23, 91
stem-cell harvesting 200
sterilisation, forced 203
Stevenson, Robert Louis: *The Strange Case of Dr Jekyyll and Mr Hyde* 46
Stoics 211
The Strange Case of Dr Jekyyll and Mr Hyde (Stevenson) 46
Strategic Defense System 143
Strawson, P.F. 117
subject 8, 188

substance 7–8
suffering 82
suffragette movement 156–7
suicide 178, 212
superstition 72, 73
Swinburne, Richard 78–9
Switzerland 68, 177–8
syllogistic argument 12, 15–17, 18

Taoism 75
Taylor, Charles 127–8
Teflon 86
teleological argument 78, 237
terminally ill people 51, 166–7
terrorism 106, 120, 138, 140, 144–5, 147, 149, 157
Thatcher, Margaret 129
theodicies 81
theories 89–91
Thigpen, Corbett H.: *The Three Faces of Eve* 46
things 7–8
Thomson, Judith Jarvis 173
Thoreau, Henry David 105, 130, 157
thought experiments 21
thoughts 42, 43–4
The Three Faces of Eve (Thigpen & Cleckley) 46
time 95–6, 97–9, 101, 227–8, 239
time travel 99–100, 102
time-tunnelling 101
token-identity theory 43
Tolstoy, Leo 105, 140, 143
torture 140, 146, 165
totalitarianism 128
totipotency 168
truth 88
truth-values 14
Tucker, Albert 64
Turing test 1
Twin Towers attack 145, 149
twins 199
 see also conjoined twins
type-identity theory 42

unconsciousness 211
understanding 1, 188
uniformitarianism 224

United Nations
 Cancun Agreement 132
 Convention against Torture 110–11
 Convention on Biological Diversity 131
 Convention on the Elimination of all Forms of Discrimination against Women 111
 Convention on the Prevention and Punishment of the Crime of Genocide 110
 Convention on the Rights of the Child 111–12, 113, 114
 Conventions and Covenants 108–11
 Framework Convention on Climate Change 131
 human rights 106
United Nations Decade of Biodiversity 131
United Nations Security Council 137–8
United States of America
 Civil Rights Movement 106
 Constitution 141
 Declaration of Independence 105
 FBI CODIS 205
 policing the world 147
universal consent argument 80
Universal Declaration of Human Rights 106, 107, 112–13
Universal Gravitation, Law of 30, 91, 239
universe
 expanding 235, 236, 237
 origins of 220
utilitarianism
 Bentham 54–6, 105, 153
 equality 63
 euthanasia 177
 Mill 54, 105, 120, 127, 153, 177
 negative 56
 preference 193
 punishment 153–4
utopia 125–6

validity 13
variation 224
vegetarianism 183–4, 191–2
verification 90–1
victim's rights 154

Vienna School 29
Vietnam War 106, 113, 150, 156
view from nowhere concept 41
violence 144
virtue theory 56
viruses 199, 208, 229
voting 68, 128–9

Wallace, Alfred Russell 222, 224
warfare
    casualties 149–51
    defined 137
    ethics 57, 138–9
    euphemisms 143–4
    human motivation 136–7
    media 143
    motivation 136–7
    proportionality 140
    self-defence 142
    state 136–7, 139

see also just war argument
Warfarin 228
waste disposal 132
Watson, J.D. 196
Wegener, Alfred Lothar 222–3
Weinberg, William 224–5
Weismann, August 224
Williams, Bernard 210
Wilmut, Ian 199
Wilson, Robert Woodrow 236
Wittgenstein, Ludwig 29, 188, 210, 211
Wollstonecraft, Mary 69
women's movement 106
words/naming 10
work, paid/unpaid 70
World War I 149
World War II 145–6, 149–50
wormholes 101
Wright, Sewall 225
Wright, Thomas 235

For Product Safety Concerns and Information please contact our EU
representative GPSR@taylorandfrancis.com
Taylor & Francis Verlag GmbH, Kaufingerstraße 24, 80331 München, Germany

www.ingramcontent.com/pod-product-compliance
Lightning Source LLC
Chambersburg PA
CBHW071814300426
44116CB00009B/1311